DUKE'S MIXTURE

Books by Frederick Manfred

The Golden Bowl 1944
Boy Almighty 1945
This Is the Year 1947
The Chokecherry Tree 1948
The Primitive 1949
The Brother 1950
The Giant* 1951
Lord Grizzly 1954
Morning Red 1956
Riders of Judgment 1957
Conquering Horse 1959
Arrow of Love (stories) 1961
Wanderlust (trilogy)** 1962
Scarlet Plume 1964
The Man Who Looked Like the Prince of Wales*** 1965
Winter Count (poems) 1966
King of Spades 1966
Apples of Paradise (stories) 1968
Eden Prairie 1968
Conversations 1974
Milk of Wolves 1976
The Manly-Hearted Woman 1976
Green Earth 1977
The Wind Blows Free (reminiscence) 1979
Sons of Adam 1980
Winter Count II (poems) 1987
Prime Fathers (portraits) 1989
The Selected Letters of Frederick Manfred (1932-1954) 1989
Flowers of Desire 1989
No Fun on Sunday 1990
Of Lizards and Angels 1992
Duke's Mixture (miscellany) 1994

*Mr. Manfred wrote under the name of Feike Feikema from 1944 through 1951.

**A new revised version of three novels, The Primitive, The Brother, The Giant, and published in one volume.

***Reprinted in paperback as The Secret Place.

DUKE'S MIXTURE

by
FREDERICK MANFRED

The Center for Western Studies

The Prairie Plains Series

Published by The Center for Western Studies
Box 727, Augustana College
Sioux Falls, South Dakota 57197

The Center for Western Studies is an archives, library, museum, and publishing house concerned principally with collecting, preserving, and interpreting prehistoric, historic, and contemporary materials that document native and immigrant cultures of the northern prairie plains. The Center promotes understanding of the region through exhibits, publications, art shows, conferences, and academic programs. It is committed, ultimately, to defining the contribution of the region to American civilization.

Library of Congress Cataloging-in-Publication Data:

Manfred, Frederick Feikema, 1912-
    Duke's mixture / by Frederick Manfred.
      p. cm. – (The Prairie plains series)
    ISBN 0-931170-55-9
    1. Manfred, Frederick Feikema, 1912-   . 2. Authors, American – 20th century – Biography. 3. Great Plains in literature. 4. West (U.S.) in literature. I. Title. II. Series.
PS3525.A52233Z474 1993
813'.54 – dc20
[B]   93-28553
                                         CIP

Printed in United States of America

PINE HILL PRESS, INC.
Freeman, S. Dak. 57029

Table of Contents

v

Foreword

"Duke's mixture, hell of a mess, holy or pretty mess, mell of a hess, mess-up, mix, mix-up, muss, mux, omnium gatherum, piggledy-higgledy, razzle-dazzle, risraz, rookery, rummage, splutter, topsyturvydom, tumble, what the cat brought in."

The American Thesaurus of Slang
by Lester V. Berrey and Melvin Van Den Bark, 1942

It has been my dream for many years to be able to finish a long hallway of pictures in fiction dealing with the country I call Siouxland (located in the center of the Upper Midlands, USA) from 1800 and on to the day I die. Not only must the history be fairly accurate, and the description of the flora and fauna fairly precise, and the use of the language of the place and time beautiful, but the delineation of the people by way of characterization living and illuminating. It has long been my thought that a "place" finally selects the people who best reflect it, give it voice, and allow it to make a cultural contribution to the sum of all world culture under the sun. In fact, it is the sun beating on a certain place in a certain time that at last causes that place to flower into literature, the highest expression of intelligence (and not necessarily human intelligence).

It has been my feeling for some time that Middle America is more apt to speak with a clear voice from this continent than are either of the two American seaboards, the East with New York as the center and the West with Los Angeles as the center. The East in New York (and Boston and Washington, etc.) still speaks in part with an alien voice. It is not clear. It is muddy. It is as polluted with foreign sounds as is the air with foreign particles. And the West in Los Angeles (and

vii

all other California points) speaks with a most artificial voice, that of Hollywood, of the sudden uncultured rich. Only the Upper Midlands (and in my case, only my Siouxland) has a chance to speak with as clear a separate voice within the whole Western Culture complex as say Madrid for Spain and Paris for France and London for England.

The final test of good fiction rests with how well the characters come through, their reality, their meaning, their stature, their durability, no matter what the situation may be. The characters should be so well done that the reader should not be aware of plot or the unraveling of time in the work. The reader should be lost in the story. The plot should be hidden like a skeleton is in a flying eagle.

If a "place" truly finds voice at last, the ultimate sacred force speaks.

And in the USA, Western American literature does this the best.

Frederick Manfred

Charles Montagu Doughty, 1843-1926

Why do I persist in talking about Doughty's poetry? Because I think that *The Dawn in Britain,* a six-volume massive epic, first published in 1906, is the Mt. Everest of all literature.

My interest in Doughty was awakened by a *Time* article, 1943, the same year that the entire epic was reissued in England in commemoration of his birth. A quote from his at the moment best-known work, *Travels in Arabia Deserta,* caught my eye:

> A new voice hailed me of an old friend when, first returned from the Peninsula, I paced again in that long street of Damascus which is called Straight; and suddenly taking me wonderingly by the hand, 'Tell me,' said he, 'since thou art here again in the peace and assurance of Ullah, and whilst we walk, as in the former years, toward the new blossoming orchards, full of sweet spring, as the Garden of God, what moved thee, or how couldst thou take such journeys into the fanatic Arabia?'

The paragraph haunted me, and so I got the work from the local library and started in. For the first 300 pages or so I couldn't make up my mind whether I was reading the work of a crackpot or a genius. What kept getting in the way was his armchair Chaucerian "style." But gradually, as I went along, as I became weathered to his manner, as I learned his language, I began to see that he was in deadly earnest about his resolve to restore to strength and purity the English which he believed had been debased by all writers since Edmund Spenser. And furthermore, I saw that his emphasis on such English was peculiarly apt as a medium with which to describe the primitive and Biblical Arabians. It took me six months to penetrate that

1

veil of language, but once inside, I found a great man, and
a great monumental work of art, a literary Stonehenge. I brought
the book back to the library and persuaded my wife, despite
the fact that we were very hard up at the time, to buy an
expensive, large-type edition. And so I continued to study and
to marvel.

Finished with *Arabia Deserta*, I wondered what his poetry
was like. It was almost too much to expect Doughty to be
equally great as a poet, especially since I had trouble imagining
subject matter for his peculiar style. At great expense and trouble, I managed to get hold of *The Dawn in Britain*, *The Cliffs*,
The Clouds, *Mansoul*, and a biography by D. G. Hogarth. The
first volume of *The Dawn in Britain* was missing, and so I
asked the U.S. Library of Congress to let me use a copy of
theirs. I took off a month from my writing and painstakingly
retyped it in a looseleaf notebook. And not only came to understand and to know Doughty the poet, but to respect him as
one of the immortals. I learned, in the concrete, just what went
into that poem. Finished typing, I read on, plunging into a
land and a time I had only vaguely heard of, a land and a
time which had almost meant nothing to me. I met Brennus
and the Romans 300 B.C. I watched the struggle between the
Occident and the primitive Britons and Gauls and Celts, saw
the barbarians temporary victor, saw Christianity in the end
prevail in the year 200 A.D. Every day I read a little, read
it like a Bible—for you do not race through Doughty, you taste
and sip and swallow and ponder, and wonder on the origins
of life, and come to understand, a little, about who you are
and where you came from. Doughty asked the big questions,
as witness the following quotation from *The Cliffs*:

> . . .I do ask myself
> What is our human orphan littleness?
> To weigh what yonder starbright infinite Gulf:
> This inconceivable Majesty of the high heavens!
> Whence that immeasurable Star-frame? yond Frost
> Of suns? From what All-Parent it derives;
> Through never-ending years? Whence have we breath;
> This reasonable soul, cloaked in with flesh?

Warm pulsing flesh! And when man's kind is dead;
Cold too this living world, dead, void and ended;
Shall (far transcending our now living thought)
It hang unchanged, and everlasting still.

Doughty is more real to me than a grandfather: wise, a
sage in control of his power and his virility, a man who rides
easy with his genius. For me, an American who writes American
and not English, he is something to shoot for, besides giving
me a frame of reference with which to estimate my own great
Melville and Whitman.

I have since read *The Cliffs* and *The Clouds* and *Mansoul*,
and find that, though these books do not come up to *The Dawn
in Britain* (he wrote them when he was an old man), they are
in the same majestic vain. I am anxiously looking forward to
reading his *Adam Cast Forth* and *The Titans*. (So far I have
simply been unable to find any copies in this country! They
are out of print in Britain.)

I have tried to talk to people about Doughty. A few have
read his *Arabia Deserta*, and no one seems to have read his
poetry. (One would think that the American university English
departments would make a great fuss over this most English
of English writers!) People stare at me with cautious eyes when
I talk about him as being as great as Shakespeare, and that
in one work, Shakespeare does not match him, that he is as
great as Homer and Dante and Goethe. Sometimes I am on
the point of deciding to keep this all to myself, for fear of
being committed. But how can one keep such a wonderful
discovery to one's self? It's impossible. Impossible.

A few have noted his greatness. A few. Bridges, T. E.
Lawrence, Barker Fairlay, Ellery Sedgewick. One or two have
even taken potshots at him: one in particular, a "poetry reviewer"
for an eminent New York magazine who read him over a weekend
and then reported to a publisher that he was just a Victorian.
Imagine! Doughty, a Victorian, when he had set as one of his
goals to make no compromise with the English he called "Victorian and Costermongery"?

A couple of months ago, I read the Postscript to a new
edition of Shaw's *Back to Methusaleh*. In it, Shaw listed three

great literary titans: himself, Doughty, and Shakespeare. Buried
in his comment was the following: "...his [Doughty's] travel
diary, *Arabia Deserta,* is a world classic...there must have
been something majestic and gigantic about the man that made
him a classic in himself...and when he came home [from Arabia]
he spent the rest of his life in writing immense prophetic epics
in blank verse of a Himalayan magnificence and natural eminence
that would have made Milton gasp. Englishmen who met him
have described him to me as a 'mountain of a man' and extant
portraits bear them out as far as portraits can."

Shaw thinks that Doughty's contradictory statements about
the hostility and the gentleness of the Bedouins reveals an un-
thinking art. But this is clearly wrong. What Doughty had
in mind was to show the effect of the desert on the human
mind, how it destroyed the civilized emphasis on consistency
of mental effort, how logic and judgment vanish, replaced by
whimsicality, by caprice. And he gives this to excuse the
behavior of the Arabs, who he says sometimes seem to have
the brains of birds, hopping from one object to another without
any logic.

Reading *Deserta* I did not find that Doughty thought of
the Arabs as damned heathens; he felt for them a deep sad
commiseration, that he like them was a wanderer on an indif-
ferent planet. He refused to pose as a Mohammedan because
that would not be honest, but he was not particularly a Christian. In fact, his poems show, even with those written in old
age, when one could expect him to make his peace with God
because of fear of death, that he felt that science might one
day give the answer to the why of our pulsing here, and that
religion at best would always remain but a solace needful for
some of the more anguished folk. He carried a revolver at the
behest of friends; the idea was repugnant to him; and never
once in *Deserta* does he indicate he felt a murderous impulse
to use it. In fact in the writing and the living of the book
there is evidence he wished he'd never carried it.

Shaw says the style "suggests the simplicity of a man who
had never read a book in his life except the Bible." I find this
untrue. His vocabulary is more complex than Shaw's. He'll use,
with logic rightness, as word doctors now find, coin all the

way from ancient English times to our own American times. He is an inventor, a coiner of words in his own right. His style is intellectually complex. At times a single sentence carries four or five loads of thought. Curiously enough, records at libraries prove that he was an unusual student of the language. His use of the Bible is given to show that its descriptions are correct, but it also shows a true poet's appreciation of the Bible.

One must be careful with Shaw's comments. Shaw often reminds one of the "brights," the "brilliants" one meets in cultured centers, who for a while capture the limelight and are known as a particular generation's geniuses. They are just smart enough to notice that things are complicated, and they resent simple statements, and think simplicity naive. In most cases they are right. Except that such men as Einstein and Schrödinger see a step beyond them, to the point where complexity once more focuses into single patterns.

How could Doughty, the poet of "Himalayan magnificence," have avoided putting poetry into *Arabia Deserta*, a volume it took him ten years to write from scanty notes and a very brief diary?

Doughty made Arabia and early Britain so real for me that I am often lonesome for these lands and those times, as lonesome as I am for the days of my own youth. Often as I walk around on my yard here, or in the cities, whole Doughty scenes arise in my mind, and my heart beats, and my eyes cloud over in memory. Yes, I lived then.

May 27, 1947

A Modest Proposal Concerning the "Rume"

Behold! I do not give lectures, or a little charity;
When I give, I give myself.

—Walt Whitman

Let me begin by saying that I have trouble calling certain of my books novels.* And if I read the record right, I am not the only one who has that difficulty. Conrad, Faulkner, Joyce, D. H. Lawrence, Mann, Melville, Wolfe, to mention a few, also were reluctant to call certain of their works "novels."

As a start I'd like to take two steady looks at this difficulty of mine: first by examining the term "novel" as to its fitness to do the job given it; second, by examining the objects or particulars it is supposed to find its meaning in. And I propose to take the steady looks from a personal point of view, that is, as it seems to me, both as reader-liver and as writer-liver of "novels."

To me, the term "novel" has a cheap look and a cheap sound and a cheap etymology. It has seemed cheap to me as far back as I can remember. I have never liked it, both before I began writing and after. I happen to like words that have roots, both

---

*Webster says:
> Novel [OF. (nouvel, nouveau), fr. L. novellus, dim. of novus new.] A fictitious prose tale of considerable length in which characters and actions professing to represent those of real life are portrayed in a plot.

Abel Chevalley in his *Le Roman Anglais de Notre* (Oxford University Press, New York) writes, in the next best definition to be found:
> Novel (une fiction en prose d'une certaine étendue) a fiction in prose of a certain extent.

into reality and into the past, that give the appearance of having direct contact with life or nature, as if the word itself were the flower or the face of a growing process or stalk whose origin goes back to roots which get their start in the soil. "Novel" does not have nor can ever have that rich texture of meaning for me. I am all too aware that in the first place it is a word borrowed from another language (which in itself is not too serious an objection provided the Anglo-Saxon does not have a candidate of its own for the job), that in the second place it was originally employed as an emergency or temporary word (the "novel" tells of the strange, of the new, of that which has not been written about before) (which again is not too serious an objection provided that as a temporary fill-in it is able to play the role of the regular), and that in the third place it is an abstract term or a clerk's term that has to be re-defined or recharged or refilled with meaning each time a newcomer wants to use it (which makes it a sort of empty can or container rather than, say, a tree or a plant.) (Though of course I realize that it is sometimes an advantage to have elastic terms. They help make order, give meaning, to a field of disparate objects or things. But there is a point at which too much elasticity is a definite hindrance. And I'm afraid that that is what has happened with the term "novel." It includes too much, to a point where a category becomes a miscellany.)

For me the term "novel" has none of that passionate and holy quality which "rime," "sage" (sagu, sawe), "wordhoard" had for the old Frisian-Anglo-Saxons when they spoke of the written word. It does not even hit like the latinate words "bible," "chronicle," "testament" do. And it seems to me that if an author is serious about his calling, he should use terms describing it that evoke at least a little reverence. God knows that in these days of cheap and expendable life we need to ring all the holy bells we can.

But perhaps this term "novel" has this inutile quality for me because of the kind of background and the kind of life I have had. I am a young man of Frisian descent born and raised in a midland American community. As such I have been trained to have little or no time for frippery, for nonsense, for junk. Ideas, books, things, people, must be "real" for me. When I'm asked to choose between "grace" and "point" I choose "point" every time since "grace" assumes that "grace" really in the fine does represent "point," just as "breeding" and "aristocracy" assume that "breeding" really in the fine does represent "superior brains" or "singing brains" or "poetic brains," that "breeding" can reproduce Plato's "philosopher-kings" generation after generation. In any case, I try not to carry around any foolish or unnecessary baggage. I have approximately (and optimistically) but some seventy years to spend on this earth and haven't got the time to waste if I want to come within a thousandth of living my potential.

In examining the particulars or the books the term "novel" is supposed to find its meaning in, I may best be able to make my point by describing my own dilemma when I came to naming my books. The titles came of themselves, arose naturally out of the material, as all good titles should, but the answer to the question "what is it?" did not come too easily.

In the spring of 1944, when my first book, *The Golden Bowl* (title from the Bible as quoted by one of the characters and not from noble Henry James) (my first title for the book was *The Golden Bowl Be Broken* — would that I had kept it!), was ready for publication, I was faced with the problem of giving it a name. "Was it a 'novel' or not?" The publisher had to know. The dust jacket at least had to say what it was. Very grudgingly, because I couldn't think of anything better, or anything equally serviceable, I had to let him tag it as was customary, "a novel," so that he could send it on its way.

But when my second book, *Boy Almighty,* was ready in 1945, I objected to its being called "a novel." For I felt that while *Bowl* could be called one (it was "made up," it was a narration of something that might have happened to me, a pointing up of a "life" I had not lived myself, "a fictitious prose narrative"), *Boy* was a personal and a vital truth, a testament of suffering and of faith in life, a tale with roots that went back to my private inner life, an odyssey created out of my very flesh and blood, as if the words were my cells and the phrases my tissues and the paragraphs my organs and the book my body.

When I expressed my idea on the matter to my publisher, he snapped, "So what? People still call such books 'novels.'" That had me stopped. People did call such creations "novels." They lacked a term just as I did. And so, after some talk together, I finally let him call it "a novel" so he could catalogue and peddle it, while he in turn compromised a bit by writing on the jacket the curious introductory phrase, *"Boy Almighty* is the saga, chronicle, scripture, what you will, of a human being . . . ."

From that day on, I set my mind to the task of finding a new term for the kind of book *Boy Almighty* was and of defining the area the term was to describe. Moreover, I felt that once I found the term it would also serve to define the term "novel" as it applied to my book, *The Golden Bowl,* or better yet, perhaps help me and others invent a new term for that category also.

During the next three years, I worked *This Is the Year* (1947) and *The Chokecherry Tree* (1948) into shape and had both published. Fortunately, both books were similar in kind to *Bowl,* not to *Boy,* and both were, more or less, "novels" as Dickens, Dreiser, Lewis, and Warren, to list a few, wrote them.

With those two books out of the way, I took up the next project, *Wanderlust,* a trilogy (*The Primitive, The Brother, The Giant,* whose working title was *World's Wanderer,* from Doughty), a project that had been brewing in still another corner of my mind as well as in separate and ever-fattening notebooks) for many years. Here, truly, I was back in the *Boy* tradition, only more so than ever, because I was not only taking the major arch of my life (as lived so far) as the germ idea for the work, but was also externalizing it, making of it an "objective correlative," so as to catch overtones of vital personal experience and, if possible, to express a truth larger than my life truth. Thus while I worked away at the note-taking and the planning and the dreaming and the writing of *Wanderlust,* I also kept a steady eye out for candidate terms.

Some of the terms that passed under my scrutiny were amen, autode (auto and ode), autogram, echode (echo and ode), egode (ego and ode), egogram, egologue, epode (epic and ode), gospel, gram, graph, homode, homolude, life, monode (mono and ode), monolude, monosode, proem, rune, selah, spel, spiel, sonode, tablet, telling, testament, voice, witnessing, and many many others.

Of that entire list only two caught my eye. They were "autogram" and "rune." Both had the sound and the feel of terms that hit close to expressing what I was doing in *Boy Almighty* and *Wanderlust*.

But both also had defects. "Rune" already had a well-defined place in our language, and so, no matter how apt, would always be wrestling with its old meanings. "Autogram" seemed too latinate for me, too clumsy, and a term that did not fit too well with its brothers-to-be such as epic, poem, rime, roman, saga.

Meantime, while trying to decide on the new term, I had a look around to see how my fellow "novelists" were making out with the old term "novel." To my surprise I found that they were just as unsure about its use as I was. Some denied that they wrote "novels," some hedged on its use, others admitted they wrote "novels" but admitted it with the air of not knowing precisely what they meant by it, some tried to get around it by claiming they wrote "historical novels," or "biographical novels," or "romantic novels," or "Gothic novels," or "autobiographical novels" (very few admitted this one, though many were quite eager to point out that others wrote such), or "bucolic novels," or "picaresque novels," or "satirical novels," or "novels of manners," etc. There seemed to be, to quote Shakespeare's Polonius, all sorts of novels, novels of "tragedy, comedy, history, pastoral, pastoral-comical, historical-pastoral, tragical-historical, tragical-comical-historical-pastoral, scene individable, or poem unlimited: Seneca cannot be too heavy nor Plautus too light."

When I went to the critics (it is occasionally permissable for an original writer to consult the critics, permissable as long as he does not go to them for advice on his own work) and the scholars (a fine place for the original writer to go to since the scholar almost always helps open a door to the past—how could I ever have read merry majestic Chaucer without the help of wonderful Walter W. Skeat?), I found even more confusion despite an increase in learning and research. The definitions they gave were either too narrow or too broad, too shallow

or too deep, too lofty or too pedestrian. No matter how brilliantly
one critic might work out the perfect definition for the term
"novel," another critic in equally brilliant fashion would come
along to demolish it and in turn set up his rules for the term
"novel." And so on and on. My search as well as the critic-
scholar's search for the "true novel" began to look like a search
for the swamp "will o' the wisp" by a posse of hunters, each
hunter carrying a lantern and yelling "I see it!" "Here! here!"
"No, now it's over here!" "No, no, now it's over here!" with the
"will o' the wisp" vanishing the moment light approached it —
except those times when the "wisp" turned out to be another
hunter's lantern.

Yet, despite all the uncertainty, I began to notice as I went
along that certain of the "first source" or the "novels" I was
reading began to fall into the same two general kinds of writing
I found in my own work. One of the kinds, the *Wanderlust*
type, was a fairly definite kind, the other, the *This Is the Year*
type, was a little less so.

Perhaps I can best indicate what I mean by listing the
two kinds of books I thought I was finding:

Wanderlust type:
Butler, *The Way of All Flesh*
Cervantes, *Don Quixote*
Dickens, *David Copperfield*
Farrell, *Danny O'Neill*
Faulkner, *Sartoris*
Goethe, *Sorrows of Werther*
Joyce, *The Portrait of the Artist as a Young Man*
Lawrence, *Sons and Lovers*
Mann, *Buddenbrooks*
Maugham, *Of Human Bondage*
Thackeray, *Pendennis*
Wolfe, *Look Homeward, Angel.*

This Is the Year type:
Crane, *The Red Badge of Courage*
Dickens, *A Tale of Two Cities*
Dos Passos, *U.S.A.*

Farrell, *Studs Lonigan*
Faulkner, *As I Lay Dying*
Flaubert, *Madame Bovary*
Hamsun, *Growth of the Soil*
Lewis, *Arrowsmith*
Mann, *Joseph and His Brothers*
Steinbeck, *The Grapes of Wrath*
Thackeray, *Vanity Fair*
Zola, *Germinal*

In basic germ, tone, mood, strike, attack, strategy, throw there was, I felt, a difference, a big difference, between the two kinds of book.

The more I kept running into these two kinds of fiction, the more sure I was that I was right to want to distinguish between them. Thus, I continued to hunt for the term. Beg, borrow, or steal it, as the old saw goes, I had to have it, had to have a convenient term to help me explore a promising area of creation. I felt that the more firmly and solidly I had in mind the outlines of the medium or form I was to work in, the more freedom I would have. (The absence of boundaries, or outlines, leaves one in a world of nothing, or rather, with "no thing" since, first, the word "world" no longer applies, second, there is "no thing" without boundaries.)

My list of possible terms grew and grew until I had some twenty pages scribbled full, including those mentioned above. And still, out of them all, "rune" and "autogram" were the only ones to catch my eye.

For some reason "rune" continued to be the most attractive of the two, though, truth to tell, there had been no more than the usual mention of the word either in my general reading or in the Frisian (the language of my eldfathers) I was studying during hobbytime, nor had it ever been used in my boyhood, the time when impressions on the human mind are supposed to be the most powerful and lasting. For some reason it continued to ring in my mind like a bell heard tolling far in the distance.

I decided to concentrate on the term.

In Webster I found:

Rune, (roon;242), [A.S., Dan., and O.N.; A. S. *run,* a rune, a secret, a mystery; akin to Dan. *rune,* O.N. *run,* O.H.G. & Goth. *rune,* a secret, secret colloquy, O.Ir. *run,* a secret, and L. *rumor,* noise, report, *raucus,* hoarse, Skr. *rauti,* he roars, cries. Cf. *alraun, raucous, roun, rumor, rut* of animals.]

1. Character or signs of alphabet.

2. Speech; conversation; language, counsel, Obs.

3. Mystery, espec. as connected with the invisible world of spirits; hence, craft in magic, magic.

4. Pl. Old Finnish poetry expressed in runes; sometimes Old Norse poetry. Combinations are: rune-bearing, runecraft, runefolk, runesmith, rune-inscribed, runesword.

Then I glanced in the *New English Dictionary,* Oxford:

Rune (I) Obs. forms: 1. *ryne, rene,* 2. *rine, rune.* [O.E. *ryne, rene,* Old Frisic *rene,* f, *run* - the weak grade of the stem *rin* - *Run* v.]

1. Course, onward movement, espec. of the heavenly bodies; running (of persons).

2. A flow of blood.

3. A watercourse.

Rune (II) (rūn) [In origin the same word as Roun, mystery, etc., but in sense 1 adopted in the 17 cent. (through Danish writers on Northern antiquities) from ON (norse) and Icel. *rún,* pl. *runar,* later *runir* (Da. *rune,* pl. *runer;* Sw. *runa,* pl. *runor*). Hence also G. and Du. *rune,* pl. *runen,* F. *rune,* pl. *runes,* etc. In sense 2 the immediate source is the Finnish *runo,* itself an adoption of the ON. word.]

1. A letter or character of the earliest Teutonic alphabet, which was most extensively used (in various forms) by the Scandinavians and Anglo-Saxons. Also, a similar character or mark having mysterious or magical powers attributed to it.

2. a. An incantation or charm denoted by magic signs. Obs.

   b. A Finnish poem, or a division of a poem, esp. one of the separate songs of the Kalevala. Also incorrectly applied to the old Scandinavian poems.

   c. Any song, poem, or verse.

3. Attributes and combinations: rune-bearer, -carver, -rister (cutter), -writer; runc bearing; rune-clog, -stone, -stick; rune-craft, -folk, -magic, -smith, -word.

Next I turned to Skeats' *Etymological Dictionary of the English Language:*

Rune, one of the old characters used for cutting inscriptions on stone. (E.) M.E. *rune,* counsel, a letter, Layamon, 253332, 25340, 32000; later *roun,* whence *roun* or *round* in Shakespeare; see Roun. −A.S. *rún,* a rune, mystery, secret colloquy, whisper; Grein, ii. 385. The orig. sense seems to be 'whisper' or 'buzz'; hence, a low talk, secret colloquy, a mystery, and lastly a writing, because written characters were regarded as a mystery known to the few. + Icel. *rún,* a secret, a rune. + Goth.

runa, a mystery, counsel. +O.H.G. *rúna*, a secret, counsel; whence
G. *raunen*, to whisper. B. All from the Teut. base RÛ-NA, a murmur,
whisper; formed (like Lat. *rummor*, a rumor) from RU, to buzz, hum,
bray; see *Rumour*. Der. *Run-ic*, *roun*.

The words "runa," "roun," "rumor," all intrigued me, so I
looked up RU in Skeats' List of Aryan Words (in the back
of his *Etymological Dictionary*, and discovered:

RU, to sound, cry out, bray, yell; whence the extended form *RUG*,
to bellow, Sanskrit *ru*, to sound, bray, yell; Gk. ẃ-pú-eojal, to bellow;
Lat. *ru-mor*, a noise, *rau-cus*, hoarse; A.S. *ru-n*, a rune (orig. a murmur,
whisper, secret.) Also Lat. *rug-ire*, to roar; *ru-men (rug-men)*, the throat.
Ex. *rumour, ruminate, rut; rune, rumble*.

As I pored over these definitions, I began to feel that
I was hot on the trail, that the game was just ahead and around
the next turn. I began to feel like a Lewis and Clark about
to trek into a Great Northwest, like a Balboa about to discover
a Pacific, like a jetplane pilot about to punch through into
a supersonic zone. It had always been there and only needed
exploring.

I looked up all the derivations of the word "rune," noting
that "rut" originally meant the noise of deer in rut-time, that
"rugitus" once meant the roaring of lions, that "rumor" struck
a glancing blow at what I wanted, that "ruminate" in one sense
made a bathic strike at it and in another sense a direct approach to it, that "rumen" in Latin meant "the throat."

It was at "rumen" that my eye really stopped, perhaps
because it was so close in appearance and sound to the constellation of such literary terms as "theme," "poem," "mime,"
"roman," "drama," "tome," "volume," and to such hoary and
evocative words as "time" and "clime." It occurred to me to
drop the letter "n" from the word. And then it was as if a
lightblue northwest breeze was clearing my literary skies for
that day. For there it was, "rume," a forceful yet tuneful word.
Quickly I looked to see if it had ever been used before. There
was only one reference to it in the *Oxford English Dictionary*,
and that was a misspelling by Shakespeare for the word "room."

So I had it. A newly coined word that almost rhymed with
word "poem." Here was now a neglected shoot growing out of

an old and powerful cluster of roots that could become mature in its own right. Given time and usage a possible tree. The rume. After deep rumination, after long inner musing, a man cries out, "RU-es" "rhues" forth among men that thus and so has he felt about living. "I was here," he cries, "and I had this happen to me, and this I did, and these things I saw and discovered, and this is what I think it all means in these times and in this place on this earth in this galaxy in this universe."

Yes. That was it. I had been trying to write a rume in *Boy Almighty,* was writing one in *Wanderlust.* On occasion I wrote rumes. So had Wolfe (or, tried to in his blind way), so had Tolstoi in *The Kreutzer Sonata,* Maugham in *Of Human Bondage.* (When I first ran into Maugham's character Philip I had the very odd feeling that Philip's limp did not belong to him or did not become him, but that instead his real defect seemed to be that he had trouble talking. It wasn't until later that I discovered Maugham the author had once had some sort of speech difficulty. Had Maugham been able to work out of his auto-truth instead of beside it, what might he not have made had he struck out boldly to write a rume. He might have made out of the speech defect something larger than just a handicap, he might have made some telling and intimate remark to the effect that his whole generation had trouble talking frankly and openly, that perhaps his whole race or species had a speech difficulty. The germ-idea lay there in his very flesh. Perhaps too had Maugham deliberately set out to write a rume, he might have become more of an openhearted and openhanded man, a man such as Gide became in his *Journals.* Perhaps too had Thomas Wolfe known about the rume, we could have had clear smokeless bright flames from him instead of the fuliginous conflagration we got.) *Boy Almighty* and *Wanderlust* were rumes, the first a single rume, the second a trilogy of rumes. Because I felt when I worked at them that I was doing something holy and passionate, doing something with the great high seriousness that the writers of the Bible felt when they bent bloodied feather to papyrus, like the old runesters felt when they slashed their single strokes on tree or stone, thinking to themselves as they did so: "Here, this now, this we must record. Today. It is not all of our lives. But it catches up as much as a single stroke

can what is most us in this singular moment." Cuts in the
stone of time. *The Golden Bowl, This Is the Year, The
Chokecherry Tree*, on the other hand, were more in the way
of being invention, of being tales of speculation, of being accounts of the fancied life of others.

This distinction is somewhat similar to the one found in
stonecutting. The hewing of architectural monuments into rooted
rocks (such as Charles Montagu Doughty saw at Medain Salih
and about which he observes in his majestic Himalayan *Travels
in Arabia Deserta*, "where art is seen thus in strange alliance
with the chaotic eternity of nature") is like the cutting of a
rume into the mountain of autobiography (a lonely mountain
accidentally singularized by some turmoil of nature's to which
our attention has been directed) while the shaping of a statue
or statues or a temple out of loose stones and boulders is like
the fashioning of "novels" out of a field of facts and experiences
not necessarily the author's. Which is another way of saying
that a rume-writer (or rumester, or rumerister, or rumesmith,
or rumemaker) sets out to give a view all the way back to
the fundaments of a reality he finds in himself, that he sets
out to make a direct tap into the nature of Old Man Reality.
(Like all figures of speech, the foregoing suggests the direction
of the argument, not its proof or even its exemplification.)

Rume.

In the following days that part of my mind which occasionally enjoys being pessimistic and cynical tossed up all sorts
of snide comments to discredit the discovery. Even the cautious
side of me threw up warnings all over the place that academes
would deride my contribution since they might feel that I was
trying to break up their neat little doctoral pedagogical
categories, that authors themselves, who had a vast investment
in the old scheme of things, would thumb their brains at me.
The cynical side of me especially warned that New York City's
rootless witcrackers, Tom and Tabby Sophisticat, "the screwed-
up New York brights," the boys and gals who make puns out
of the helpless stumblings of their own grandmothers, would
try to sneer me out of countenance. Even the hypochondriac
side of me which is always fussing about throat colds and chest
pains and gallbladder twinges tried to get rid of the term by

pointing out that it sounded too much like the word "rheum" and that it might lend itself to endless balloon-pricking puns.

I tried it out on a fellow craftsman, a writer young enough to be still interested in change. He liked it; wanted to use it immediately.

I tried it out on a publisher. He wondered if it might not give my work a precious air, that it would set up another barrier between my work and potential buyers.

Yet, despite various heats and freezes, rains and droughts, winds and calms, the term "rume" lived in my mind. I just simply could not get rid of it. It lived. It was a truth I could not destroy. It had outgrown me. It no longer was mine to give or withhold.

Of course once I was awake to the problem of what to call *Wanderlust,* awake to the idea of the rume, I began to notice in my reading that other writers were throwing out hints on the same theme.

Among the many pertinent suggestions I found were the following:

Critic V.S. Pritchett wrote in his *The Living Novel:* "It is interesting to contrast a very consciously made novel like Bennett's *The Old Wives' Tale* with Lawrence's *Sons and Lovers.* Both novels cover a life-time of family life and truthfully recreated English sentiment. Bennett feels from the outside. He puts down what he has known. He sympathizes, pities and invents. And he condescends. In the mind's eye the characters of any novel can be measured for height, and Bennett's characters always seem to me small people, miniatures seen from a height, as Bennett looks down upon them on the writing-table. The characters of *Sons and Lovers* are less complete in their detail, there is a blur in many of them so that we are not always sure of the focus; but they are life-size. They are as big as Lawrence is. He has got inside them until they have grown to normal size. We *follow* Constance in *The Old Wives' Tale;* we walk *with* Mrs. Morel in *Sons and Lovers.* We are as uncertain as she is, from day to day . . . . *Sons and Lovers* goes wrong when Lawrence begins telling lies, that is to say when he starts arguing, as in the Miriam episode, which is often boring and obscure. English novelists are afraid and ashamed

of adolescence because, later in life, to be serious about oneself
is considered priggish and conceited. The young prig is taken
at his own valuation in French literature—see Stendhal and
Flaubert's *Sentimental Education*—and is generally admired
because the French respect the gradual formation of the mature
nature. They are also interested in the formation of artists.
But Lawrence grew up in a community and indeed in a country
where the biography of an imagination embarrasses and is despis-
ed .... *Sons and Lovers* is patchy—it was rewritten—and
English novelists who write autobiographical novels seem to
plunge in and have no idea where to bring their life story to
an end."

Glenway Wescott wrote of F. Scott Fitzgerald in *The Crack-
Up:* "...The great thing about Fritzgerald was his candor; ver-
bal courage; simplicity. One little man with eyes really witnessing; objective in all he uttered, even about himself in a subjec-
tive slump; arrogant in just one connection, for one purpose
only, to make his meaning clear. The thing, I think, that a
number of recent critics have most disliked about him is his
confessional way, the personal tone, the tete-a-tete or man-to-
man style, first person singular. He remarked it himself in *The
Crack-up:* 'There are always those to whom all self-revelation
is contemptible.' I on the other hand feel a real approval and
emulation of just that; and I recommend that all our writers
give it serious consideration. It might be the next esthetic issue
and new mode of American letters. It is American enough; our
greatest fellows, such as Franklin and Audubon and Thoreau
and Whitman, were self-expressers in so far as they knew
themselves. This is a time of greater knowledge, otherwise worse;
an era which has as many evil earmarks as, for example, the
Renaissance: awful political genius running amok and clashing,
migrations, races whipped together as it were by a titanic egg-
beater, impatient sexuality and love of stimulants and cruelty,
sacks, burnings, and plagues. Fine things eventually may be
achieved amid all this, as in that other century. I suggest revela-
tions of man as he appears to himself in his mirror—not as
he poses or wishes or idealizes—as one thing to try a revival
of, this time. Naked truth about man's nature in unmistakable
English .... And for clarity's sake, let us often use, and sanction

the use of, words of one syllable. The shortest and most poetic is the personal pronoun: *I*. The sanctified priest knows that, he says, *credo,* and the trustworthy physician only gives his opinion, not a panacea. The witness in the courtroom does not indulge in the editorial we; the judge and the lawyers will not allow it; and indeed, if the case is important, if there is life or liberty or even a large amount of money at stake, not even supposition or hearsay is admitted as evidence."

Thoreau wrote in the opening pages of his *Walden:* "In most books, the *I,* or first person, is omitted; in this it will be retained; that, in respect to egotism, is the main difference. We commonly do not remember that it is, after all, always the first person that is speaking. I should not talk so much about myself if there were anybody else whom I knew as well. Unfortunately, I am confined to this theme by the narrowness of my experience. Moreover, I, on my side, require of every writer, first or last, a simple and sincere account of his life; and not merely what he has heard of other men's lives; some such account as he would send to his kindred from a distant land; for if he has lived sincerely, it must have been in a distant land to me."

Thoreau also wrote in his essay *Life Without Principle:* "At a lyceum, not long since, I felt that the lecturer had chosen a theme too foreign to himself, and so failed to interest me as much as he might have done. He described things not in or near to his heart, but toward his extremities and superficies. There was, in this sense, no truly central or centralizing thought in the lecture. I would have had him deal with privatest experience, as the poet does. The greatest compliment that was ever paid me was when one asked me what *I thought,* and attended to my answer. I am surprised, as well as delighted, when this happens, it is such a rare use he would make of me, as if he were acquainted with the tool. Commonly, if men want anything of me, it is only to know how many acres I make of their land — since I am a surveyor — or, at most, what trivial news I have burdened myself with. They never will go to law for my meat; they prefer the shell. A man once came a considerable distance to ask me to lecture on Slavery; but on conversing with him, I found that he and his clique expected

seven eighths of the lecture to be theirs, but only one eighth
mine; so I declined. I take it for granted, when I am invited
to lecture anywhere — for I have had a little experience in that
business — that there is a desire to hear what *I think* on some
subject, though I may be the greatest fool in the country, and
not that I should say pleasant things merely, or such as the
audience will assent to; and I resolve, accordingly, that I will
give them a strong dose of myself. They have sent for me,
and engaged to pay for me, and I am determined that they
shall have me, though I bore them beyond all precedent . . . . So
now I would say something similar to you, my readers. Since
you are my readers, and I have not been much of a traveler,
I will not talk about people a thousand miles off, but come
as near home as I can. As the time is short, I will leave out
all the flattery, and retain all the criticism . . . . Let us consider
the way in which we spend our lives."

John A. Kouwenhoven said in his *Made in America:* "Think,
for a moment, of the eminent American writers of the nineteenth century and notice how many of them are difficult to
classify in terms of the literary forms in which they worked.
Was Melville a novelist? Certainly not in the sense that
Thackeray, Flaubert, or even Tolstoy were novelists. *Typee,*
Omoo, and *Mardi* are not novels by any definition, and *Moby*
Dick itself is — in form — altogether unlike any other ever written, a compound of tragic drama, treatise on whaling technology,
allegory, philosophical speculations, adventure narrative, and
seamanship manual. Were Emerson and Thoreau essayists and
poets? But Emerson's essays are really oral lectures, and his
stature as a writer depends fully as much on the *Journals* as
upon the essays; it is the *Journals* after all which come closest
to being the kind of 'Montaigne's book' he wanted, 'full of fun,
poetry, business, divinity, philosophy, anecdote, smut.' Thoreau's
masterpiece, *Walden,* is part poetic record of a personal adventure, part a philosophy of rebellion against social conformity,
and part the record of a reporter-naturalist. For years Whitman's *Leaves of Grass* was only reluctantly admitted to be
poetry. ('Confused, inarticulate, and surging in a mad kind of
rhythm which sounds as if hexameters were trying to bubble
through sewage,' Professor Barrett Wendell of Harvard's English

department called it in his *Literary History of America* in 1900.) The author of *Huckleberry Finn, Life on the Mississippi, Personal Recollection of Joan of Arc,* and *Roughing It* is hard to label in terms of forms he worked in. Even Hawthorne and Poe, who on first thought are easily classified as writers of fiction, were the creators of a new form: the modern short story."

Malcolm Cowley the critic noted in his introduction to the *Portable Faulkner:* "Faulkner is another author who has to wait for the spirit and the voice. Essentially he is not a novelist, in the sense of not being a writer who sets out to observe actions and characters, then fits them into the architectural framework of a story . . . he is an epic or bardic poet in prose . . . ."

John Horne Burns the "novelist" said in his *The Gallery:* "They [the Neapolitan artists] told me that they worked from their hearts, after they'd tested those hearts. They said that every human heart contained a key to other hearts. But the artist's gaze must be within, after a long time of looking about outside. These Neapolitan artists told me that a man knows if he ever puts down the truth. It hurts as it's being torn out of the heart. But once set down, undeformed and whole, it will lie on the paper forever – more or less. It should never be warped into what the artist thinks *may* or *should* be the truth . . . . The American artists had no such counsel to give me. They spoke of fitting oneself into movements. They talked of periods and tendencies and lucky shots and literary agents."

Novelist Wallace Stegner was moved to write in *The Saturday Review of Literature* (April 22, 1950): ". . . too often overlooked is something which I can call only 'intense acquaintance.' In all our wandering through real or fictional worlds it is probably ourselves to seek, and since that encounter is impossible we want the next best thing – the completely intimate contact which may show us another like ourselves. I am willing if necessary to risk condemnation as an advocate of what C. S. Lewis has called the 'personal heresy,' though it is certainly no such biographical hunger as Mr. Lewis deplores that I speak of here. It is utterly irrelevant that Milton misused his daughters or that Conrad had a habit of flipping bread pellets around the dinner table. What is relevant is the artist himself, or his refined and distilled spirit, the totality of his understanding. Acquaintance on that level is a thing found very rarely in life, but a book which has profoundly and intensely moved us is a most intimate experience, perhaps more intimate than marriage and more revealing than fifty years of friendship. We can make closer contact in fiction than in reality; more surely than we know the secrets of our friends we know how this writer who is something like ourselves looks upon himself, how he fronts his life, how he, another waif in a bewildering world, has made out to survive and perhaps be at peace. Ultimately, I am convinced, he is what we read for. The work of art is not a gem, as some schools of criticism would insist, but truly a lens. We look through it for the purified and honestly offered spirit of the artist. The ghosts of meaning that flit past the windows of his fictional house wear his face. And the reward of a lifetime of reading is a rich acquaintanceship with those gentle or powerful or rebellious or acceptant, those greatly mixed and humanly various but always greatly human ghosts."

E. M. Forster the "novelist" in his *Aspects of the Novel* mentioned with approval an anonymous scholar who "classified novels by their tones. 'There are only two tones, personal and impersonal.' And having given examples of each he [the scholar] grew pensive and said, 'Yes, but you must have genius too, or neither tone will profit.'"

The Foreword to Hemingway's *Green Hills of Africa* announced: "Unlike many novels, none of the characters or incidents in this book is imaginary. Any one not finding sufficient love interest is at liberty, while reading it, to insert whatever love interest he or she may have at the time. The writer has attempted to write an absolutely true book to see whether the shape of a country and the pattern of a month's action can, if truly presented, compete with a work of the imagination."

Joseph Conrad wrote in his rume *Heart of Darkness* (Marlow speaking): " 'I don't want to bother you much with what happened to me personally,' he began, showing in this remark the weakness of many tellers of tales who seem so often unaware of what their audience would best like to hear; 'yet to understand the effect of it on me you ought to know how I got there, what I saw, how I went up that river to the place where I first met the poor chap. It was the farthest point of navigation and the culminating point of my experience. It seemed somehow to throw a kind of light on everything about me – and into my thoughts. It was sombre enough, too – and pitiful – not extraordinary in any way – not very clear either. No, not very clear. And yet it seemed to throw a kind of light.' "

W. Somerset Maugham remarked in his *A Writer's Notebook:* "Truth is not only stranger than fiction, it is more telling. To know that a thing actually happened gives it a poignant touch, a chord, which a piece of acknowledged fiction misses. It is to touch this chord that some authors have done everything they could to give you the impression that they are telling the plain truth."

Bernard Shaw in his *Sixteen Self Sketches* wrote of Goethe (the Goethe who made of his own life his major work and who said of his own poems that they were fragments of a great confession and who is reported to have said, "If I were young and daring enough I would purposely violate all these technical crochets, I would use alliteration, assonance, false rime, to suit my caprice and purpose"): "The best autobiographies are confessions; but if a man is a deep writer all his works are confessions. One of the greatest men who ever attempted an autobiography was Goethe. After his childhood, which is the readablest part of even the worst autobiography, his attempts to escape from his subject are pitiable. He takes refuge in sketches of all the Toms, Dicks, and Harrys he knew in his youth, persons utterly unmemorable, until the book drops from your hand and is not picked up again."

André Gide noted in his *Journals:* "I often imagine . . . a preface . . . that would set forth what I mean by fictional objectivity, that would establish two sorts of novels, or at least two ways of looking at and depicting life, which in certain novels (Dostoyevsky's) are joined. The first, exterior and commonly called objective, which begins by visualizing others' acts and events and then interprets them. The second, which begins by paying attention to emotions and thoughts and runs the risk of being powerless to depict anything that the author has not first felt himself . . . . A book really interests me only if I feel it born of some inner necessity and if that necessity can find some echo in me. Many authors write rather good books today who could write different ones that would be just as good. I do not feel any secret relationship between them and their work, and they themselves do not interest me; they remain *littérateurs* and instead of listening to their demon they listen to the public taste.... I came to understand that *objective depiction* often means a superficial representation; but, for a profound depiction, the poet must experience in himself what is to be the subject of his picture.... It is not at all that I feel more 'human' today than at the time when no trace of such preoccupations could be found in my work. I simply took care to forbid them access to it, judging that they had nothing to do with art. I am no longer so sure of this, nor that anything can and must remain foreign to art; it runs the risk of becoming, it necessarily becomes, artifice if what is closest to the artist's heart is banished from it."

Kenneth Burke wrote in his article "Three Definitions," published in *The Kenyon Review,* Spring, 1951:

"The third [definition] will be the narrowest. It was designed solely to provide a formula for Joyce's *Portrait of the Artist as a Young Man.* This single work was considered somewhat 'angelically,' as a kind all by itself. We say 'angelically,' thinking of Aquinas' doctrine that each individual angel is a distinct species, and the only member of its kind. But though we treat the work as *sui generis,* we necessarily define it in terms of some *classification.* Tentatively, we propose 'lyric novel' as the generic name for this work, considered as a species .... A serious prose narrative, imitating an agent's spiritual adventures, in the development of a new attitude, with its corresponding doctrine; it employs an intense, elevated, or otherwise exceptional diction (involving a principal of selectivity that makes it representative in the *culminative* sense rather than as tested by *statistical averages);* the unity of action centers in the unity of the main character, whose transformations coincide with the stages of the plot; like the lyric proper, it places great reliance upon sensory images, not merely for purposes of vividness (enargeia) but to serve structural ends (the images thus taking on "mythic" dimensions that transcend their specifically sensory significance); the seriousness of the agent and the magnitude of his trials serve to dignify the development towards which the work is directed."

Thus I felt my way along, writing and exploring and sifting my inner life, reading and exploring and sifting the inner life of other craftsmen.

Thinking that I might be able to come to a clearer understanding of what I meant by the term rume, I began to list various distinctions between the rume and the "novel" that occurred to me from time to time.

Here are a few of them:

Writing the rume is more the discovery and the channeling of an inward gusher; writing the "novel" is more the discovery and the description of gushers outside oneself.

Rumes are autobiographies made universal by exalting and transmuting personal agonies; "novels" are biographies made universal by exalting or transmuting other people's agonies.

The rume is the peculiarly intense and highly personal vision of a subject which comes out of what the artist feels in his heart; the "novel" is the dispassionate vision of a subject which comes out of what the artist sees in the hearts of others.

The rume is a passionate avowal; the "novel" is an objective statement.

With the rume the author comes forth as poet and prophet; with the "novel" the author comes forth as narrator and program commentator.

The rume has a natural inner consistency; the "novel" has an artifically imposed consistency.

The rume is the work of fiction built in retrospect out of materials gathered from personal experience; the "novel" is a work of fiction built in retrospect out of materials gathered from the lives of others.

The rume is a personal looking-within fiction in prose (usually) of a certain length; the "novel" is an impersonal looking-without fiction in prose of a certain length.

The rume is a narrative credo, usually in prose though occasionally or in part in free verse, of considerable length in which characters and actions representing those of real life are portrayed by means of a plot (or structure, or form, or symbol, or myth, or prophecy); a "novel" is a narrative impersonal tale, almost always in prose, of considerable length in which characters and actions representing those of real life are portrayed by means of a plot (or structure, or form, or symbol, or myth).

A writer is more likely to write rumes if he wants to give a truthful echo of his day as he felt it; or write "novels" if he wants to give a truthful echo of his day as he thinks others felt it.

The rumesmith is more likely to stick to the truth; the "novelist" to invent it.

The impetus of the rumester's creation is toward the true and the real; the impetus of the "novelist's" creation is toward the artificial.

The rumist takes a truth about himself as a particular and invests it with "singular" meaning. The "novelist" takes truths about others as particulars and invests them with "general" meaning.

The rumesmith takes the inner logic of his life as a model or central idea for a rume; the "novelist" takes the inner logic of the lives of others as a model or central idea for a novel.

The rumester starts out with a truth of his life and, using the building devices and skills society has at hand for him, constructs an edifice from his personal (and on occasion his general) knowledge and embellishes it with his imagination. The "novelist" starts with a truth he has found in the lives of others and, also using the building devices and skills society has at hand for him, constructs an edifice from his general (and on occasion his personal) knowledge and embellishes it with his imagination.

The rumist sits down in the middle of his life; the "novelist" sits down in the middle of the lives of others.

And so on and on.

As these distinctions and contrasted definitions kept coming to me, the concept of what a rume was began to exist ever more clearly and firmly in my mind, began to mean something so definite that I used it in my conversation with friends. And once they caught on to what I meant by it, they used it to describe "a certain type of novel." We knew instantly what was meant when we said, "So-and-so wrote rumes" or "So-and-so wrote 'novels.'" It was that simple. And, after all, that is really the final test: usage, practical applicability. Once the reader catches on to the term, it will help him when he wants to buy a certain type of book, to buy the "here-is-what-the-author-really-thinks-and-feels" kind of fiction as distinguished from the serious contemporary-history (or the frivolous, or the merely entertaining, or the historical, or the biographical) kind of fiction, to buy the author's narrative *Ecclesiastes,* his narrative *Isaiah,* instead of his entertaining *Decameron.* People still buy more non-fiction books than they do fiction. And there is a reason for it. They seek truth more than they do entertainment. And what can be better for these serious-minded folk than that they can buy an author's, a man's, own narrative *Job*?

Again and again it has happened to me, after having given a talk either before friends or strangers, that afterwards one of the friends or one of the strangers comes up to me and pulls me by the sleeve to ask, "I've heard what you've had to say before the others—but what do you really think when you're alone and off by yourself? What does your true heart say?" The first time the question was thrown at me I was stumped by it. I didn't particularly want to give the confidential questioner a detailed diary of my intimate thoughts. Yet I felt I should give him something. He was serious. He was earnest. He only lived once too and wanted to know. He wanted to be enlightened; not just entertained.

Well, I think I now have an answer for him. I can tell him to go search my rumes. Because the rumes contain both my selective story and my well-considered summation of how I have fronted life.

This means that my rumes are not mere autobiographical novels, that they are not literal transcripts of my life. (Though actually, even in strict autobiography, one does not tell what really happened, but what one remembers as having happened, or what one has been told has happened, or what one cares to remember as having happened, and this is in itself already a start toward art. Even in Thoreau's wonderful *Walden* and in Charles Montagu Doughty's *Travels in Arabia Deserta* we do not get strict diary or strict daily journal or strict autobiography. In those two works there is a great deal of imagination and selection at work. In both cases we get a general but altogether truthful account of two years of wandering.)

This means that my rumes are built up out of autobiographical elements, both as to material and as to structure. Mostly. And in particular with respect to the structure, with regard to the throw or the arch of the work. (It is that first complex, that first set of the frame, that first arrangement, which molds all subsequent incoming and outgoing experiences. It is like the story of the New Englanders setting their stamp on the Midlands with their town halls and such and then the later incoming ones having to fit themselves to it. It is that first jump, that first arch, that first construction that is important.) (Truth to tell, the prospect of writing an autobiography doesn't stir me very much. It sounds like a lot of hard plodding pedestrian work. But the thought of writing a rume delights me even as it agonizes me. Because it means to me that as a human being I have a chance to tell my personal deep truth with greater freedom than I would have if I were to write either "an autobiographical novel" or "an objective novel.")

This means that Thurs as a person in *Wanderlust* was created in my own image, after my own likeness. This means that the life or the span of life of Thurs was created after my own span or way of life. In the beginning there was my life, or the "real life," or the "first" life; and then there was Thurs's life, or the "New Life" (Aristotle's "imitation"), or the "second" life. (Like God, an author can create a man after his own image.)

This means that to write *Wanderlust* I deliberately set out to examine my self and my life record, that I approached it freely, even boldly (instead of obliquely as in the old days when it wasn't considered "good taste" to write autobiographically), to seek a curve or an arch in it (after a few years of living almost any thinking person begins to see lines and meanings and echoes developing in it as if it had been laid down beforehand by God or by a supra-reasoning being), and, finding the arch, finding "God's meaning in it," proceeded to make it the backbone or the structure of a work of art. (In the old days the "novelist" who willynilly found himself using his own life as a model all too often tried to hide what really happened. He was afraid to create "out of what had happened.")

This means that I have found in my life a certain meaning, a certain drift or structure, a distilled essence, which I think interesting and important enough to write about. (On the face of it why shouldn't my account of my own life be as interesting and as important as my account of someone else's? I have spent more time trying to understand who I am than I have trying to understand who any one else is. It has been my duty as a citizen of the human swarm to know "my self" as well as I can. This is "my self." I know it better than "thy self." And I can only and truly know more about "thy self" if thou wilt also write rumes of "thy self."

Let me repeat it. This does not mean that Thurs is exactly I, nor I Thurs, but it does mean that Thurs and Thurs's life grew out of my person and my personal experience.

For example (and this is written expressly for those maggot-savoring goooips who will go through *Wanderlust* with malicious intent to point the finger and say: "That Frederick-Thurs fellow has sure been around all right") when a hair falls from Thurs's head, or when he falls over a crack in the walk, or when he witnesses a sparrow falling from the skies, it does not mean that these things happened exactly and precisely the same way to the author—but it does mean that the author intended that "in these terrible times" such accidents and witnessings as he ran into and chose to record were to have a peculiar influence on Thurs's personality, that they were to help make him what he became in the end when he was "at the top of his battle." Which is another way of saying that the rumemaker wrote *Wanderlust* not to confess his individual sins (individual acts) but to confess his general emotions. Which is still another way of saying that while God-the-Author can be held accountable for any hairs falling from Frederick's head, Frederick the-creator in turn can be held accountable for any hairs falling from Thurs's head. (God's reasons for writing His rume or universe are given in His various *Postscripts* or *Bibles*.)

Too often when this kind of naked writing has appeared in "novels" the reader has been embarrassed. And he has been

embarrassed because he does not expect it in "novels," because
he has found such things only in laments, in lyrics, in poetry,
in testaments, only in holy self singings, only in products of
ecstasy, only in certain kinds of poetry precisely because the
poet has deliberately written them in. In that fine collection
titled *Criticism* by Mark Schorer the poet Stephen Spender
writes in "The Making of a Poem": "All one can do is to achieve
nakedness, to be what one is with all one's faculties and percep-
tions, strengthened by all the skill which one can acquire, and
then to stand before the judgment of time."

Rume-writing, ruming, is a witnessing. And while you do
not necessarily tell the literal truth of your life in a witnessing,
you do tell the real truth of it before men and before God.

It might be well, at this point, to tell a little just how
Thurs and his book did come about.

The germ for *Wanderlust* had its origin all the way back
in my childhood days when I craved for music and for a musical
instrument with a wild and unnatural hunger. But we were
poor, my parents could not afford either instrument or lessons,
so that the only things around on which I could exercise my
talent were a broken and discarded hired man's mouth organ
and my father's battered accordion. I blew and diddled a little
on both. When finally my aunt gave me her old violin, it was
too late, since by that time I already had huge work-stiffened
baseball-gnarled hands. (Even today to shake hands with me
is to thrust a hand into a bushel of warty potatoes.) Just the
same I continued to dream of music, I continued to be moved
more profoundly by a phrase of music than by a phrase of
poetry. (And, ah! even today this is true—certain themes in
music make me so wild inside I fear for others who may be
near me. I want to yell and strike out, to seize and crush,
to run, dance, and soar, to sing and poetize, to ascend the
heavens and direct the course of the sun and stars, to know
What Is is finally and at last, to become Old Man Reality
Himself.)

Somewhere along in the late '30's, sometime after I had
gotten my first real job with the old Minneapolis *Journal,* I
ran into a lonely man who had once been a fine musician, both
as interpreter and as creator of music, but who had left it.

In fact, he had also been a writer for a while, but had left that too. And, further, was about to leave the life he was living at the time I met him. In each case, his leaving of music, and his leaving of writing, and his leaving of politicking, had come about because the three forms of expression had gotten him into trouble.

I would not have observed all this, at least not so sharply and so clearly, if it had not been that I had observed almost the same thing about myself. I had left behind me two separate ways of living because my own demon had gotten me into trouble too. There was more than casual meaning in the fact that my demon had driven me to live, in the main, in three separate places—out of Siouxland into Michigan, out of Michigan into the New York City area, out of the New York City area into the Upper Midlands; that I had moved from home to college, from college to job-hunting, from job-hunting to settled occupation.

The more I considered these facts the more I saw that I had left a primitive (farm) kind of life for a Christian life, then had left a Christian life for a Marxist-Capitalist life, then had left a Marxist-Capitalist life for a Scientific life; that, in fact, what had happened to my creative bent was also the story or the synopsis of the general creative bent of American Man, as writer not only but also as musician and as theoretical scientist and as painter and as inventor—that whole constellation of creators—; that, even in greater fact, what had happened to me in this short life, was also the story of Man-on-earth. Systems and ways of life came and went, but Man, man as beast and man as social animal and man as social creature and man as creative soul, Man always seemed to survive no matter how many physical and mental and spiritual fevers he might have had, no matter how much wandering he might have done in this world. Man Himself was the Thing. The human being lasted "forever," if there was any "forever" at all, and conventions, religions, styles, way of life, momentummed through the sea of humanity like waves sliding through the ocean. (If I have any religion at all it is that I have reverence for the life I live as man. I'm glad to get at least this life, these seventy years.)

Thus the idea grew. I began to see all sorts of supra-meanings and subconscious-meanings both in my life and in the idea. In actual life I had five brothers and a father and mother, whom I loved very much, but amongst whom, as a singer, as a potential rumemaker, I always felt lonesome; in the idea *Wanderlust* I became myself-the-creator as fatherless and motherless and brotherless (as most creators have felt at times, even those born advantageously). Hence, Thurs became an orphan who was to spend a share of his life looking for his parents, just as Man-on-earth in his religious and anthropological researches spends a share of his time looking for primitive and pre-primitive ancestors. In actual life I had no sisters, only brothers; in the idea I became Thurs as raised in a for-boys-only orphanage. Et cetera.

All along I had been terribly aware of my size, of course. People just never let me forget it. I had got used to it, but my fellowman had not. I had even got used to his not-getting-used-to-it. But for purposes of art it had never meant very much to me — until one day I happened onto the idea that modern man, no matter what his individual height might be, was a giant too. His fist and arm had become, by means of extension, by means of his science, the fist and arm of great greatgiant, a greatgiant such as the earth had never known before. This became especially true when he constructed the successful atomic fission reactor, when he "successfully" dropped a bomb on Hiroshima. We all had a hand in that violence.

Then I had it. I could make a symbol, a myth, of my size. Because, actually, a creator is the average man, the animal man, writ-large. My troubles with my strength, my troubles with my personal demon-who-went-crazy-in-the-presence-of-music, my troubles as a lonely American and as lonely Earth artist, all these could be employed, employed straight, so that while telling one story I would also be telling a number of other stories — with the main story being Thurs's (Modern Man's) attempt to find a Love that could control his Violence. Hitherto, it had been possible for Mankind to survive self-generated violence, but the time was rapidly approaching when Mankind might not. Love had never been able to stay the violent hand of Man, but it was time that Love did or Man might perish. Love had to become strong enough and still remain Love. Love had to be sought in ourselves (who else has it?), and found, and developed, and made persuasive enough to stay Violence.

This did not mean that I made out of Thurs a six-foot-nine giant weighing two hundred fifty pounds because I measured and weighed that. But it did mean that I made of Thurs a giant of some considerable height and weight. Nowhere, as a matter of fact, nowhere in the entire trilogy is mention of Thurs's exact height or weight. This was done quite deliberately, and one hopes artistically, since I wanted each reader to image Thurs as being just a little larger than himself, so as to make the reader identify himself with "the great man he might have become," so that a five-footer would make of Thurs a six-footer, a six-footer would make of him a seven-footer, so that Thurs would become each man writ-large, as Thurs was for me once he was on his own. (Though I realize that if the reader is too small to begin with this whole scheme of identification backfires, since the small man's concern with "power" starts from his being on the receiving end of it rather than on his exercising it.)

There still remains the question, "But just how did you visualize Thurs? Does he look like your reflection in a mirror? Or what you think you look like?"

The answer to me happens to be surprisingly simple. Thurs came to me in dream; and not in daydream so much as in nightdream.

Let me explain. Thurs had occupied my thoughts for so many years that by the time I was about to begin writing *Wanderlust*, I could see him in my mind's eye. This in itself would have been enough to start with, since once the writer begins writing, mysterious processes associated with writing, "creativity," as Robert Penn Warren calls it, fill in whatever is lacking, the filling-in, of course, depending on the power of the mind of the creator. But I was fortunate enough to have a visitation in addition. Some two weeks before the first line was written I dreamt of him. And in my dream he showed up with rusty hair and a whitelock, with shoulders slightly bulkier than my own, with calves slightly heavier than mine, with a height that exceeded my own by just a little (actually, the reason I can't give his exact height is that I really don't know), with hands just as quick as mine, and without parents. He was so real that first night, I woke up. And I continued to see him in the dark black of our bedroom. And the name Thurs fit him exactly.

The next night I dreamt of him again. And the next night. He became so real to me during the writing of *Wanderlust* that often, when stepping for a second before a mirror to comb my hair, I had to blink twice to realize that I was not looking at myself as Thurs but myself as Frederick. And once I saw him out walking when I went for one of my strolls, saw him so real that I quit writing for a few days to make sure I wasn't going crazy. In fact, Thurs had such a power over me that he often made me write things I would ordinarily never express in public, let alone rarely think of in private. With the result that many passages in *Wanderlust* embarrass me a little, as they probably also do the reader—mostly because too much is revealed of our sinful or beastly nature, despite all our talk of being "human beings" or "children of God."

While I'm at it, I might also tell a little about where the other characters come from. Are they drawn from real life? Well, most of the marginal or secondary characters are, those that you meet but for a moment or two—though all of them have been subjected to a careful screening as they went through my mind. And the major characters? Well, they came from my nightdreams too. For example. There is Eva, wife of Thurs. Is she my wife? My answer is, No. Though in part, Yes. Let me explain. Obviously, the moment I were to marry my wife to Thurs, I could no longer report her as she appears to me. Because her life with Thurs would have been much different from (and perhaps happier than) the one she lived with me. Moreover, I couldn't marry her to Thurs, because my wife has a right to her own life, to make up her own mind about such matters. She has a life of her own. So what to do then? Well, find Thurs another. But from where? I, Frederick, have only been married once and that to Maryanna and so hence my knowledge of married life is limited.

I thought about this a long time, brewing on it, passing through my mind all the eligible women I had met at one time or another, marrying them in imagination to myself first, then to Thurs. Of course this was wrong, since I was making up Thurs's mind for him.

My mind did fasten on three women, however. One was an only daughter of a widow, both of whom were musicians. Another was also an only daughter of a divorcee who had gone for a while with a close friend of mine. Another was a girl in New England who I saw a couple of times for the length of a week and that only socially (very politely, at that). Somehow they felt one to my conscious mind, though each time I sought to make them one, they remained part of a composite. I also noted that these particular women, or this composite, seemed to be related in "feel" or in spirit to my mother (who I remember often as a slim pale goddess of evening singing hymns to herself at the organ in our parlor on a Sunday), to a neighbor girl who walked to country school with me, to a pale blond girl who went to town school with me, to another blond in high school whom I had worshipped from a distance, and to a tiny blond in college. Still, after all this, Thurs's wife-to-be, Eva Nordling as I had named her, wasn't alive to me.

What finally did it, I think, was my decision to have Thurs meet Eva in a library. Afterall, I thought, Thurs had once led Hero, his college sweetheart, from a library on a certain "fatal" night and had lost her forever and for good because of it. He had also been frustrated when he tried squiring Ilse the New Jersey librarian. Moreover, Thurs was a frequent visitor to libraries, which increased the chance that eventually he might meet an Eva in one. It was also time to think of re-employing one of the old themes of the trilogy. Thus the demands of the plot and of the New Life did it.

Because the very night after I thought of having him meet her in the University Library, I dreamt of her. I saw her whole, complete, alive, and so wondrously herself that I could not tell what part of her was my mother, or all the other women mentioned above. She too I've seen in real life, once caught a quick glimpse of her in a crowd at the symphony, once downtown in a department store, once out walking a mile ahead of me, a number of times across from me at the breakfast table. Eva came from the deeps.

Naturally, as I went about describing Thurs's and Eva's married life, I laid hands on any information I could get a hold of, from my own as well as from (and mostly from) the married lives of friends. Where else can a man get it from? Real life is always the first source. Even the genie who composes my nightdreams, let alone my daydreams, has to draw from that.

Of course, to write about music, I had to do some researching. And again, to my stunned surprise, at least to my stunned conscious surprise, when I began to study the piano and composition and musical history, I discovered that a talent of a sort had lain dormant all these years. (Can you blame me when I shiver and say, "It was as if 'a God' were directing my eyes and my hands as I planned and wrote *Wanderlust*? That it was 'a God' who revealed to me the idea of the rume as I went along so that I could all the more tell His truth by telling 'my' truth?")

From that point on everything I touched seemed to help the project along. In studying music I also got precise ideas as to just how I should work out the form, the structure, of *Wanderlust*. I saw that I could build it as a vast three-movement symphony, that, if I so fancied, I could add prelude, interludes, postludes, introductions, and codas, that I could have principal themes, transition themes, second themes, and closing themes, that I could play around with harmony and echo, with melody and counterpoint to my heart's content. (See the passage near the end of Part Two, The Nexing, in Rume III, The Giant, where Thurs "discovers" or "uncovers" that he has again and again seen the same face, the same idea, the same chord, echoing and reechoing, in the people and the events and the happenings he has known up to that point.) The very sounds of the words themselves, I saw, could be employed as if they were notes of music. (My sense of hearing, smell, taste, touch are sharp because of heredity and because of the competitive life I had to live in the country during boyhood, but especially my hearing. I "hear" much of my life. In fact, I often seem to "hear" things before I "see" them. Hence, if that is one of my strong suits, why shouldn't I play it out down to the ace? Why wait around for a precedent when one can be the precedent itself?) (It is perhaps because of this acute sense of hearing that coining words comes easy to me. I often coin them right on the spot, as if my Mother Tongue had secretly planted in me at birth a hoard of neologisms so that as life unfolded they would always be ready to hand when I would have need of them. Some have criticized this in my work. Why? Why shouldn't I exercise this gift too? In baseball no handicap is imposed on the Dizzy Dean who can come up with a new kind of natural pitch. Any writer worth his salt makes some little contribution to the language, sometimes as a coiner of new words, sometimes as inventor of a new style, and so on. Chaucer, Shakespeare, Twain, all coined words with glorious abandon. In that respect they have no more rights than I. (One more parenthetical remark: if you hear odd or broken or clashing sounds in my work it is just possible that I may have heard odd or broken or clashing sounds in my lifetime. If you run into passages where everything is played deadpan, and then into passages of warm irony, and then into passages where the heart lies open and pulsing, and then into passages of dark bardic brooding, and then into passages wild, and then into passages passive, and then, perhaps, into a section where all these passages are woven together at once, it is just possible that I may have had to cultivate such mental attitudes to tolerate, to stay afloat in, my own lifetime.)

A rumemaker can make the claim that his rume is, for once, as lifelike and as universal a story as a human being can write. The rumesmith is more likely than the "novelist" to get Old Man Reality to say a few words for him in his work—and who can be as fertile in ideas and as deep in thought and as inventive in plot as the Old Man Himself? (whether the Old Man be Chaos or Cosmos or a combination of both?) The "novelist," the inventor, is more handicapped than is the rumester in getting at submerged truth, a submerged truth that often escapes the notice of the author as well as generations of readers. It is this submerged truth that all creators are hunting for, that Gertrude Stein, for one, was trying to give voice.

The rumemaker is in effect saying the following when he offers up his rume: Here, in this offering, there is a good chance that the human mind, as evaluating and as symbolizing instrument, has at last recorded the receiving of as true a message as it is possible to get from the All-Wise Subconscious, from the Leviathan that lurks below and off the wings of the conscious stage of the brain, from the "giant" who all along has known more than we the seen actors. A good rumester, if he has trained himself sufficiently, will do all he can as a conscious being to encourage this mysterious greater self to speak freely (often by tearing down inhibitions and controls necessary to the good citizens), and when he does this, this is what happens— the Deep Sea, armed with symbols from "land of literacy" above, given a job to do, a question to answer, will quietly explore itself, going down many a pathway and opening many a buried tomb of horrid truth, quietly searching and exploring, until it hits the exact thing needed, and then, stomping and jumping on its genie-huge legs in joy, will draw down the attention of the actor on the stage. Hence the stunned feeling we often have when we discover some great revelation within ourselves, as if we have been engulfed in a terrible passion, as if we have been in a grotesque and terrible and wonderful other-world. Have you ever noted how much you can see of your Deep Self after orgasm, after those veils off the wings have been momentarily rent?

Thinking is a physiological process of the whole body, not just the brain. The brain thinks for the body just as the bowels defecate for the body, just as the heart pumps blood for the body. Each does its particular bit of systemic work.

The brain, the mind, is only (to make a guess) a thousandth part of the total personality. For it to match wits with the other nine hundred ninety-nine parts, or to match wits with a God, is a risky business. Looking up from the bottom end of the evolutionary telescope, from the vantage point of the unicell's abode, the difference between a moron and a genius is seen to be negligible. Thus, to become the great artist, one must so train the brain as to make it a fluent and eloquent medium or tongue for the other nine hundred ninety-nine parts, for the real and big you, for the God that lives in you. Thus,

too, I, this whole I, is highly suspicious of the sophomoric young
or the quickly trained or the precocious artist. Thus, I, the
whole I, is more than a little wary of the emanations of the
brain, more than it is of the emanations of the instincts. The
use of the brain by the human being is a high calling. All too
often the brain deludes itself into thinking it is the whole human
being. Thus there are times when a moron is more sensible
and more sensitive than a genius. For a time a genius may
blur his deep native feelings, his deep native bents. But in the
long run his native feelings will out because they actually have
more wisdom to fight with than does sheer brain. The human
species has spent billions of years at trial-and-error living to
get here, has been proven by fire and flood and vast frost,
while the Johnny-come-lately sophisticated brain or mind has
not. It is categorically foolhardy to forget the great wisdom
of our fathers, to neglect the knowledges of the successful animal
our ancestor, which he has accumulated all these years both
in tissue and in book.

I believe a man, man by himself, means littlo, that when
he thinks he can run things, even in this awe-ful and wonder-ful
atomic age, even in the next even more awe-ful and wonder-ful
cosmic age, he is not only vain but somewhat ridiculous. At
the same time, however, I believe too that deep in a man, in
man, there lies a behemoth, a vast truth of nature, the Old
Man Reality mentioned above, and that it is this truth, this
Old Man Reality, that occasionally speaks by means of the
tongues of men, through the mouth of the lowly as well as
through the mouth of the mighty, in moments of great distress,
or massive stress in labor, or inhuman excitement. Thus I say,
yes, develop your mind, your sensibilities, as well as you can,
but always with a mind that it is to be the voice for this greater
self, not its strawboss. When you become the voice you become
the rumester writing the rume. (In fact, it might be said that
man himself is a sort of rume, if it is true that a Mind is
slowly coming to expression through the medium of Matter.)
The true rumester, then, presents a maximum of vital life and
vital truth along with a maximum of art.

One thing we must insist on again, insist on to the point
of boring the patient reader and the aspiring writer, even to

the point of insulting them, and that is that the good rume can only be written by the good artist, never by an artless one; a good rume can only be written by a mature artist, rarely by a young one. The true rumester must be a highly developed and civilized being to make of his auto-story a work of art. No matter how autobiographical in source the rume may be, it must, in the end, once it is done, stand by itself. It must be free of the author, as free of temporary literary movements and schools as it is possible for any work to be. It must be a New Life, a life apart by itself, a world that, if it were all we had, would explain itself about as well as the world we live in explains or reveals itself to us. And to say that, of course, is to say that rumesters are rare, since it is the travel from non-knowing to knowing that breaks many a delicate animal brain. The integral artist in a highly developed society is as much a wonder of the world as is the literate man in a primitive society.

A rume, just as a "novel," just as any full art form, must have structure, must have art. Just as in the writing of drama a man must begin with experience (in this case deep personal and private experience), and then must find in it a subject, and then from the subject must find a theme, and, in relation to the theme, must revalue his experience, and then, ah, then must create. It is that last step that all hunger to achieve, and since it is much like faith, that is, you know you have it only when you have it, few attain it.

There is a reason for my interest in writing rumes, a profound reason. In this very relative world of atomic fission and fusion, of cosmic-ray power, of scientific doubting that the fundamental nature of the universe is not "orderly," people are asking for rumic truth, for more Life in their reading. They ask for new testaments, new bibles, new rumes, for self-expression and for self-revelation. They are intelligent enough to know that in this touch-and-go age too much ignorance of the explosive properties of the human self may be as dangerous to the human swarm as too much ignorance of the explosive properties of uranium. So let us open hearts and have a long look in.

Thus, imperfect and all too human as it is, here is the term rume. May it be a fruitful suggestion to others, to writers as well as to readers.

At Wrâlda
1950-1951

The Evolution of a Name

I was baptized as Frederick Feikema, despite strenuous objections from all the old Fiekema great-uncles who claimed I should be given the name of Feike Feikes Feikema, the customary name of the family *stamhalder* (oldest male child born to the oldest male ad infinitum). But my father (who was born Feike Feikes Feikema but who used the first name of Frank) was for Americanizing it some, and for honoring his wife's (my mother's) father, Frederick Van Engen. So Frederick I became. However, I was called Feike by many relatives and bore this as a nickname all through high school and college and into life, though I was always called Fred or Frederick by my intimates, such as mother, brothers, father, wife.

When it came time to publish my first book, the old question of what to do with my last name, Feikema, came up. People just would not pronounce it correctly. They'd say Fy-keem'-ah, Fy-kame'-ah, or Fee-keem'-ah, or Feek'-a-ma, or Fyk'-ma, etc. My editor suggested using my nickname, Feike, along with Feikema. This would help pronounce my last name, he thought. But not so. They'd get the first right, but mangle the second as usual. At the same time, I regretted losing Frederick. A nickname is one thing (it is a casual catch at your being), but your real name is the one your mother and father and your wife, and very close friends use. I wanted Frederick back. But I also decided that in taking it back I'd add a new name which Americans would be able to pronounce.

I began to look around, ask around. I asked all the relatives if they knew what Feike and Feikema meant. None seemed to know. I next asked Professor Konstantin Reichardt, who taught in the Foreign Language Department at the University of Minnesota here. (He's now at Yale University.) Konstantin spent some time digging and came up with the following: that "Frederick" and "Feike" and "freedom" and "friend" had the same

Indo-European root in *fri-du* and *pri-tu* with *pri* meaning 'love,' 'friendship,' 'peace,' that over the centuries through a process of vocal nicknaming or petnaming in the Frisian language (possibly also in other Teutonic dialects) the Germanic or Old Frisic-Anglo-Saxon name of "Fridurik" became "Feike" – "Fridurik" became "Friducho" which became "Friccho" which became "Ficco" which became "Feike," that the ending of "Feikema" was still the old *ma* from ancient times (the old Aryan root for the word we now use as 'man'), that therefore Feikema meant, anglicized, Fredman, (Frederickman), or Manfred. I liked the last very much. It was as Anglo-Saxon as a man could make it. Even morons couldn't help but pronounce it, or spell it right. A perfect name for one who wanted a trademark that the American and English public could pronounce. At about the same time my wife and I heard Tchaikovsky's *Manfred* played on the radio, and the ease with which the announcer pronounced the name convinced us. Armed with this information, I attended the next family (Feikema) reunion in Sioux Falls.

Upon closer inquiry I discovered that the great-uncle and great-aunt still alive remembered that my grampa's translation of Feike as Frank was wrong, that good Frisians didn't do so because the Franks had once been hated enemies, that Frank had been given to my father's father by the immigration officer at the port of entry. The officer told my grandfather that Feike and Feikema would be too tough to pronounce in America, that he had better adopt an American name. When grandfather didn't know what to choose, the officer asked where he came from. "Franeker," said grampa. "Well, that's it. Make it Frank." And so it became Frank, and after that all the firstborns or Feikes in the United States were called Frank! The great-uncle and great-aunt also remembered that the Feikes in the other families, upon coming to the America, always translated it to Fred or Frederick, e.g., Feike Groene now called himself Frederick Green. This tied it down. And it was a case of where scholarship helped awaken the memory of aged immigrants as to old customs back in the Old Country. When I told them that because of business reasons I was going to *add* (not change) Manfred to my legal name of Frederick Feikema, they agreed that it was a good translation and a good sounding name in their ears. Some of the younger Feikemas, who had dealings with the world (most Feikemas are farmers and so don't feel the need for a change), accepted it enthusiastically, and one family beat me to it, that is, adding Manfred to their name. I suggested that all male children be given the middle name of Feikema so that our descendants would always know where Manfred came from. In my own case I was going to give my son, when he came, the name of Frederick Feikema Manfred which would be the *stamhalder's* name, which would have the same meaning as Feike Feikes Feikema, that is, Frederick the-Feike-man of the Manfreds. As the great-uncle explained to me, Feike Feikes Feikema meant Feike Feike's 'feike'-man, that is, Feike has a son meaning 'peace' 'friend,' and besides being a nickname for Frederick, also meant 'firstborn male of the firstborn male.' (Incidentally, this was the only meaning the family remembered: Feike meant 'the first one.' My mother's people believed that Frederick meant 'head of the house.') Thus Feike Feike's Feikema means the 'Firstborn First-born's *firstborn manchild.'*

The long Feike line began back in the early 1700's. A fellow named Feike Sierks, a *huisman* or *boer,* of Klein-Lankum, Friesland, started it off. He died in 1767. He was married in Franeker and lived near it. He named his son Feike Feikema, II. And so on, until my grampa was named Feike Feikes Feikema, V, and my father Feike Feikes Feikema, VI, and I, well, I was supposed to have been Feike Feikes Feikema, VII, but instead am now calling myself Frederick Feikema Manfred, VII, and will name my son Frederick Feikema Manfred, VIII. It is also interesting to note that for those seven generations the firstborn child was always male, that there was a heavy predominance of males in all those families, that my father, for example, had seven sons (one died at birth) and no daughters, but that now dad has six granddaughters and no grandsons! (I have two daughters, Freya and Marya.) It is also interesting to contemplate the odd historical accident that gave me a grandfather on my mother's side with the name of Frederick, a name which was given me, and which, by great luck, turns out to be the original for Feike.

West of the Mississippi:
An Interview with Frederick Manfred

On July 13, 1958, four editors of *Critique* interviewed
Frederick Manfred at his home outside Minneapolis and
overlooking the Minnesota River valley. Their purpose was
to discuss with Mr. Manfred the writer as a product of
the area west of the Mississippi, his use of that area in
his fiction, and his relations with his contemporaries. The
interview, recorded on tape, has necessarily been edited
somewhat to meet limitations of space; every effort was
made, however, to retain the conversational tone of the
original discussion. (In the interview, "E" refers to the question or comment of an *editor*, "M" to Mr. *Manfred's* response.)

E: Mr. Manfred, would you tell us something about your
introduction to the writers of this area?

M: My first real contact with any Midwest writer was some
time during college.* I was home in the summer on vacation,
and had just enough English in college to feel very depressed
about my background. Having heard the English prof, two profs,
there exalt the Lake country and all the walks and paths there,
and all of Hardy's Wessex, and so on—I began to feel those
men were very lucky—they had a great country to write about,
whereas what I had was nothing. I felt quite depressed because
even at that time I had already made up my mind that I was
going, some time, to be a writer. It happened that we had
a doctor who loaned me books in the summertime. He had the
complete set of Jack London and I had the complete works
of Shakespeare. Well, I finished the Jack London that summer

*Calvin College, Michigan

45

and asked him for more books and he gave me a book by
Rölvaag. I had never heard of him, I hadn't even heard of him
in college. That was *Giants in the Earth.* I got into it about
fifty or sixty pages when suddenly to my great astonishment
I saw that Per Hansa's trek was going right across the very
farm I was sitting on, probably went over the very house I
was sitting in, and went west to Split Rock Creek, and it dawned
on me that this was famous country, that it was classic country
because it had been written about.

E: This was where, specifically?

M: This was in northwest Iowa. I was sitting in my father's
home in Doon, Iowa. That was the first key, the first opening
door in my mind that it wasn't all lost, that my past wasn't
for nothing. I think that's one of the things that I ran into
as a teacher at Macalester, that these poor kids had the feeling
they were to cut off everything they had been up to the time
they came to college and to adopt a new life, a new past, because
everything they read about or were given first came from other
countries – England, France, Italy, Greece, and so on – and that
they weren't given enough in high school about their *own* writers
and their *own* heroes. That was the first big jump in my life,
and I read *Peder Victorious* and the other part of the trilogy.
(That was the only book of Rölvaag I cared very much for,
though – *Giants in the Earth* – and I read it once since. I think
he's a good writer, but he isn't as great a writer as Lewis;
he was my hero then but he isn't any more.)

The next author I ran into was in sociology in college. This
was much later, in my senior year, I think it was – I wasn't
taking a course in sociology but my roommate was, and he
talked to me about his course a lot and kept mentioning Veblen
and one day I heard that Veblen was from the Northfield area;
I dug into *The Theory of the Leisure Class* and I had a terrible
time with it. But I liked all of it, the feel of it and the mood
of it: he wrote like an old saga writer and he reminded me
a lot – his air and his manner – of my uncles, my great uncles,
who spoke Frisian, and of their stories about the Frisian past,
about the time in the old country.

The next step was Lewis. Someone told me I should read
Elmer Gantry; I read it and I liked it very much. I enjoyed

that book probably most of his. Later on when I got to read *Arrowsmith* and *Main Street* I saw that they were greater books, but while I can see where other people think Lewis is a great writer, he never really awakened my harp. (I often think of human beings as being like the harp in a piano.) Somehow the keys that Lewis played in his novels didn't waken any echoes in my harp – not too many, just a few of them here and there. We were different kinds of people as I mentioned earlier; I always had the feeling he was kind of like a tomcat while I was more, say, in the dog or the bear field. Lewis had a fierce yellow mind that leaped. He was just in a different category.

The next contact with a Western writer was reading Herbert Krause's novel *Wind Without Rain,* which I thought was quite a good evocation of the West. Because of reading that book I got acquainted with Herb Krause. I've read all his books since. I think he's doing some interesting work about the West, and I feel somewhat a kinship with him in the sense of trying to preserve the first attempt to establish the nuclei of a civilization out here.

E: You're going from the Midwest to the West now, is that right?

M: He's still Midwest. Herb Krause is still Midwest. I got to know him and like him, and we got along quite well, but we're different again, quite different people. The only thing we have in common is this attempt to put down the sort of single experience which separate families here in the Midwest, and in their first attempt to begin a society. I was interested in that too. Later on I ran into Stegner's books and I liked *Big Rock Candy Mountain* very, very much. It was a tremendously moving book to me and I felt that here was somebody who, like me, wanted to get down the arch of a life as lived in the *whole* West, not just the Midwest but the idea of living west of the Mississippi River.

My Pier in *This Is The Year* – there is almost a whole arch there in his life, the big strong man with great potential but who had a fatal weakness, an Achilles' heel – he had basically the brains but he did not yet have a trained mind to handle his environment. The culture wasn't old enough yet to tell him how to use his talent. I have one man in *This Is The Year*

(the dreamer, I call him Peterson the dreamer) who tells Pier
to practice soil conservation, and I use him as a kind of a
voice of the new age. Not that I was particularly interested
in soil conservation as such — Peterson's is just a new voice
coming on, but Pier wouldn't hear this voice (Stegner's hero
Bo Mason had the same problem) — he heard advice in the air
around him, coming at him a little bit, but he just didn't have
enough background built up as a member of a flourishing society to hear it so it would nick in, would stay in.

Then I ran across Guthrie's book, *The Big Sky*. I can see
why other people like his books; I think they're very good and
I like to read them, but somehow I don't feel akin to him as
I do to Stegner or Krause or any of the other ones. I feel
much closer to Wright Morris, who describes people who have
lived just long enough to have that first regret about having
lived in the West. Say like married couples who by the third
or fourth or sixth year finally see everything as it really is,
and then there's a little period where they both think about
getting a divorce but most of the time they don't; they go
on living and then they discover new values behind, which are
richer than the first ones they ever thought of. And Wright
Morris is in the middle of that section. He's busy showing disillu-
sionment in most of his books but also giving hints that there
is some real stuff coming up behind that. I felt a real kinship
there. I won't say it was close — I feel like he's — like in the old
days, when you saw a neighbor's smoke, he was already too
close, twenty miles off. Not that I want to move off, or Wright
Morris wants to move off, but I can see his smoke, say, ten
miles off at work and I think I know what he's doing over
there. That's about as close as I feel to him. I like him very
much too.

E: Why, particularly?

M: In his case? Well, for one thing, I like the style, because
it comes out of Nebraska just as Mark Twain's style came
out of his life. Henry James has a style which comes out of
Boston and England. And Mark Twain has his style which
mostly comes out of the West, and which much later on, as
Cowley and these people have been telling us, Hemingway has
followed and Faulkner has followed. It's an idiom that comes

out of the West. And they use this as a base, as a web or matrix, of their style and their way of presenting their feelings and so on, and I like that part of it. I think too I like the people he describes because I'm acquainted with them.

E: Do you feel that you belong to a kind of a group of Midwestern or Western writers?

M: Well, I have to say that at first I felt I was working pretty much alone. As far as, say, Stegner or Wright Morris or Guthrie, or any of those were concerned, it wasn't until the last two or three years that I began to feel that perhaps they were working near me. There was no close relationship such as the Fugitive group had—they all knew each other and inspired each other and so on—we were too far apart ever to meet. I had one letter from Stegner; I never had any correspondence from either Guthrie or Morris. There has never been any direct communication.

E: Do you think that you do not like Guthrie's work as much or are not so much in sympathy with his work because even when you write about the same subjects you treat them differently—what you seek to do is somewhat different from what Guthrie seeks to do?

M: I might say that the reason I wrote *Lord Grizzly* and since then *Riders of Judgment* and am now at work on a new one— which you might say are Western books (people are beginning to call them Western books; I'm stuck with that; I myself didn't want to call them that)—my reason for writing them was primarily that I began to feel a thinness in my own heroes. No matter how hard I worked, how much I thought about them, somehow they did not have all the dimensions for me. They lacked something; they lacked a—what's the expression the critics throw around?—a "usable past" within themselves; there wasn't enough history or country or culture for me to throw it up to use as a background, for me to throw my characters against, to deepen them in *that* sense. Some of the novels that we think are great take on an added greatness because we're acquainted with the culture from which they come so that the least little gesture of the author or the hero inside that book instantly evokes part of the whole background and, if that background isn't there and the author is busy pushing the front part of the book with not much background, there's always an empty hole. So I went out – I was interested then to find the heroes or the ancestors of my men like Pier and Maury, Elof and Eric. I thought, well, maybe I should look a little more to find, not just who were their fathers and mothers, but who the people were before them on the land – furtrappers, the first mountainmen, and so on. Perhaps these people left some residue in the air, not only left their marks on the soil but left them in the air and the way they handled the new thing they hit first which transmitted itself down, say, to my grandfather and so on. And it happened that when I was doing *The Golden Bowl* I ran across a reference to Hugh Glass in the *South Dakota Guide Book* and it instantly caught my eye – this man fighting the bear alone – it struck me that here was the first real contact of the white man with the raw West. This typified it, this was the first bumping into it. And since then there has been a series of generations; they don't necessarily follow one another directly, say, in a family, but in sequence they are sitting behind these, and even further back behind the first furtrappers are the Indians who really lived here first.

Once I had that in mind, then I decided that some day I was going to write about Hugh Glass. But I didn't know how to end the story. Hugh Glass, according to history, is supposed to have forgiven the men who deserted him, and I couldn't. I could see intellectually why he'd forgive them, but I could not feel it emotionally. I had to go into his mind, into his kind of psychology, to see why he should do it, and it took me ten years before I ran into something in my own experience – something about which I became terribly enraged and had to overcome my rage and look at it dispassionately to see that it was just. I finally had the personal experience before I could find out the end of that book, *Lord Grizzly*. Then I got right at it. By that time Siouxland had come to me – the concept of Siouxland came to me when I was writing *This Is the Year* – that that would be my core, my center, from which all other novels would gradually work out because I knew that country and the people best – and that somewhere in every book there would be someone related to Siouxland or someone who would live in Siouxland. And then I decided that some day I would write a series of books (like a painter who wants to fill a hall with murals, one after the other) so that when I got through I'd have something all the way from 1800 on to the day I die. *Lord Grizzly* fit part of that pattern and that helped me make up my mind to do it. That's a different reason from Guthrie's, I think.

E: You conceive then that this becomes a part of a saga-like pattern?

M: The whole thing. Say, like Balzac's *Human Comedy;* he tried to do all four aspects of French society – the city and the peasants and the workers and – what was the other? Mine was mostly that I wanted to get everything that I could get – a sampling of various decades from 1800 on. And I felt too that if I did three or four in the back there, then when I went back to some modern problems that I wanted to do later on, that that would help me write a better book. I have two or three ideas I've saved all this time that I hadn't been able to do because I didn't know how to handle them. They're great stories, far better stories than any I've done so far but I did not know how to handle them or how to do them justice. I thought I had to know more about them in the past and that's why I went after it.

E: Now there are a couple of things I'm not clear about. You've admitted that *Lord Grizzly* can be classified as a western book, and I gather from what you've said that you believe there is more validity to the Western tradition than the Midwestern in literature and that this is what caused you to go back to the past, the mountainmen and furtrappers; and yet on the other hand you've spoken of Siouxland as a kind of center from which all the rest of the novels radiate?

M: Yes. Well, Hugh Glass and those men did work through Siouxland. If you widen Siouxland, if you make Siouxland a little larger, it includes Fort Kiowa where most of this took place; it's on the western outskirts of Siouxland. When I was very young I used to sit on Saturday afternoon in front of the billiard hall and hear these old men talk about the days when they used to trap in South Dakota in the spring and in the fall – in the winters and summers they'd come back home. And they used to speak of the old trappers beyond who'd taught

them the tricks—where the beavers were, where the mink were—
so in my mind that was always related, Hugh Glass was part
of my experience, that those men who became furtrappers and
so on left the outposts of the advancing civilization, went over
there, and then came back periodically to the Midwest, but
they became heroes of the West. To me, somehow, Pier and
Hugh Glass are somewhat similar men except that one lived
at a time when there were no farms—not many farms around—
and when Pier lived he had to fight his bear in the land.

E: What was West then is now Midwest.

M: Yes, the line keeps moving further back.

E: You speak then of the West in terms of frontier, the
westering movement?

M: Yes.

E: Do you believe then, so far as literary traditions are
concerned, that the Midwest and the West have different
traditions?

M: I've tried to put them together. I understand that Mr.
Webb, who wrote a book called *The Great Plains,* tries to
separate them. He says that there is a distinct literature that
you can call "short grass" and another that you can call "long
grass" or high plains literature. The "short grass" man is the
sodder, the sod-buster, the one that built the farm. He likes
to go out in the field and stick his hand in the soil and lift
it up and love it and smell it and to him that's everything.
The high plains boy sits on a horse and rides over it, doesn't
want to touch it at all. His attitude is something like the Indian's. He [Webb] divides them up. But I think they are all
part of a larger sense of the white man taming this country
and each section you tame differently.

E: Well, granted you have tried to put the traditions together
for yourself. Do you believe that for others the two traditions
are distinct?

M: I think they are for Guthrie.

E: Do you think that people like Walter Van Tilburg Clark
and Wright Morris are writing in the same tradition?

M: No, I think those two are apart. Wright Morris is writing
about the short grass country and its breaking up, somewhat
the disillusioning process—whereas Clark is quite distinctly

writing (certainly in *The Ox-Bow Incident* and *The Track of the Cat*) about the Far West, the great untillable soil. The difference between tilling and non-tilling; I think there's a great difference there. You'd have some trouble putting them together.

E: Well, in the early period, say, when there's actually Lord Grizzly fighting the bear and similarly fighting with the land, the struggle would take different forms, perhaps, but it would be the same struggle – the Western struggle?

M: Yes.

E: But by now – would you feel that somehow during the period between the present and the struggling period there was a change in the characteristics so that, on the one hand, you get Sinclair Lewis writing about small towns and farmland, things like that; on the other hand you have, say, Willa Cather writing about the tremendous sweep, the desert, the arid places, and the Mexican tradition?

M: She sort of puts them together, doesn't she? There's a definite influence from the Southwest moving into her work; the wind is southwest in her books, west and southwest. For Lewis, there wasn't any wind – there was a pull to get away and then to look back and to pick it apart. Cather really loved it and was full of longing for it even though she didn't live there much afterwards. I think in her novels the West and Midwest come together somewhat as in mine; I think she liked it all. I know Red Cloud quite well because part of the new book I'm writing takes place there, curiously enough – the last half of it takes place out there. It's still tillable country – it's short grass country. But Cather also writes about the Southwest, Mexico; there is a Western atmosphere in her books.

E: Of course, part of that difference might be attributable to Lewis's temperament as a satirist.

M: Yes. A poet tends to fix his feelings and his imagination to a certain country and to exalt it, even when sometimes he's a little rough on it. Lewis speared it and cut it; in a way he always claimed he loved it too, but he didn't operate the way that Cather did – he was a satirist.

E: Well, you've spoken now of some of the influences on you as a writer, particularly about some of the writers that

you came across as you were beginning your career. What about
Walter Van Tilburg Clark?

M: I read Clark quite a few years ago. *The Ox-Box Incident,* I think, helped me go after *Lord Grizzly.* Knowing that
he had done it, I had the feeling that then I could do it too.
In fact, I got more out of that book than I did out of Guthrie's;
the general tone and attack appealed to me. That is what I
felt about Clark – he tried to find in the flow of life a knot
or a problem that would catch up a particular feeling, a particular web of life that those men lived in those days. They
had to set up their own society. Some rudimentary sense of
justice came along with them out there; but here they had this
trouble, and what were they going to do about it. He tried
to pin down the first formations of society out there, just as
I tried to do in *Lord Grizzly.* He was interested in justice – it's
a key to his book – and I was interested in justice in *Lord Grizzly.* I didn't read the book at the time I did *Lord Grizzly;* I
made a point of staying away from it because I unfortunately
am one of these people who, if I read someone, find he moves
in on me.

E: What do you think of Vardis Fisher?

M: I didn't read Vardis Fisher early in my life and so he
could never have the impact on me that he would have had
if I'd read him earlier. But I've read him in the last ten years,
and I like much of what he does. *The Mothers,* I thought, was
a marvelous novel, very fine. It's about the Donner party going
through the Sierra Nevadas. A real fine study of the many
kinds of things that I'm interested in: of people having suddenly a sort of moving community coming out of the East and
having to go into a narrow pass and suddenly having to face
nature for a while, and then later on having to face their own
souls, their own internal natures – some of them are cannibals
and some are not – and what finally saves them. It's a very
fundamental study of what makes up a human being. The new
book, *Tale of Valor,* is as fine a recasting as you could possibly
do in the field, in the novel of well-documented historical event.
It wrote itself through him more than he took it over and wrote
it, but that's something he couldn't help. It's just a tremendous
theme, epic in its own right; he couldn't tamper very much

with it. But he did fill it out. Fisher is interesting. He first wrote about people he knew and then took up themes farther away from home—you might almost call them Western books, Western novels. That didn't quite satisfy him, he wanted to probe even deeper, so then he began this long Testament of Man series in which he went all the way back into primitive times, in Indo-Europe, and has followed that all the way out into the time of Christ. And we're now about to get into modern times, so he's going to take it into America. He's been restless as a writer out there in Idaho, and he's been somewhat unhappy with what he's found. Not only is he unhappy with the people he found, he's been somewhat unhappy with the themes he's had to deal with, so he's gone further back, beyond America, into and beyond even European civilization and the roots of European civilization—he's jumped all the way back.

E: May I interject one other name? What about Frank Norris? Did you ever read him, or has he had any influence on you?

M: I've read *The Pit* and the one before that, *The Octopus;* there's another. You know, the style of those books never appealed to me. It didn't hit me. I read those with great interest and I was intrigued by the idea, by the largeness of the concept, but somehow the style didn't catch me. And I never pursued them; I never went on.

E: We've been looking at the end of *The Golden Bowl*, and in the italized section at the end there is the same kind of celebration of the new life coming up again, that you find when Norris is hitting his stride.

M: I don't remember that at all. But of course it might have caught in; I don't know. I might tell you how the ending of *The Golden Bowl* came about. I didn't know how to end that book. I didn't want to leave it in total defeat; at the same time I was working toward the center of the cyclone, not only in the book, but in a cyclone of living on the plain. Of course, living here, I'm very intrigued by the weather, tornadoes and cyclone systems, and so on, and I had in mind somewhat the device of a cyclone for this book; it never came off completely, except in the last chapter when it comes in again. And it occurred to me that I had stopped exactly in the eye of the cyclone; this was a good time for a pause, and also a good time to

end the book; in the center of the cyclone there is calm, and
in a calm moment after a lot of commotion, people have a tendency either to let their spirits go down or to soar, and mine,
mine soar. That occurred to me, and then I said, now I know
how to end it. I wrote it in about a half hour; to me it's perfect,
I wouldn't want anything else. That symbol came up out of
the country.

   Could I go on about using materials out of my area for
the structure of my books? I think that's pertinent to the inquiry here. *This Is the Year* — the version that was finally
published — was actually the third version; the other two versions I destroyed except for four chapters I still have here
in my files. The only thing I kept was the terrain but I destroyed
the people, everything — started fresh each time. The third time
I decided that my problem was the plot; what kind of a plot
was I going to use? One of the twenty-six conventional plots
or one out of the *Decameron* or should I try to work out a
plot of my own out of my own country as Rölvaag sort of
haphazardly did? I was studying weather bureau records one
day when I noticed — I made a graph of them — when I noticed
five interesting different swings in weather cycles and I thought,
why not use this interesting weaving of the ups and downs
of the particular year; I'll take one year up and one year down,
one year up and two down — because I was going to make it
a tragedy, of course. I found these years quite easily; they
happened to fit the most dramatic years that I remembered
my uncles' and my father's living. And so I fitted that all over
the top and then I decided that the words, as much as I possibly
could, and the actions and the height of the man as opposed
to the flat lands, and the stiff upright buildings, and trees and
so on — that all would help build up this concept I had, first,
of time flowing over a vast expanse. Whenever I found myself
using a technique out of Hardy or someone else I would quite
consciously throw it away and make a sheer guess into the
next chapter so that it would be as if it came right up out
of the ground. This was my concept: the flowing seasons over
the soil, rolling on almost like a cycle again. I've tried to do
that consciously with every book since. I read everybody —
Conrad, Thackeray, Smollett, all of them. Dickens, Irving — and

when I'm all done I turn my back on them as much as I possibly can and try to find things in my own life, or my own way of doing things, the way I might garden or the way I might, say, live with my wife or the way I get along with my relatives. I use that as web or a line of going; I put it in my books. My feeling is that it's very difficult to be original, it's very difficult to add your little bit to the ant heap, but the more you try to be on your own, totally so, the more you might finally contribute one little bit of grain to the pile. But I think that that is an expression of Western America too; I find that amongst cowboys and lonely trappers and lonely sheepherders and lonely farmers—and, incidentally, in Cather and in Lewis. Lewis had that sense too of being a definite "apart" fellow. Apartness—I think you find it in Clark and in Krause too. I think that comes up out of this Midwestern region; you don't care to know your neighbor, the writer, too much.

E: This seems to me what you've been saying right along—that these people have not given you anything you want to imitate but you like the kind of thinking that they're doing and in your own way you do the same sort of thinking. You admire the same things they admire.

M: Yes, and I like them being lonesome. I don't mind being lonesome myself—I enjoy being lonesome. I like the old sense that my father had, and my grandfather had, of the family as a unit, of being very close; yet at the same time, how I enjoy getting into my car alone and going out West, to drive out away from town and to have experiences for myself. I enjoy them thoroughly without telling anybody about them, having a good time with it all, reading a good book alone, having a good time with the author so that I meet him in the book almost on his own ground. I enjoy that tremendously. I enjoy both things: I like people and, on the other hand, I like being alone and I like people who like being alone. I like lonesomeness.

E: That's different from loneliness.

M: Yes, much. Much so.

E: One of the reasons we've asked you about some of these contemporary writers like Stegner, Clark, and so forth, is to get your reactions to other writers. You've said that you think people like Clark have influenced you. Some others have not. Can you think of any other writers you especially like?

M: No, but I think if you're making a real inquiry about writers who "worked" on me or had some influence on me, I think we should not overlook three people – or things: the Bible and Shakespeare and Chaucer. The Bible had a great influence on me because it fell upon me to read the Bible at the table. So I read the Bible seven times through before I was seventeen, and knew it backwards and forwards, loved a lot of it, and read it in between times because I liked reading about the battles and I liked Job and I liked some of the prophets and some of the psalms. When I got to be sixteen or seventeen, I began to read the Song of Solomon over and over again. Wonderful thing for me.

When I was sixteen years old – between high school and college I stayed home two years – I bought a complete set of Shakespeare which I still have. I read them through on the farm while working. When I hitchhiked I took the Bible and Shakespeare and Walt Whitman with me; those three travelled with me everywhere in the suitcase, and they're battered and they're full of road dust from every state in the Union (except the South where I didn't go – I was afraid of the chain gangs, so I didn't go to the South; I'm sorry I didn't now). The old Bible I got when I got through grade school, the Shakespeare I got in high school, and the *Leaves of Grass* I bought just as I graduated from college.

I mentioned Chaucer; I didn't know much about Chaucer until college, and there I had a course in English, and when the prof there read Chaucer it hit me suddenly that the sound of this language was similar to the Frisian that my uncles spoke. That was the first time that it dawned on me that being a Frisian was an honorable thing. You see, I grew up in a community where there were New Englanders; they were the ones who settled Doon, Iowa. They controlled the community. Later on the Dutch moved in, or the Hollanders; among the Hollanders were Frisians. The Dutchmen let you know quite soon that to be Frisian was something to be looked down upon, because in Friesland, back home in Holland at least, they were farmers or sailors, and they never got beyond that. (I might add quickly

here that my father was a West Frisian from Holland but my
mother originally was part Saxon and part East Frisian from
Germany, which is different; I mean they're both Frisians, but
one is from the German side and one is from the other side.)
So I went out into life thinking, first, I was a minority amongst
Hollanders, and then Hollanders were a minority amongst
Americans, and I had to punch up through two layers to get
out to where there were Americans, when all along my father
already felt like an American and talked like it. Yet when I
went into life I always had a sort of double inhibition to break
through. But in college I first heard that the Frisian language
was really Old English. To my great joy, I then started going
into it further and further, and when I lived at the University,
Red Warren helped me—suggested a few books I should get
if I was interested in Chaucer. I now have an old set of Chaucer
which is as worked over as the Bible; and those four [the Bible,
Chaucer, Shakespeare, and Whitman] really had as much to
do with my life as Lewis and Cather and some of the other
ones have probably more. They were probably the entering
spear of culture from The East into me.

E: Did reading Chaucer and Shakespeare give you a sense
of being soaked in an English as well as an American literary
tradition?

M: No. For one thing, Shakespeare writes about Julius
Caesar and Hamlet—subject matter that isn't always English
and except for having, say, a longing to see Stratford-on-Avon,
I don't think it worked on me particularly that he was English.
Just that he was a very great writer and also that he used
strong racy language. At times this appealed to me as a man
from the West, so that, for example, I wouldn't care at all
for Ben Jonson, but I would like Shakespeare very much. As
a Western man, I like those direct expressions. The same thing
with Chaucer. The thing that Chaucer did for me was to sort
of help me throw off that yoke of being called a Hollander
and a Dutchman which I had in the name of Feikema. I'd never
felt like a Dutchman; my family very strictly taught us that
we were not Hollanders. We were Frisians if anything, but
Grandpa loved being an American—could speak the language
very well; he had little difficulty learning it because in the Frisian

language the basic words are very similar to the English words. For *through* they say *troch;* for *stone* they say *stein;* for *cheese* they say *tsiis.* So Grandpa taught us early that we were American; yet people were calling us Hollanders. That always disturbed me. Chaucer helped me get rid of that sense of particular race or ethnic group by discovering—well, if it came down to it, I was actually as English as you could *possibly* get, and I still loved being a Western American.

E: Now we move on to a couple of other things. Are you in communication with any of your contemporary American writers?

M: No. None of them, as far as I can think. I've met them all off and on more or less, at one time or another, but I don't correspond much with any of them. I *have* corresponded with—I have to think about that—that answers your question right there. I have to think and scratch my mind. I have written and do correspond occasionally with Van Wyck Brooks; I've had letters from him—a dozen or so over a period of ten years—in which he has scolded me for not soaking up and sort of investing my plot or relating my plot with the environment and filling it in and tying it in with the sense of the rest of the country. But you see I can't do that. Mr. Van Wyck Brooks lives in New England, a much older section, and he feels part of it and part of its history. We're still busy building it out here. It is difficult for me to feel as tied to what I'm supposed to be tied to as he is to what he's got.

E: It's really because you wanted some usable past, as you mentioned, that you wanted to do things like *Lord Grizzly?* You don't sense any presentness of the past—in the Midwest especially?

M: Every mile I go west, I do. When I take a trip out, the further west I go, the more I feel that those people remember the old days more than they do, say, in the town of Minneapolis. I think the town of Minneapolis looks east and looks to Paris and New York on almost every scale, and to Europe more and more as the years go by. They have centennials and they try to remind you of the old days and so on, but I think that's mostly water off a duck's back in the larger towns here. But in the smaller towns and in the open country, I think they do remember the past.

E: That's what you find attractive in Walter Van Tilburg Clark's work?

M: Yes, and that's what I find attractive in leaving town and driving West, why I like to go back to my home, which is just a short ways away from here, and visit. I want it to be a great place and therefore I look for heroes in it and I try to celebrate them.

E: This may overlap somewheat with some of the other questions, but we'd like to ask you again about the matter of ethnic groups. You've already talked some about the Frisians.

M: Well, you know in the beginning many little towns had them—say New Ulm would be solid German; Orange City, Iowa, would be solid Dutch; Holdingford would be Norwegian; Askov, Minnesota, would be Danish; Floodwood would be Finnish—in the beginning when they were first settled. As time goes on, though, a *great* intermarriage has been going on continually; that has intrigued me about Siouxland because you'll have these little spotted centers over Siouxland which were originally separated but now they're pretty much intermarried and I notice that—I get the three weeklies from down there—and I watch the marriages, and I notice a great intermingling of marriages. Now, when I wrote *This Is the Year,* I didn't mean particularly to celebrate the Frisians as Frisians; it just happened that I knew something about them and I thought it would be intriguing to describe such a small embryo settlement which never really will take hold. Eventually it will break up, as it did, and as is happening now. This is part of my reason for it, but I could as well have written about the Norwegians or any other one. I didn't particularly mean to celebrate any one group. I wanted to show that eventually they do intermarry. Even Pier the hero. He marries a Norwegian girl from the north a ways. And the legends that his father had disappeared—pieces of them remain and they're transformed and taken over much the way that the Christians took the pagan beliefs in the old days and adopted them into the Christians' religion; so, too, I think that the general American stamp will eventually make these people a homogeneous group. It's continually going on.

E: I believe in *The Primitive* you speak of the ethnic groups coming and taking over the tradition of the New Englanders who first settled. Do you believe this is all part of the melting process?

M: Yes. They're all fitting into the mold. The New Englanders set it; they put the town hall in, the constables, and the relationship of the township to the country and so on; and these other people come in and they fill that gap. For a little while they hold on to their religions, their little private house gods, and the way they run their weddings. Going back to your observation about the difference between books about the Midwest and the Far West – what I meant to do a little bit in *Riders of Judgment* was to pull the two together, in my mind anyway. I took people – or the feel of people that I have – that I know back home in Siouxland and I put them in Wyoming. The hero and his family all came out of Siouxland and I had an intention for that in this sense, that people, if they're unhappy in Siouxland, if they're a little on the roisterous side or the community is a little too tight for them or close, where people are living as too close neighbors, then . . . .

E: Is Siouxland a way of designating a geographical location and of suggesting an intense midwesternness, or do you feel the peculiar Indianness in the background somehow? This occurs to me because I know that someone like Walter Van Tilburg Clark has been quite explicit about his feelings toward the Indians. Someone like Joe Sam in *The Track of the Cat*. Clark said once he had come increasingly to feel that the most important man on the North American continent was the Indian.

M: Well, I'd almost say that even today. I use the word "Siouxland" definitely because the Sioux lived there. My grandfather told me that when he first came here he ran into the Sioux, and one of my relatives, some three or four generations back, when they came in their wagons, rather late in the summer, knew it was too late to plant any corn or wheat, yet wondered if he couldn't get in some garden produce like, say, radishes or lettuce. When he talked about this, an Indian overheard him – a man named Yellowsmoke – and showed him where to go to plant. They didn't have a plow and the sod was too tough to break up with a spade. So he told him to go to these mounds that the pocket gophers made and to sow their radish seeds and lettuce there. And I remember very vividly, when they told me that as a boy, that really put the Indian right into my mind.

Then as part of my process, which I talked about earlier, of going back to find heroes, or pre-heroes, or early-day heroes to my modern-day heroes, I discovered in studying Hugh Glass that he was in many ways part Indian himself. In fact, of course, the fur trappers and mountain men lived with the Indians and married them and got along very well with the Indians. There wasn't any argument there. The argument came later on, when the traders, that is, the merchant men came in, and the missionaries came in; then with the ledgerman and the storekeeper, that's when the trouble set in, but in the early days the Indian got along very well with the white man. Hugh Glass had some Indian in him, and behaved somewhat like an Indian, lived like an Indian; well, then I knew that some day I'd have to go back before his time to write a book about that. That occurred about fifteen-twenty years ago in my mind; and I began to collect things in my memory and also in my notebooks about some possible book about Indians and about my country, Siouxland—a book which I'm now writing. It's a book about the Yankton Sioux before the white man reached them.

E: Well, how does this all fit in with the other ethnic groups that figure in your work, which are all openly of European stock?

M: Well, for one thing, the Indian is related to, closely and warmly related to, the soil of this country; he was part of the ecology and got along with it and was doing fine and I think was slowly evolving up the ladder of becoming civilized. He was many years behind the ladder in Europe, which had begun earlier; but he was moving up on his own speed here, probably about as fast. Suddenly we broke in on that and disrupted it completely and for a little while we had to contend with him as well as the environment. After we had dispersed him—we think—we discover we too have come to terms with the same environment that he came to terms with—only we have different tools. We discover that if we're not careful with the land it runs away on us, erodes away or is washed away. We're just now learning a little bit about how to build a house that is warm in the winter and as snug and comfortable as his was, the tepee in his days. Then, maybe I'm a little bit of a mystic here, but what brings them together in my mind is that you're continually running into the ghosts of the old boys around here. It's as if this land has its own souls and it evolves its own souls—the Indian has his particular soul and now the white man has come in and he has to forget the soul he has and—this is treacherous ground, by the way. I realize it. I'm not a philosopher and I'm not a professional psychologist, but I nevertheless still feel very strongly that there is something going on in the relationship of the human being to his environment. Eventually it makes his soul. I think you're given the nervous equipment to have a soul; that's all you're given at birth. After that your environment makes you whatever you are, makes your soul. And I think that we're beginning to have our soul out here. And I find in my mind some conflict whenever I listen *too* sharply to Chaucer, or too sharply to Shakespeare— that then I lose a feeling for what I am out here, as Fred from Siouxland; and naming that country Siouxland helped sort of crystallize a lot of things in my mind. When I built this mural, I could see the first people almost—the land remained the same, but the animals keep changing as you go on. You see all the way in here from the early things that come out of the sea and gradually some four-legged animals, then upright, and so on. The soil always remains the same but the creatures change a little bit; the outside of the creatures may change a little bit but the inside, I think, remains the same.

E: This is all tied up with lonesomeness in a way, isn't it?

M: Yes.

E: In other words, being out here is a way of identifying yourself?

M: Yes. That's exactly right, because if you get too sociable then the other stuff comes in, pours in on you, that doesn't belong here quite yet. We have to be our own kind of roughnecks in this country before we can develop our set of manners. That's the way I feel. Ransom wrote an article some time ago about the rednecks, or the roughnecks, in American letters. I thought, well, so what, the British were known as big eaters and strong ale drinkers and were ruffians of the first order and it took them five hundred years before they developed this very high-toned Oxonian accent and set of manners. And we've got to have about the same amount of time to develop our particular set and I think there is a distinct difference between the kind of guy that's going to develop out of the Midwest as well as the far West in time to come, who will be a distinct fellow with a peculiar and separate way of behaving, and the English gentleman, as well as, say, the French cavalier, and the Spanish caballero. We aren't old enough out here to have our own set of manners.

E: But then Siouxland for you is not only geographical, it's spiritual?

M: It's spiritual, *oh*, yes! Oh, yes. To me it isn't just Minnesota. It's a piece of four states; and so that sort of lifts it even geographically above just being one state. It becomes the upper part of the Mississippi valley. I have the feeling – I haven't pinned this down yet by enough reading – but I have the feeling that the writers from the northern half of the Mississippi valley and the writers of the southern half feel more as a group, more brotherly towards each other, than do, say, the writers of the South Mississippi valley and the writers of the Piedmont. I heard Allen Tate talk a little bit about that one night; I didn't catch all of it, but he had somewhat the same feeling. I feel a great deal of kinship to Tate and Warren and Faulkner; different as we are, they are lonesome too. And I think part of my feeling is due to the fact that all my life I've regarded the Mississippi valley as *one* entity. If you look at the Mississippi, it's like a tree with branches going out, and we all pour into it, even though we did come in from the east to settle it, some of us; many of us also came up the river and gradually branched out over these rivers; as time went on, we set up civilizations in these river towns, and they were there first. I think that's part of the reason why I'm interested in Hugh Glass and in some of these other western themes, that they came in via the river, whereas some of the older people that I write about came in from the East as immigrants. But they still have to come together on these rivers and get caught in this vast interlocking web. And I think that America has in the Mississippi River a sort of Nile of Egypt. We even have some towns named alike – Memphis, and Cairo, what is it, Illinois? – and we have a great seaport down at the far end – very similar to the seaport off the end of the Nile; the Nile periodically overflows its banks and reawakens the land over there, and our Mississippi periodically overflows – there are *many* similarities of the two rivers, in the way they affect the people. And I think the Nile tends to unite the people in Egypt, just as I think the Mississippi tends to unite everybody here.

E: I noticed that *Morning Red* is dedicated to Faulkner; is that part of your attempt to express that kinship?

M: Yes, it is. I like him a lot. There's much in him that appeals to me. I'd say a good half of his work is *warm* to me. I'm immediately in it, and it's as if a better part of me could have written it – not that I could do it, but a better part of me could have written it. The other half I don't quite get. It may be that it's due to the fact that Mississippi is warm and humid and has bayous and mosquitos and so on and is damper; the air is muggy and sort of unclear most of the day, whereas up here the air most of the time, or about half of the time, is very clear with clean, strong north Canadian winds and so on; there's a difference there and that causes me to feel a little uneasy about half of it. Or it may be in the character of Faulkner himself as a person.

E: Do you know him?

M: No. I've never met him. I wrote him that I was dedicating the book to him, but he didn't acknowledge it or anything. He plays possum a lot, you know. His smoke signal is almost out of sight. But there's something that appeals to me. I haven't done too much of it – I'd like to; maybe he has more daring than I to do it. If a human mind can be considered to be, say, a four-walled room or a walled room, then Faulkner has a three-walled room with one room open to nature – to the wilds. And you're not aware of it, by the way. You know, you're used to reading the proper Thackeray, or Mr. Conrad who hid a lot of things he saw, in his style and so on, and you've read all these proper people who have conventional walls around what they are doing. And so you get into Faulkner's room and you sit there a little while and you're reading and all of a sudden it dawns on you that there are some strange things going on: you look at the floor and there's an alligator crawling right past your chair and there goes a vine lifting and crawling and moving. It's very horrifying for a little while, that this nature is just sort of breathing, pulsing, in and out of that wall that's gone, into this room, and it gives you the terrible shivers. He really lets the old dinosaurs get into his books, the old *far* past times; they get in sort of automatically in that man. And I think that helps explain some of his style once in a while, these serpentine sentences, you know.

E: Something terribly primitive, like Stravinsky's music.

M: Yes ... Yes ... It's *quiet!* as nature is at first. Until the jump, see, until the pounce.

Friends...Intervention at PEN*

Friends. I am an American. From Minnesota. We are all members of the human hive. And all of us are interested in truth. In honey. And this is true of us whether we're the queen bee type, or the drone bee, or the worker bee, or, lately, the computer bee. Now the computer bee has been telling us that he can package our honey in marvelous new shapes and forms, so that if the queen bee and the drone bee desire it they can wax fatter than ever. In fact, the computer bee tells us that because of his inventions, life for us in the hive is going to be completely changed, is never going to be the same again. This prediction has thrown some of us into a state of shock. But the truth is that when all is said and done, we've still got to have our honey. And it will still take the worker bee, the writer bee (poet, playwright, novelist), to find the original nectar from which the honey is made.

*An "intervention" or short speech given at the 1966 international convention of PEN held in New York.

Doon, Iowa: Magic Place

Doon is the magic place for me. It is the town of my childhood as well as my young manhood. I need only to come over the brow of the hill and a host of recollections come flooding to my mind. When I used to drive the horse and buggy to school in town I saw it often in the pink morning light so that the church steeples and the water tower would gleam like the pink turrets of some fabled castle. I loved going to school and always hurried toward those pink spires. Doon is the town where we used to wait eagerly on Saturday nights for the train from the north to come in with packages from the mail order houses in the Twin Cities. It is the place where we played baseball, where we met at church on Sundays, where on still other Saturday nights I and a buddy would divide a quart of ice cream between us. Memories inexhaustible – and I shall no doubt be mining the aura and the magic of them all the rest of my life in my books.

I've skated on both the Big Rock and the Little Rock; I've swum in all the swimming holes around, including the ice-cold sandpit south of town; I've raided watermelon patches when just a lad; I've gone on long hikes through the back-country pastures and "wild lands"; I've cut my name on a boulder north of town; I've gone slumming down the various lover's lanes.

I've learned such manhood as I have in the good old town: going to school on horseback when it was thirty below, picking corn on cold wet freezing mornings, scooping out the road for miles, thawing out a frozen car, pitching straw onto a rack from an old strawbutt in freezing driving snow, fixing my old tin lizzie with some bailing wire and fresh water for the radiator.

I was born on a farm near Doon and I hope to be buried in the cemetery near Doon. It's my true home town. I've come to like my adopted home town too, Luverne, but Doon I cannot escape because I spent my first years there.

Blue Mounds, 1967

Our Mother River Has Diarrhea

A Talk Given at the University of South Dakota

The subject specifically was the Missouri River, its dams, and Corps of Army Engineers' plans to straighten the channel from Yankton to Sioux City – the last of the Old Missouri that had not been touched by man. Since the Mississippi-Missouri River Basin is the great mother of us all, perhaps my defense of keeping that stretch of Missouri wild applies elsewhere as well.

The first thing that catches my eye is that our old mother river has a very bad case of the diarrhea. One good look at the silted water tells us that it is indeed serious. Attempts to treat the diarrhea with six huge plugs, to wit, the six earthen dams now straddling the Missouri above Yankton, S.D., haven't helped a bit. The plugs are rapidly silting full and in some eighty years will be of little value in controlling floods.

My recommendation would be to discontinue the present treatment and instead attack the other end of the alimentary canal of our midland mother. We should try to stop that drop of water where it falls, wherever that may be, in the whole Mississippi-Missouri River watershed. Holding that drop of water where it falls, as much as we possibly can, will cure the old lady of this silting disease.

I've long been against having the earthen dams. Engineers admit they will eventually fill with silt. Engineers have never been able to assure me that a minor tremor of an earthquake will not crack the dams. Should one of the upper dams ever break due to a minor earthquake the destruction below would be a catastrophe. Much good river bottom land has been lost and has not yet been replaced by irrigated land on the plateaus above. We stole land (yes, once again) from the Indians to put in the dams.

It is too bad we're descendants of bogtrotters and peat-diggers and polder-makers. We come from people whose experience was solely with flat lands. We knew nothing about

70

tilling rolling lands, yes, even steep hillsides. How much better wouldn't it have been if we could have come from Taiwan, or Japan, or China, where they knew about terracing long before man invented the alphabet, let alone the printed word. We would have known how to keep the best soil in place. We would have treated our midlands as truly our mother.

When the mother is sick, everybody in the family is sick.

It is a vain hope to think that somehow or other the Corps of Army Engineers will just go away and disappear. I'm afraid they're here to stay. Once a bureaucracy, especially one of the Army, has been established, it is almost impossible to get rid of it. They'll fight to perpetuate themselves. They'll come at us with plan after plan of make-work. So, we might as well resign ourselves to having them.

But, having them, let's give them a project that we can all approve of. And I have a suggestion to make. Instead of building more earthen dams, I think we should ask them to convert their equipment and material into barges and trucks, and have them go down to the delta of the Mississippi River, which is some fifteen miles wide and forty-five miles long, and have them bring all that good mud and dirt back up the river and distribute it on the eroded yellow hills of our uplands. This should keep them busy for years and years. And in addition we should ask them to visit every farmer, every manager of a forest preserve, etc., to educate them into holding that drop of water where it falls.

If we could just get the Army to do that, our Army would go down in history as one of the great ones of all time, even greater than Alexander's army, which as a by-product hellenized the then known world.

Think it over. This suggestion is not as crazy as you might think. What we're allowing the Corps to do now is even crazier.

Place

Frederick Manfred, who writes under his own name and as Feike Feikema, lives at Luverne, Minnesota, and has been described as "the Faulkner of the Great Plains." His many novels have a strong regional feeling, and The Primitive, The Brother *and* The Giant, *all published by Doubleday, were gathered later into a massive trilogy.*

The question should be rather how do I think The Place is affected – if at all – by my living in the Midwest. The Place is the boss and when it finally decided to use me to be a voice for it, I had to do what it pretty well wanted. Had I been raised in, say, Passaic, New Jersey (where I worked for a while for the U.S. Rubber Company), I would have written much different work, perhaps in the direction of William Carlos Williams's various "Patersons." Or had I been raised in Pacific Palisades (where I lived for some six months at the Huntington Hartford Foundation), I would have written still other kinds of work, perhaps in the direction of John Steinbeck's *Pastures of Heaven* or *East of Eden.*

I do see other writers occasionally. They sometimes drop in on me here on the Blue Mounds, or I go to see them. One of the best times I ever had in my life took place at Robert Bly's home near Madison, Minnesota. We (Robert Bly, James Wright, Thomas McGrath) talked about everything but our own writings for three days. We went swimming together. We took long walks across the prairies together. Generally, however, we prefer living apart from each other, as all good writers have always done.

Critics and good readers often have the idea that writers need to fraternize a lot, need to fire each other up, to get the writing done. Perhaps for critics and good readers to write original things, fraternizing is necessary. But a good writer is a self-starter and an outrider. (Outwardly he tends to be a good citizen of his community; inwardly he is an outrider.) Downtown he coffees with the farmer and merchant; at home he sits at the desk of judgment. Critics and good readers like to talk about schools of writers, forgetting that Dickens and Thackeray, though members of the same club, rarely ever talked to each other, forgetting that Hemingway and Faulkner and Steinbeck never met, forgetting that there is some doubt that Aeschylus, Sophocles and Euripides were friends (Euripides, in fact, turned his back on Athens and went to live alone by the sea.). Writers shouldn't see each other too often — it leads to intellectual inbreeding, when to widen the cultural spectrum of a society there should be creative outbreeding.

I do agree though that there should be a center for publishers and agents and critics. It is too bad that in this country it is in New York and not, say, in St. Louis. I consider most people living in New York as aliens in what I think of as my country.

What Makes a True Soul Mate?

I've often asked myself: what two people are most apt to make good friends, make true soul-mates? What two individuals have basic natures that are in near-perfect correspondence with each other? What two human spheres come closest to overlapping each other? Is it husband and wife? Father and daughter? Mother and son? Father and son? Mother and daughter? Brother and sister? Twins, dissimilar and identical? Cousins? Grandparents and grandchildren? Where, in all those different relationships, is one most apt to find those people who naturally and spontaneously understand each other at all times? Who discover and have true human bonding?

Already when I was a little boy, I remember asking my father and mother on our way over to visit a neighbor or a relative, "Do they have a little boy there I can play with? Who's like me?" When we went to a Fourth of July picnic, or attended church in another town, or if I was sent to a new country school, the first thing I did was to look around for a possible chum.

I wanted a confidant to whom I could tell all. I wanted to share all my secrets. I wanted a chum with whom I might do great things: explore the creek in our pasture, build an airplane, breed centaurs, read special books, win baseball games.

Later on, as I became older, as I grew up through puberty and young manhood, I began to look for that perfect friend in a girl. I hoped to find in her that perfect complement mate, in which the man in me would love the woman in her, while the woman in me would love the man in her. And vice versa. By doubling our eyes we would quadruple our insights into The Darks and magnify our ecstasies into The Lights.

Of course, all too sadly over the years, I've come to doubt that I will ever be able to spell out the magic of a true human bonding, describe its origins and its workings, its fusing and

74

its shapings. And I'm also afraid that no such thing as a true bonding has ever existed. It is probably impossible for any one person to know another person completely. We are all such very complicated flesh prisms, with our endless facets and sides, and whether it's love or friendship, we can light up only so many of each other's facets, those facets that our light falls on. The facets on the far side of another person's prism remain dark for us. Yet it is in the very nature of the human being that we continue to hope, to dream, to fantasize, we will somehow light up all the facets of our chum-friend-love, that our chum-friend-love's light will illuminate up all our facets. If we are in love, we strive to light up the dark side of the moon of the other person. We truly hope, for a season, that we can reach a full understanding of each other.

Lacking that perfect friend, we sometimes settle for the next best thing. We cultivate a circle of friends. We need more than one friend to light up all our facets at one time or another. When a novelist uses someone he knows as a model for a character, he never really gets him or her down exactly as they are, but has to fill in the dark side of the moon of that person with imaginative material taken from his general knowledge of human beings to create the fully rounded character.

The search for the perfect soul mate has been going on for a long long time. There are the quests of David and Jonathan, Paris and Helen, Achilles and Patrocles, Pericles and Aspasia, Tristan and Iseult, Lancelot and Guinevere, Romeo and Juliet, Aucassin and Nicolette, Abelard and Heloise, Frankie and Johnnie. The search for the perfect love is one of the dominant themes in all literature.

I've pursued this lovely problem in every one of my books, sometimes quite openly, sometimes indirectly. Taking just the five books in *The Buckskin Man Tales* we find, *among other things,* the following:

In *Conquering Horse* the hero No Name is told by his mother's brother, Moon Dreamer (who was in love with his mother), that his vision, interpreted, contains two instructions: one, he must capture a white stallion, and two, kill his beloved father.

In *Lord Grizzly* old Hugh Glass takes a liking to Jim and Fitz, mostly because they reminded him of his own two boys back home in Pennsylvania. Further, Hugh Glass marries Bending Reed, an Indian woman, mostly because her heyoka or contrary behavior reminds him, subconsciously, of his former sherip of a wife Maggie. And there is also his and the white race's addiction in wanting to touch strange skin, either to love it or destroy it, or both.

In *Scarlet Plume* comely Judith Raveling, a woman from a white civilization, one of the first bloomer girls, falls in love with Scarlet Plume, a man from a Stone Age culture, a Yankton Dakota Sioux, when he tries to help return her to the white settlements. Scarlet Plume's uncle, Whitebone, has already forced himself upon her, and other Indian men have already ravished her, yet some powerful man-woman draw was to work between them. It was more than just the usual animal attraction between man and woman, more even than the white woman's fascination with colored skin. It was as if both suddenly found themselves caught up in an archetypal kind of bonding.

In *Riders of Judgment* a dark tie exists between the cousins Cain, Harry, Dale, and Rosemary. There is also the counsel that a father had better kill his first-born son if he wanted peace in his home. In cattle country times some strange ties were permitted. There weren't many women around and men were often gone for months at a time during cattle drives.

It was while I was looking for some material in back files of the 1890 *Review* in Rock Rapids, Iowa, which I later used in the novel *Eden Prairie,* that I came across the germ term for *King of Spades.* In a local news column there was an item about a man of the town who wanted it to be known he'd spotted a fellow hanging around his home. He announced that he was taking measures to see that it was stopped. He said he'd also instructed his wife and young son to keep the doors locked.

Reading on through the files I found further references to the story. The man had bought a gun and said that the next time he caught the intruder hanging around his home he was going to shoot him.

Finally I came upon the news item telling about the murder. Some of the phrasing in the account were eye-catching. "He threatened to murder me unless I acknowledged I had been a bad woman." "He repeatedly and publicly accused his wife of infidelity and charged her with relations with men, when nothing less than madness could imagine grounds for suspicion." "Strong men could not gaze upon it without a thrill of horror!" "The ball entered her right breast just below the nipple." "The monster emptied another chamber of the weapon."

It struck me, as I read all that, that the intruder was in the man's own home. The older the son became the more tormented the father became. The mother-wife was lavishing too much of her affection upon their son and not enough on him.

I had already explored, in part, the tie that existed between my father and a brother in the novel *This Is the Year*. And I knew that I would explore it further along with the tie that existed between my mother and myself in a later book. (Which I did in the rume *Green Earth*, published in 1977.) I pretty much understood what had been going on in my own family with my father and mother and with my five brothers, but the bizarre murder-and-suicide that took place in Rock Rapids, Iowa, threw me back on my heels. What in God's name had gone on there back in that previous century?

I began to speculate as follows. In those days it was not unusual for a mature girl of thirteen or fourteen to get married. There were few women around in frontier towns, and the moment a girl was nubile she was subjected to pressure to get married. Let's suppose she had a baby boy at fourteen. By the time the boy was fully grown at seventeen she would still be only thirty-one. If she wore a long dress it would hide possible varicose veins on her legs and if she put on flour make-up she could pass for a woman of twenty-four. If the young man let his beard grow he could pass for twenty-three.

Suppose further that when the boy was seven, something climatic happened in the family, so that father, mother, and son were suddenly ejected into the world, with none of the three knowing where the other two had gone. Suppose still further that some ten years later mother and son ran into each other in some far Western city. More than likely, after all that time, they would not recognize each other. The boy would look like any other cowboy come to town to raise hijinks and the mother would resemble any other housewife window shopping along the board walk. Meeting on the streets of Cheyenne, would they be drawn towards each other in the ordinary natural man-and-woman way, or would they be drawn towards each other because of a one-time mother-baby tie? Would a subconscious kind of bonding be at work in them?

Well, when I'd gotten that far in my speculations, I remembered that two other writers had been there, Sophocles and Shakespeare. What to do. I was sure that some critic somewhere would accuse me of arrogance to think that I could tackle the oedipal problem on equal grounds with them. And someone was bound to argue that I was ruining the genre of the Western novel by unnaturally thrusting a Freudian concept into it.

I had read Sophocles (in translation) a number of times and I had read Shakespeare many times. I had learned that Sophocles had actually borrowed the oedipal idea for his *Oedipus Rex* from Egypt. And I knew that Shakespeare had borrowed his idea for *Hamlet* from the Danes. In both instances the original germ had not come from the author's place. It came to me that I probably had more right to use the oedipal problem than did either Sophocles and Shakespeare. A love affair between mother and son was more apt to happen in our West than in either Sophocles time or in Shakespeare time. As was mentioned above, the women were few and far between. Also, the frontier was in a continual turmoil as a new people tried to come to grips with a strange and sometimes hostile environment about which they knew little or nothing. And the few people going west were an outlandish lot. Anything was possible.

After pondering it all some more, and with a bow of apology to the ghosts of Sophocles and Shakespeare, I decided to go ahead anyway.

I'd add a new aspect to the story. In *Oedipus Rex* the father Laius is mistakenly killed by the son of Oedipus off stage and we never get to see the father. In *Hamlet* the son Hamlet doesn't kill the father, the uncle does it for him, but we still get a glimpse of the father when Hamlet sees his father's ghost on the platform of the castle at Elsinore. In my novel I'd have the father Magnus King survive the attempt on his life and

I'd let him come in on the scene at the end. I was curious to know what the father Magnus King would think about all this mother-son stuff. It might give still another sounding of that hoary old tabu, one that might be of value to help us understand the profound ties inside a nuclear family.

And, while I was at it, I'd try to deepen the problem so that at the end we wouldn't just ask what the father thought about all that unnatural affection, but we'd ask, what did the stallions think of it? For me the word "stallion" is a much richer word than the word "father." "When a son's blood is finally spilled, which mother weeps most? The stallions."

What helped drive the whole thing home, as I was writing the book, was the sudden appearance of the young maiden Erden Aldridge, whose Indian name was Blue Swallow, rising like a jinn from the end of my pen. She came all unbidden. She was not in the original plan for the book. But once I saw her, I knew she belonged. She helped set up the tragedy of the Ransom-Katherine tie. Erden was the girl Ransom should have married, not Katherine. Erden should have been his true love, his romantic ideal. And interesting enough, with Erden coming in on the scene, she also helped tie the whole quintology, *The Buckskin Man Tales,* together. Carrying Ransom's baby, she disappears, going farther west.

By having the father Magnus King come in on the scene when Ransom is about to be hanged for shooting his wife Katherine, Ransom hears from his father that his wife was also his mother. It convinces Ransom all the more that life was not worth living. So he kicks the barrel out from under his feet and hangs himself.

(The reader will notice that not once did I use the word "incest." That's because I didn't think "incest" to begin with. I was first of all interested in the problem of human bonding.)

And what did the stallion Magnus King think about all that mother-son bonding? That's the mystery I tried to unravel.

All through the writing of *King of Spades* it was as if I was possessed by a Better Writer, as if some kind of Holy Hand were guiding my hand. This was especially true after Erden appeared on the scene. Nights when I went to bed I

couldn't wait until morning to find out more about what was
to happen to Ransom and Erden. Every night I looked forward
to breakfast and work.

                                    Roundwind, September 11, 1979

Space, Yes: Time, No

Lecture given at the University of South Dakota
March 31, 1981

I'm mostly known as a person who writes stories and a few poems, but I do have some hobbies, and one of my hobbies has been, for many years, to read in the fields of physics, astronomy, and anthropology. I like to know where we came from, and how. Every once in a while I think I see something that the boys in those fields have missed. I think, shucks, I ought to do something about it, I ought to remark on it in some way, but then in a week or two I forget about it and I never do it.

Before I go any further, I want to say that in addition to the various magazines and books that I've read in those fields, in the last month or so I've read one book with much interest, and every now and then tonight I'll be leaning on it some. It is *The Dancing Wu Li Masters* by Gary Zukav. Wu Li is the Chinese word for physics, meaning "patterns of organic energy." That rightaway tells you something.

I feel a little bit like the student who's going to take a final exam in a subject he doesn't know very well, because who am I really to make observations in the field of physics? I'm supposed to be somewhat of an expert in making plots, somewhat of an expert in using metaphors. But I plead that most fundamental ideas of knowledge, whether in science, philosophy, or literature, are essentially simple and may as a rule be expressed in a language comprehensible to everybody. So what I shall have to say tonight will be essentially simple.

I approach the "time problem" in a child-like manner—try to see the world as it is with a beginner's mind, free of the harness of the expert. It's a little bit like the story of the emperor's clothes. Everybody knows and expects the emperor to be wearing splendid clothes. So when one day he comes down

mainstreet in a parade, everybody cheers him, all of them convinced without question that he is wearing regal clothes. But
there's a little boy in the crowd, on the sideline, who's never
been to the parade before, who has never seen the emperor.
He sees what there is to see – that the emperor, an eccentric,
has taken to going without clothes. The emperor is naked. The
same for us. We see everybody around us wearing and using
time. When actually, if we will only look around us with a
child's pure uncontaminated honest eyes, we will see that so
far as time goes we are naked.

I also approach the "time problem" with the confidence that
I think I've seen something, that it would be wrong of me
not to speak up. Henry Miller once wrote in his *Wisdom of
the Heart:* "I obey only my own instincts and intuition, I know
nothing in advance. Often I put down things which I do not
understand myself, secure in the knowledge that later they will
become clear and meaningful to me. I have faith in the man
who is writing, who is myself and the writer." Speaking from
my own experience, I sometimes do have a plot fairly well worked
out before I begin a book. But it often happens, when I'm about
a third of the way into it, that I desert the plot and follow
what I find in my head, on the grounds that what I find there,
as I go along, is going to be a whole lot better than that
preconceived plot. When I run into an area in which I seem
to feel stuck, and I don't know what's coming next, I usually
rub my hands in glee – because I have come to know that I've
come upon something I don't want to look at. If I go ahead
and push in anyway I'll write something very well.

I also remember that Max Planck, who was the first to
see that the basic structure of nature was granular, discontinuous, quanta which were discontinuous, realized that what
he had to say might undermine foundations of old Newtonian
physics. But Planck went ahead anyway, and today is known
as the father of quantum mechanics. Einstein too was very
disturbed by some of the conclusions that could be drawn from
both his special theory of relativity and his general theory of
relativity: that black holes were possible, a singularity; that
there was no stable spot in the universe, a point of reference
"on solid ground," from which we could measure other things

in motion. Yet he never backed down once he found what he considered to be a truth. His relativity theories spurred on Niels Bohr to come up with his complementarity theory, or quantum mechanics.

Once you know something you never back away from it.

This talk is going to be a little bit like taking a jump on the sack swing. My father helped me build my first sack swing. You know how they make it — you find a tall tree with a powerful limb, a strong rope, a good tough gunnysack. You fill the gunnysack with straw. You tie one end of the rope to the limb and the other end to the gunnysack. Then you can take a little run at it and jump on it and get a little ride, like a hobby horse. Or you can have someone push you, preferably someone tall, so you get a good ride. Or you can jump off of a step ladder — onto the sack swing.

Or you could do what I once did. Look for another limb in a nearby tree. You tie a string to a corner of the sack, a long twine string, tie the string around your middle, climb that nearby tree onto the other limb and reel in the sack swing. There you stand on the edge of that limb, not quite having a good hold of that sack swing. You don't know what to do. If you teeter, you may fall off and break your neck, so you've got to jump and catch the sack swing. The first time I made one of those jumps, I just barely nipped onto the sack swing with my knees. Part of me scraped the earth, and on the way back my brother told me he could see a lot of pimples. Maybe tonight that's what's going to happen too.

One time I went so high that when I got to the other end of the arc the rope slacked on me a bit as I rode up into some leaves. One leaf lay right over my eye with the sun shining through it. I could see the purple veins of the leaf right in my eye for a fleeting second. And then I fell back.

There was one time I didn't make that jump, when I should have. We were invited to a party at Mark Graubard's house. He taught science at the University of Minnesota. It was one of those buffet-style dinner parties. A few minutes into the evening and I realized that I was out of my element. Most there were scientists. I began to wonder why I was there. I finally decided I was the token artist. In those days it was fashionable to have at parties a token Negro, a token Indian, a token professor of literature, a token writer, and so on.

It wasn't long though before I started listening carefully to the scientists. The discussion got around to pairings in nature. If there is a negative charge around somewhere, there will be a positive charge. For the male there's a female. If someone advances a thesis, then someone will advance an anti-thesis. Idealism versus materialism. Body and soul. Action and reaction. Yin and yang. It was mentioned that our language was full of it: the long and short of it, up and down, black and white, to and fro, back and forth, seesaw. There was also much talk about matter and what it was made of.

It struck me, as I was listening to all this, that if the universe was full of pairings, opposites attracting each other, then this matter that we find ourselves in must have its opposite too. So, waiting for a pause in the talk, I finally cleared my throat and offered my observation.

Well, there were looks of embarrassment all around. What was this boor doing here? What did this farmer think he was saying? All agreed there was only one kind of matter. The matter we were in, the one we knew here and now. And anyway, suppose there might be an opposite to our matter, what would you call it? I said, thinking of Hegel's logic, and thinking that the law of symmetry demanded it, if there is matter then there must be anti-matter. "No, no, impossible, impossible. There's only one matter." This party took place in the late 1940's. On the way home, my wife chided me for the presumption that I would have anything valuable to say amongst such an august body of physicists. So I fell silent. Some six or seven years later Emilio Segre and Owen Chamberlain of the University of California came up with some evidence that indeed there was anti-matter. Later on I found out that another man in 1928, Paul Dirac, had wondered if there might not be anti-matter. No one at the Graubard party, however, had ever heard of Dirac's speculation. That's how I once before missed seeing the sun shine through a green leaf lying across my eyes when I didn't take that jump on the sack swing. Tonight, though, I'm going to take that jump and we will see at the end of this talk if I made it or if I fell with a loud bellyflop on the ground.

Once early in 1960, listening to my neighbor farmer grousing about Daylight Savings Time, that we were monkeying around with God's time and that God might punish us by giving us a drought or tornado, my Interior Commentator suddenly spoke up. It said: "What's God's time? God didn't make the clock, we did. God just gave us day and night."

I might explain what I mean by Interior Commentator. You meet a friend on the street, you're glad to see him, you shake hands with him, you smile at him, you ask him how he is, all the while right in the middle of all this, a voice in the back of your head speaks up and says, "You know, he looks pretty pale this morning. Dark splotches under his eyes. Aha. He was out late last night, carousing." Or, "He has an odd color. Aha. Heart trouble. Isn't going to live very long." Of course, you don't say this out loud. You might when you're five years old. But you don't after you're thirty. Or "fifty" like myself. You see, your Interior Commentator, your IC, if we've kept it alive, is always brutally and wonderfully honest. It is at once child-like in its directness and ancient in its wisdom. It is the honest lizard in us talking. By the way, the initials, IC, make for a nice play on words. "I see."

Julian Jaynes in his wonderful book, *The Origin of Consciousness in the Breakdown of the Bicameral Mind*, suggests that maybe one's IC lives in the right hemisphere of our brain, where other voices also live, the kind of voices that once qualified a man to become a priest or soothsayer, or the voice at Delphi, but which today qualifies him for the nut house as a schizophrenic. I often have fun by myself at parties wondering what other people's IC's are saying. (Not what the people are saying socially. Even in their catty remarks. Catty remarks are often actually pleasant if you look at them right.) What for example is a doctor's IC saying when he sees a man with a certain kind of pallor? He'll right away make some kind of medical comment to himself: "He is going to be coming to my office within a month." Or what a psychologist's IC is saying, when he sees a fellow with a tic. Or a lecher's IC is saying when he looks at a young lady. Or a preacher's IC is saying when he sees a gross sinner.

Over the years I've thought about my neighbor's remark about tampering with God's orderly world of time. The more I thought about it, the more I was convinced that we as a thinking species invented time, not God. (Or if you don't believe there is a God, then WHAT IS did not invent time.)

Some years ago I was riding in a car across Washington, D.C., at night, past the Vice-President's house. The driver and I had just left the party where some poets had some wine after a reading. One of the poets there dropped a remark that he was suspicious of mathematicians, that if we must have inquiry, he'd much rather trust a poet's ability at metaphorical inquiry. That remark set off a whole chain of explosions in my mind — with the vigorous help of my IC.

When I got home I wrote a long poem. I'll read you just a short portion of it:

> In Chevy Chase
> we found the late party for poets,
> house lights striding across green grass,
> voices strident inside,
> souls dangling from the ceiling,
> not a rooted set of feet anywhere —
> all uprooted bushes gasping in a glass hothouse.
> Finally in a corner a poet
> chewing his mind's cud soundless
> said the following thing:
> "It's a mistake to follow the mathematicians all the way.
> They've pushed thought so far
> there's no longer any reality to fit it.
> It's better to take the route of the metaphor
> to explain Time and Space.
> At the end there
> Einstein was chasing wraiths."
> I didn't argue.
> I'd long thought the final whispers of higher mathematics
> were leading us nowhere.
> Our white days
> and our black nights
> broke continuity for us,

made us think in segments
and then call it "time."
There's no Time.
There's hardly Space.
There is only matter in motion, yeasting mass.

My lady driver broke in on my reverie. "Why so silent?"
"Oh, I was just thinking there's no Time." "You mean, time
for . . . ." Then with a laugh, she said, "Or, do you mean time
as Time?" "Time as Time. Real Time, or Einstein's relativity
Time, or quantum mechanics Time. There's only People Time."

We're caught up in who we've become, a rational people
with a strong scientific bent, so thoroughly, that we can't step
outside ourselves to see ourselves as a stranger might see us,
a stranger say, from Sirius. The stranger from Sirius would
say: "Very interesting creatures. But they're obsessed by a fiction they call Time. It is constantly on their lips. When in
reality there is no such thing as Time. Matter doesn't give
a rip about time. Everything is just Now. It is always Now
to matter."

I went on to explain that had we been born on a non-spinning
planet we would never have evolved the concept of Time. Like
the moon our planet would have been all dark on one side and
all light on the other. We would have lived along the margins
of darkness and light. The states of darkness and light would
not have come at us like an alternating current. We probably
would not have built into us a need for sleep. Life from birth
to death would have been one continuous state of illumination.
The idea of Time would not have occurred to us. We would
not have been concerned with befores and afters, but only with
nows.

Since that ride home from that party of poets, I've slowly
but surely come more and more convinced that there is no real
Time, no absolute Time, or relativity Time. There is only People
Time—and singularly, only this our People Time. To explain
further: this business of us living on the planet where there
are alternating periods of darkness and light has, over the late
millennia since we woke up to the fact that we were conscious
beings, so drilled into us that existence is broken up into

segments, that we began to give those segments names. As savages we probably spoke of day and night. Later on we broke up the day into segments called morning, forenoon, noon, afternoon, and evening. Then we broke it all up into hours, twelve hours of day and twelve hours of night. Before we had clocks, had only sundials, we had twelve hours of daylight whether it was summer or winter on any part of the globe. In Chaucer's day the days were twelve hours long in the summer and twelve hours long in the winter. They just either lengthened the hours or shortened them, depending on the season.

Once we invented precision instruments in clocks, we were truly hooked, so that even so great a free mind as Einstein was caught up in the obsession. Newton, Einstein, Planck, Bohr, all of them couldn't make a move mathematically but what they included in their equations a symbol, an "X" or a "Y," or as in the case of the speed of light, a "C" to stand for time. $E = MC^2$.

This obsession with time may very well have prevented Einstein from unifying his theory of general relativity and his theory of special relativity with the theory of quantum mechanics, from unifying the four fundamental forces in the universe: gravitation, electro-magnetism, strong nuclear force, and weak nuclear force. Einstein should have thrown out time like he once did ether. Physicists once believed that the whole universe hung in an invisible and odorless substance which existed so that light waves could move through them to get from the sun to the earth. There had to be some medium for light waves to get here. However, every attempt to find any evidence of ether failed utterly. It was an assumption; so Einstein, a pure beginner, like a young boy five years old, one day said, "Ether does not exist." And then he made his spectacular jump into his theories of relativity.

Had Einstein said the same thing about time and concentrated instead on matter to see what it is doing—is it in motion? is it at rest? if it is in motion, is it energy? if it is at rest, is it arrested motion or arrested energy?—he might have declared that the fourth dimension was motion, or dance, or wiggle, and not time. But the concept of time was so embedded in our everyday experience that he, and we, never questioned it.

The truth is that since we invented it, recently, because of our peculiar situation here on this sometimes lighted up and sometimes darkened planet, we will never find its essence, or some kind of ultimate constituent, as we can, say, of space. The constituents of space we can point at. On the macroscopic level we can point at this podium, at you, this room, our earth, our planets, the sun, galaxies. On the microscopic level we can point at photons of light. (The human eye can actually detect a photon, provided that the eye has been adapted to darkness for a period of time.) We have good reason to believe that there are gravitational waves or gravitons. We find evidence of atoms and molecules. We find evidence of neutrinos on photographic plates. In other words, matter takes up space. But we will never be able to point at a particle of time. Space was always there in the first place, but time was never there. We invented time. We didn't invent space. Space we can become aware of because we bump into matter somewhere. But you can't bump into time. What essence of time can we bump into? (Unless it's a clock, of course, and we made that.) We can speak of anti-matter and of anti-particles but we can not speak of anti-time, or of an anti-second, or anti-minute, or an anti-hour.

Should the human being and his inventive mind die out, time would vanish, but not space with its matter. Time is an illusion mankind has leaned on for a few thousand years. It is a mental construct, an abstraction. And we have lived so long in our abstraction that we no longer know we are in it. We are caught up inside the envelope of our language.

So let's throw time out. And then what do we have? Well, perhaps we can then go faster than the speed of light, 186,000 miles per second. We have locked the speed of light onto a second, which we have just said no longer exists. So there is just speed. So, therefore, the idea that you can not go faster than the speed of light may not be true at all. Also, there is a suggestion that for some of the far out galaxies to get where they are from the time of the Big Bang (if you can accept the Big Bang as a theory of the beginning of the universe) those galaxies must have traveled faster than the speed of light. Also, some subatomic particles, according to quantum mechanics, seem to know instantaneously that decisions that affect them are being made elsewhere, and know what those decisions are. That "elsewhere" can be as far away as another galaxy. The transmission of this kind of information, of course, far exceeds the speed of light.

For years early pilots were warned not to exceed the speed of sound. Break through the sonic barrier and their plane would break up. But now we do it routinely in commercial jet airplanes. So, perhaps, now we may be able to break through the speed-of-light barrier without flattening out and disappearing. Maybe we will be able to fly faster than the speed of light and will be able to visit the nearest star with its system of planets, and do it in less time than is now believed possible. Maybe we should change Einstein's famous equation, $E = MC^2$ to $E = MM^2$, that is, energy equals mass times motion^2.

The findings of quantum mechanics as invented by Planck and Bohr may have to be looked at again. At best, quantum mechanics can come up with only shrewd guesses in their experiments to account for events in man's experience. They are accurate so long as they predict probabilities, but they can't predict particular events. (By the way, this distressed Einstein. He said you should be able to predict particular events. This is what God would have intended.) By throwing out the symbol for time in their mathematical calculations, they may very well come closer to predicting particular events. I hope that the mathematics department gets busy rightaway tomorrow morning to see if that will work.

Mind you, I'm not advocating that we throw out our precious bauble "people time." It is handy to have. But may I suggest that we relax a little in the way we use it, be more like the way the Indian handles the problem. We should always remember it is merely an instrument, that it does not have any true philosophical import or scientific existence. For example, instead of looking at your watches and wondering if Manfred hasn't talked long enough, why doesn't he wind it up? you should check the seat of your pants. If your "sit-upons" are beginning to hurt, then the talk is already far too long. Discomfort has relevance, not a wrist watch.

The problem of whether or not we are observing a particle or a wave—and, according to quantum mechanics it can't be both at the same time – if you look for a particle then you can't find the wave, if you look for the wave you can't find the particle – can possibly be resolved if we throw out the symbol for time. I notice that physicists in their equations and in their experiments invariably use a symbol for time. I keep scratching that symbol out to see what it looks like. And you know, it sounds sensible to me without that symbol.

We are so hooked on time that we have been taken in by the argument that if we are not here then reality is not here either. Quantum mechanics physicists now think that reality isn't there unless there is an observer to observe it. I believe reality is there apart from whether or not I'm there to observe it. If I die, you, that fellow here, or you, that fellow there, you can go on observing it. If all of us die, reality will go on being there until another intelligent being comes along to observe it. To argue that the dinosaurs did not exist to make observations good enough for them to last three hundred million years is ridiculous. We find their bones.

We've always had a problem with the "I" which is in here, with the external world which is "out there" – when in fact it is all one and related intimately.

Perhaps we can explain what we think the word "time" describes if we say the following: Just as the water in a pond remains in the same place as waves move through it after you've thrown a stone into it, so, too, the matter of the universe remains in the same general position as motion moves through it. Or dance. Or wiggle.

Perhaps Einstein, Bohr, and Newton should have employed the metaphorical route even more than they did, perhaps even relied on poets, to help explain the expanding universe. For example, and I now quote another portion from my poem:

My mother sometimes
baked raisin bread:
a clutch of sourdough
(spook she called it)
several cups of flour,
a hand full of raisins,
melted butter.

She'd kneed it,
interweave it,
pound it down into a ball,
place it in the bread pan
on the warm reservoir on the back of the stove,
or take it into bed with her at night
under the warm quilts with Pa,
and wait for it to rise.
By noon the lid
on the bread pan would begin to quiver,
a great eyelid opening.
Mother would take all the dough out
and pound it down again.
"Just to make sure every slice had an equal share of raisins."
Mother's raising bread dough
resembles the expanding universe more
than does the astronomer's picture of a balloon filled with air.
In mother's dough all the raisins were spreading
equally fast from each other,
both inside the continuum
as well as on the surface.
In the astronomer's example
of the expanding balloon of air,
we know what's happening to the raisins on the surface,
but what's happening to them inside the balloon?
The metaphor of the rising dough
is a better one
than the example of expanding air in the balloon.
But just as a whisper is not a muon,
so a likeness is not flesh.
We need the next mind beyond Einstein
to tell us that what we are seeing,
motion in mass,
mass in motion,
yeasting matter,
the Spook in the universe.

Permit me to make some further observations. Perhaps a
mistake was made when we made a distinction between organic

and inorganic matter, between a toad and a dull brown stone. Touch the toad and it jumps. Touch the stone and it just sits there. Our American Indian believed all things were alive, that we were part of the whole, that if one listened carefully one could hear a stone speak. The fact is, so far as atoms go, there is no difference between an atom found in the toad and the atom found in the stone. Down inside that subatomic realm, inside the atom, the electrons, the protons, the positrons, the neutrons are all alike.

According to quantum mechanics there is some evidence that a strange "knowing" is going on in the subatomic world. J.S. Bell, in Switzerland, had been working on this. Bell's theory says that at a deep and fundamental level the discontinuous (that is, the unconnected) parts of the entire universe are connected in an intimate manner and are connected in an immediate way. If so, what need for time?

Take the business of sending a beam of electrons through a magnetic field. Instantly the beam will split into two smaller beams of electrons. In one of them the electrons will spin up and in the other one they will spin down. If one takes one set of these paired electrons, we know that when one particle spins up, its twin spins down. If we yet again divert the first particle by means of a second magnet, its twin, without a second magnet, will yet again be diverted exactly like the first one. How does the second particle know what the first is doing? What's the connection? Seemingly a message passes between the two. This is true across even very great distances. And it knows it with superluminant speed. That is, beyond the speed of light. A communication is going on which is so swift that time in any form is no longer involved. Maybe the particles are alive, have some kind of life we have not yet figured out, and that is why they respond to each other.

Perhaps far down in the subatomic realm there exists a form of life we've never dreamed of or ever speculated about, the final building block, bit of a bit of a bit of a particle, beyond which we no longer can reduce matter, a bit of which we can no longer subdivide, the ultimate stuff, which is alive. Perhaps it is something even more refined and tinier than hadrons, muons, leptons, pions, etc. I don't mean by this Plato's theory

of ideas. It is something different. It informs and makes go
both inorganic as well as organic matter. If enough of them
cluster together, for whatever reason, they produce in our eyes
and in our microscopes the gray edge of a mass of something.
If true (and we won't know for sure until the laboratory, or
speculators like Bell and Bohr using the methods of quantum
mechanics, find it) then we all, each in a vague way, priest,
poet, physicist, have been right in part from our particular vantage point all along. We each have caught a glimpse of it, or
caught a glimpse of a part of it. I know I have sensed, if not
perceived, a reality out there, THAT WHICH IS, which is all
of a piece, an ALL that instantaneously at any given moment
knows what any part of it is doing in all instances, and knows
it with superluminant speed. IS is IS is IS. Various religions,
for example, Buddhism, Islam, Christianity, Confucianism, et
al., haven't been all that wrong; nor of course the physicists
and the mathematicians and the astronomers. All have been
pointing at, hinting, grasping at, a truth that actually lay in
ourselves as much as it did out there. The final iridescent
building block, which for the moment I'll call a "deon" (after
the Latin word "deo" meaning "god-like" and the Greek word
"deon" or "deontos" meaning "that which is obligatory") is in
superluminal communication with all other building blocks at
all times. This would account for ESP, for premonition, pres-
cience, intuition, hunches, etc.

I've had some absolutely fantastic things happen to me
which I haven't dared tell people. I'll give you one example.
I have never been able to figure out how it came about. We
were living in Bloomington, Minnesota, at the time. My wife
went to town with my daughter, Freya, to do some shopping.
They came home late. I had gone to bed reading Rabelais and
wasn't too interested in talking to anybody. I heard Freya go
to bed at the other end of the house. Then my wife came into
our bedroom. She threw a package on her bed and said, "I
don't suppose you care to know what I bought Nemo for his
birthday." Nemo was a neighbor boy. I had never discussed
with my wife what we might buy him for a birthday present.
Still mostly paying more attention to Rabelais than my wife
(Pantagruel was cleansing the streets of Paris with a marvelous

urination), my brain thought, peripherally, "Mouse." At that point I looked up at my wife. If I said, "Mouse," she'd think I was crazy. So I said, "I don't know." She gave me the package to open. What do you think was in it? A rubber mouse. Where did I pick that up? Some part of me picked it out of the air.

When we were children we often had things like that happen to us, but we didn't dare tell our elders. They'd say, "Go out and play under the trees some more." As we get older we get more rational. We start believing in time. We have this orderly society. We ignore those voices as foolish. If you teach mathematics, or physics, yes, or even poetry, you better not talk about those kinds of things or you'll be sent to the loony bin.

But the deons, now, those last bits of indestructible matter, they know. They are always in touch. Deons are godlike. They have a life and existence all their own. Deons really run the universe. But we're not always in touch with them. Some of us are trying very hard: poets, ministers, priests, physicists, biologists, fortune tellers, and mediums.

When any one of us takes on the task of studying nature, what we are actually doing is having nature study itself, since we are already part of nature. The deons in US are identical with the deons OUT THERE. Deons know. They correspond with each other — if we let them.

Deons are never at rest. They are always in a state of dance. Deons are continually creating, annihilating, and creating. Around and in an electron there is a behive of activity. Not only particles but virtual particles. Virtual particles are enigmas. One moment they are there; the next gone; the next moment back again. Now this kind of activity is against the law of conservation of energy. We can't have something pop up, then disappear, then pop up, then disappear. It sounds like self-creating life. That surely isn't physics. Or rational. But perhaps the problem is we still don't have instruments refined enough to catch or see or witness deons, to see their waxing and waning, to get in there deep enough to see what's really going on when those **deons** are doing their work. They are alive in their own odd way. We have as yet no concept of what that aliveness of theirs is. They are the apple of paradise we haven't eaten yet.

There is only one reality, a universal yeast of telepathic deons. It is one whole. All is related in an intimate way. There are no separate parts not knowing other separate parts. There is an all-pervading unity. Therefore, there is no need for Abstract Time, Real Time, Relativity Time.

Of course, there will always be a need for People Time. Knowing students as I do, they would never arrive in class on time if there weren't People Time.

And there is a need to end this monologue because people's sit-upons are bound to have gotten restless. I don't know about you, but I think that tonight we made that jump on that sack swing. We saw the purple veins in the green leaf. I know I managed to clamp my knees onto the sack swing. Not as good as we might have, nor as high as we might have, because I have the distinct feeling that I got a bit of bruising against some part of the earth as we went by, but we made it. I hope you'll forgive me if you felt a little bruising too.

Interview with
Frederick Manfred—I

by Nancy Bunge

FM: Poems come out like angleworms: if you pull them out right, they come out perfect. A poem is put together by the dreamer in you; I don't know if it's way downstairs in the basement or way up in the attic, but wherever it is, it's all been gone over and organized. I hardly ever rewrite a poem. I'll rearrange the stanzas once in a while, although I'm beginning to question that; I should probably leave them just the way they come out. The right side of my brain is kicking those out and the left side is trying to organize them. You feel with your right side. Your left side makes you logical, social and so on; you have to be suspicious of that.

Novel writing is a completely different operation. There you can be an amateur architect and amateur carpenter. You're making a long report on a certain activity in society and that takes a long time to get organized. You worry about plot and structure and, at the same time, you're trying to suck up as much as you can from the basement or the attic. I generally have a plot worked out, a target area, because I have a tendency to digress. But if something occurs in the story that asks me to take a side path or some new person comes popping in, I welcome it and follow that; just so I get at that target area.

I rub my hands in glee whenever I hit a wall in my manuscript and I don't know where to go next. There's a damn good reason why: it's something I don't want to look at. If I can push through and get into that area, I'll find something not only about myself, but something that may be of real value to someone else. And inadvertently, everything you need, the theme, the plot, will jump right out at you as you go along. Mark Twain's *Pudd'nhead Wilson* started off being one thing and then wound up two stories; I think that makes that a very powerful novel although he should have spent more time putting all that together. He should have explored what pulled him off base. Mark Twain was a forerunner; I wish he had done more exploring of himself, but he spent too much time lecturing.

Madison Jones and I had some great talks and we remarked that we often write the novels we're next going to live out. For example, if I were to write about a roué, after the book is done, I might start chasing women. *(Laughter.)* And that's a curious thing; I did that somewhat with *Milk of Wolves*. I found myself being interested in a lot of women after I wrote that book. *(Laughter.)*

NB: You've said that as you write more your dreams improve.

FM: Yeh. The only thing you've got to be careful with is that pretty soon you self-instruct your dreamer. You want those dreams to come up naturally.

NB: Do you record your dreams?

FM: I got probably a hundred dreams I've typed up in the last six or seven years. I write them down the next day. The only ones I record are those I remember. I figure there's a reason why you remember it, just like there's a reason you never forget certain incidents in your life. Those are the ones you should write down.

NB: You also read a lot of philosophy. Do you worry about that creeping into your stories?

FM: No, it stimulates me and widens my brain and allows me to receive more. It rarely shows up in my novels. It might in my poetry because philosophy can pop into poetry quite easily; if it's done beautifully, it's very powerful. But fiction is fiction. I'm highly suspicious of authors who preach in their novels. I have trouble reading Saul Bellow; his stuff is often animated essay – which maybe is all right for the academic critic, but it's not really fiction. True fiction is where the reader, no matter what the intelligence is, gets lost in the story. You can relay profound information by the route of fiction; it's a philosophical inquiry in story form. The findings in fiction are just as legitimate as those made by a logical route and you shouldn't mix them up.

Homer wouldn't have been repeated orally for two, three, four hundred years if there had been a lot of philosophy or moral instruction in it. It was a great story. When you're sitting over the campfire after a hard day's work in a warm campaign, or conquering a new area, you don't want heavy sermons. You want a good story while you're drinking your mead or gnawing away at a roast. A good story is basic to human enjoyment, so I go for the story line. It isn't that I don't have any philosophical thoughts: I'm always booting them out when they try to sneak into my stuff. If a character wants to talk it, I won't give him much more than seven, eight lines, and then I'm going to interrupt him with some jackass talking so it doesn't get too heavy. I'm not going to let him take over.

I won't let myself get in there. I write in my journals and I occasionally give talks. March 31st I gave a talk to USD about two things. One is that science is making a terrible mistake by thinking that there is such a thing as Time. The other argument I suggested was that maybe the final indivisible building block of the universe, whether particle or wave, may be a piece of life not the way we conceive it, but of another kind that informs both organic and inorganic matter, something I call a deon. So it isn't that I don't do a lot of that kind of thinking, but unless I get a scientist in there, it'll never show up in my books.

NB: Fiction writers in particular have talked about the importance of being exposed to different ways of seeing things. Why?

FM: It's a mind stretcher, a mental muscle stretcher and at the same time a mental music builder. It gives you more options. It's a little like in baseball. If you're a pitcher, you do all kinds of stretching and running and fooling around with different pitches on the sidelines and in training period; but when the game is on, you concentrate on the one pitch to be made with the batter standing in there ready to hit your ball. If you think about all those theories at the moment you wind up, you're licked. A real athlete always operates instinctively; all that previous training and previous experience will show up automatically. And it's fun. That kind of mental play keeps your mind active and alive. Anything to keep that muscle upstairs alive and full of tensile strength helps you write fiction. That's early morning stuff, isn't it?

NB: You've talked about writers being especially nice people. "The highest a man can become is to be one of these artists. It's true that they look a little foolish to other people because they happen to be so plainspoken and because they take strong positions. But this is because they somehow manage to keep a child's innocence while looking for truth." Why do you think artists are like this?

FM: Unfortunately, Harry Stack Sullivan died a rather young man in a car accident, but he was on the way to becoming our American Freud before he got whacked and he had some marvelous things to say about writers. He felt that if mankind as a species is driving towards some ideal state of being, then all men and all women will have artistic natures. And there are hints of it already in our society. When you run into a middle class family that has aspirations for itself, let's say it's a legal family, you'll find that the older sons or daughters will be interested in law, or that general field, and do well financially and socially. But when it comes to the youngest child, the family will say, "Oh, he's terribly bright. It looks like he's going to be an artist." And then they push him and hope he's going to be the family star. This is also true of aristocratic families and poor families. So behind the facade of trying to get along, there is a secret hope in everyone that "my child is going to be special; if not a president, then maybe a Mr. Faulkner or a Charles Ives or Frank Lloyd Wright." So there's a motion in our race towards having us become a special species.

Every writer I've run into of any consequences – Robert Penn Warren, Bellow, Bly, McGrath, Lewis, Dos Passos, Fisher, Waters, Walter Clark – were all strong people with strong egos and strong drives and strong bodies. And almost in every case they felt a little odd in youth. I knew I was different from people around me. I had to nourish that and keep it alive all the while that I hid it. Because if you don't hide it you get lampooned by your buddies and by your hundred IQers. The average person didn't understand you and thought that you wrote because you were slightly crazy. But you knew better. You knew for your intelligence this was normal activity.

NB: You've said that people drink because they want to be high like an artist when he is going good; but according to legend, writers drink a lot.

FM: There's occasionally a writer who drinks. People who can't write latch on to this and say, "I'm not a great writer; but the reason he is, is that he drinks." Beach had the theory that a writer was like an oyster: if a grain of sand got in there, a pearl will develop. Something bothered him, so he wrote. Well, to begin with that's not so. I say you write because you are a superior being. This is arrogance, but I consider it permissible arrogance since that's part of who you are as a writer. You write because it's a natural thing to flower in that way, just like the male bird sings near the nest where the female is sitting on the eggs to let everybody know: "Hey, this is my area," and also, "Say, this is pretty nice. I'm singing away here and I really like it." That's why writers or artists explode into song: it's possessive, as well as a giveaway.

NB: Do you think writers could drink when they miss the high of writing well?

FM: I guess Hemingway did near the end of his life. Hemingway didn't drink in the morning when he was writing though. And Faulkner drank in between books; he had to have his head clear when he wrote. I always felt that the "fifth" I can't understand in Faulkner is Mr. Jack Daniels. There's no question that drinking alcohol in between those writing bouts affected his brain. Something happens to your brain after you drink enough alcohol: those synapses are slowly but surely being relaxed and dulled by alcohol, and writing comes out of the wonderful work of your synapses in your associative centers. So you want to have a healthy brain and healthy body so your synapses and your associative centers are sparking away like hell.

But there are just as many bankers who drink as there are writers. The day John Berryman jumped off the bridge near the University of Minnesota, a vice president of the First National Bank also jumped off the bridge a little further up the river. John Berryman got the front page in the second section; the other guy got an obituary in the back. That's not fair. That's pointing and saying, "Oh, he jumped because he's a crazy artist." What about that crazy banker? You can't say that artists are inclined to be more neurotic or eccentric or drunken or apt to have more divorces than any man in other business.

In my social schema, there are two classes of people: aristocrats, who are creative people, and the rest, who try to be. If there are any kings or queens they are creative people. But they shouldn't take on airs. From the point of view of a worm, two human beings standing above the worm, one of them a moron, the other an Einstein, look exactly alike to the worm. If there is a God, from the point of view of God, Einstein and the moron also look equally bright. So you shouldn't take on prima donna airs. If you're really good, you don't have airs. Einstein didn't have airs; Hardy didn't; Warren doesn't.

NB: Some people have suggested that having airs would get in the way of your writing.

FM: Of course. That's a bit like the pitcher who's got great stuff: fast balls, great curves, changeups, powerful physique, quick as a cat, can field grounders. If, just as he's about to pitch, he remembers the story in the paper about him four days ago when he pitched a two-hitter, he's going to get knocked out of the box. He isn't going to be concentrating on his next pitch. He's got to be totally lost in the moment of that action. He can't be thinking about his press clippings. It's the same way with a writer: he's got to be lost in the moment of writing; he can't be thinking that he's a genius.

NB: The people I've talked to have been very nice, but when I say that to other people, they say it's because I've only talked to people who've succeeded.

FM: I was at the Huntington Hartford Foundation twice. We had four categories: sculpture, painting, music, and writing. None of it was criticism. Everything had to be original. There were four to a category, two older people and two younger ones. There was some rivalry, but less than I found in any other business. The early part of the day, you are supposed to leave each other alone. But in the evening, everyone met in the commons for dinner, and one of the first questions invariably was, "Did you have a good day?" Not that silly American expression, "Have a good day," but, "Did you really write well today?" Or, "Did you sculpt well today? How did it go? Did you make something new? Can we look at it?" We all hoped that everyone would do well. They know if they do something well and if somebody else does something well, life will be richer for each of us. I've wished a Shakespeare was living in my home town of Luverne, Minnesota. He'd be greater than me, at least possibly *(laughter)*, but my life would be richer.

NB: You've said, "The ideal life is to find what's there and then to live with it." Do you think writers are better at that than other people?

FM: They're more apt to be. You learn more about yourself and then you learn how to put that down, whereas the other fellow is so busy being a social being that he won't learn that. You run into a man who is in business – it takes a long time to figure out who he really is. He's doing everything in relation to that business: will it sell, will it not sell? Will this hurt me in the community, or won't it hurt me? He's continually concerned about front room stuff, not back room stuff. That doesn't work for a writer.

NB: So how do you teach your students to be writers?

FM: I had a great teacher in philosophy, Dr. Harry Jellema at Calvin College. He always gave you a chance and he made it a game every day. It was always a thrill to go to that class. One day he started the class reading my story, "A Harvest Scene," out of *The Chimes*. And the kids in the class all started looking at me. I always sat by the window. I could feel my face being bombarded by these pairs of eyes. I looked out the window so I wouldn't see the eyes. I was thrilled and excited and embarrassed. When he got all done, he explained why he read it: that it had such and such meanings, and what it meant in relation to such and such a philosophy. And he did that with every kid in the class. It was marvelous to have that happen to you. It didn't give you the big head; it just made you think, "Say, I'm not half bad." He was a great teacher.

I try to run my writing class the way Jellema ran his Plato Club, which was not a class but a philosophy club. Every member had to give a paper before the end of the year. That was your night. You handed out copies of your paper to the members a week or two ahead of time, so everybody could read it, and when you arrived, you read it again. You spent the whole night thrashing out the ideas in the paper and the other things we ran across as we argued and talked. It started out at seven and might go on until two in the morning. It was the best "class" I ever had because it was informal and that's how I modeled my writing classes.

In turn, I hope that every one of those kids in my class, if they become teachers, run their class like I ran it. I think teaching would be a lot better. But I should make an observation here. I don't have much time for psychologists and psychiatrists. Their field is a new field; it's also a tough field to explore because you can't point at a particle like you can in science. They tend to be defensive, so they'll take dictums by Freud and Jung and Adler and Horney and then talk as if those things are actually there—when they're not really there: they're just super guesses. We've got about twenty thousand practicing psychiatrists in the country applying these critical apparati and trying to make their patients fit these categories rather than the other way around: listen to what the patient has to say and see what the patient really is and work from there. In the first instance you're doing it as a practitioner and as a kind of teacher, and in the second you're doing it as an artist. There can't be that many artists around; there can't be twenty thousand geniuses around, all located in the field of psychiatry. Well, the same in teaching. You have to be highly talented to be a good teacher and there aren't that many highly talented persons around in any society at any time, so to ask almost a million teachers to be artists is hard going. So you thank God that a few good ones did go into the teaching profession because they're handing something from one generation to another.

NB: In *The Wind Blows Free* you said you didn't want to become a teacher because teachers get dried up and over particular. Why do you think that happens?

FM: Because they're overworked. I love teachers. Teachers and librarians are terribly necessary to society. These days those people are continually overworked. But I for myself can't stand repetition. So every year I try to teach my small class different.

And that's important to a creative writer: that you have to be new all the time. A writer…you don't say "have to"; if you say, "have to," that means you're already lost. You are continually being new. It's no wonder the average teacher is dried up. Even the genius teacher finds that his classes are too large.

NB: What do you want your students to get from your classes?

FM: At least this, that after they get out of school, even if they don't write, they will know how a poem or a story is put together. If they should happen to be teachers later on, say TAs, they're that much the better comp teachers. If they teach later on the advanced creative writing course, they'll know how to teach that too. They won't come wandering in from some other discipline and try to get it from a book. They have seen an author at work.

What a joy and inspiration it would have been to me if, when I was a young man at Calvin College, I could have seen Sinclair Lewis walking across the campus once a week; how he walked and how he looked, and how he looked at the rose bushes and the girls. *(Laughter.)* We learn best by watching examples around us. Little boys imitate their fathers and little girls imitate their mothers. So it's the same way with young writers imitating…although I tell them that they've got to figure out their own way of doing something. I always tell them, "If you resist me, privately I'll admire you, provided you convince me you know what you're doing." This is not the usual English class where they have to curry a prof's favor. Once in a while they catch me up short in something, or I've overlooked something, or made the wrong observation. I always say, "By golly, I think you're right." I don't get on any high horse.

I might tell you how I run the class.

NB: Okay.

FM: I have these exercises I want them to go through first, and then they're to have one overall project. What we want at the end is an excellence inside of what they can do. The first thing they turn in is an autobiography because I like to know where they're from. They can write that in any form they want, just so I know how old they are, what their parents

were like, if they have brothers and sisters, if there have been
any deaths, if they're remarried, if they're embittered or not
embittered, and so on. That's absolutely confidential and I return
that to them.

Then I want to see a letter to their best friend that's not
aimed at me; not a letter they write after they've met me. Same
way with a page from their journal, if they keep a journal.
And a dream, if possible, one as soon as the class has started
because that dreamer in the back of your head might aim a
dream at me too. If possible try to remember an old dream
and get that down without thinking about style; try to plop
it down as it occurs to you because a real dream has odd
qualities: it isn't logical, wanders in all directions, people change
clothes without reason, faces change, bodies change, and I want
all that. See, I'm already suggesting some powerful forces at
work. They have to be aware I might be bending them a little bit.

Then they must write an opening paragraph, whether they
are fiction writers or not, and we compare it to the opening
paragraphs of *Islands in the Stream* or *A Farewell to Arms*
and we talk about whether if you were to pick up a book in
a bookstore with that opening paragraph, would that catch your
eye?

Then they're supposed to keep their ears cocked for lively
and interesting conversation around them and try to get that
down, whether it's in the women's room or in the men's room
or the student union or at home or in a hospital. Put it all
down; don't try to edit it; just stick it down; and we'll help
cut it in class and show how sometimes two pages can be con-
densed to four exchanges and you still have it all.

By the time they're through with all this, I get a pretty
good idea of what their forte is, and they learn that writing
is not getting on a literary horse, that literature is something
that comes out of you spontaneously. The reason we think
Steinbeck's style is good is because this is his natural way
of talking. And Hemingway, too. And what we want to find
is a natural way of doing things. And then we can go to town.
Not that I can teach them anything, but that the class is there
for them to explore their potential.

They oftentimes say, "What can we write about?" I tell them, if there is some memory that keeps recurring to you, there's a deep reason for it. Explore it and then you'll have everything: you'll have the theme and the whole business sitting in there. If you're human and you've got brains and you're somewhat sane, it's going to be OK.

We do it altogether. As fast as I can, I get them to operate as a peer group. After a while, they start calling me Fred and I'm just a guy with them. And just as in Jellema's philosophy club, the Plato Club, each member of the class has to come up with a final project, which the others have a chance to read beforehand, and has it examined from stem to stern, and by me. Wonderful discussions follow each read project. By the end of the semester, everybody has got tears in their eyes because they have to let up. It's true. I had the last class this past Monday and everybody was sitting there kind of hating to get up because . . . why, they interrupt each other in a friendly warm way and they all cheer when somebody gets tough about his own things or tough about somebody else's. It's a friendly, warm, but strong exchange.

NB: Why do you think that's so important to them?

FM: Because they can talk any way they want; can be themselves totally. They can't do it anywhere else.

When they're through with the class, you hope that they're on the way to becoming superior citizens. They've learned to find out who they are and what they can do and to do it enthusiastically. In that sense, it's of great value that you have only twelve or fourteen people in a class a year. Those twelve or fourteen people can be a power wherever they go.

NB: What do you think would happen if there were more teaching like that?

FM: It would revolutionize our country. I've had roughly 150 students. Suppose forty of those wound up in Congress, one-half in the House of Representatives and one-half in the Senate. You can imagine how odd they'd look to the other Senators who are always worrying about their constituency. They'd speak their minds on the theory that if their constitutents don't like what they say, they can always not vote for them the next election. But I think the constituents like to have a man or woman representative who really votes how he feels. If they've elected him, they'll tend to trust him, especially if he or she is very honest.

NB: In *Green Earth,* the principal tells Free that when he reads more and his taste gets more sophisticated, he'll realize that Joseph Conrad is a better writer than Mark Twain. Do you know where that kind of prejudice comes from? For instance, I was just editing the transcripts of interviews with three entirely different kinds of novelists and they all mentioned Dickens in a favorable way. And a couple of novelists have used Conrad as a bad example. While it seems to me that academics tend to favor...

FM: Conrad.

NB: And fiction writers talk about Dickens.

FM: Yeh, I would too. Conrad really bothers me. I've always had trouble reading him. But I finally figured out why. He was a Pole; he felt as a Pole. Then he was a Frenchman for a while; he learned to express himself in a clear logical way as a Frenchman. And then later on he became an Englishman. So he's working his way through three writing frames: feels as a Pole, thinks as a Frenchman, and writes as an Englishman. You're getting three languages coming at you in the guise of one: English. Something in you as a reader is picking up those two other echoes and throwing you off. By the time he writes his last book, it's almost pure English. He didn't have too much to say by that time, but that's the best-written book from the point of view of a complete expression in one language. I worry a little about him; he was too intellectual even though he tried not to be. I think that's why critics latch onto him. Critics are not really the best critics *(laughter)* because they go at it as critics and not either as readers or as novelists.

NB: Oh, and so they want an ideological scheme.

FM: That's right. Actually critics should be the novelists because they are so busy bringing up marvelous critical apparati.

NB: Why aren't they novelists? What's the difference?

FM: They don't know how to play, literally play. They don't know how to play in their heads. That word "play" is a rich word.

NB: You've mentioned that it was probably good for Faulkner, Steinbeck, and Hemingway not to have much schooling:

"I think college and graduate school is for the critical teacher, but if you are creative something goes wrong there, even if you have the most marvelous teacher in the United States. Something goes wrong in that critical atmosphere in the classroom." I don't quite understand what you're saying there because I don't see why a classroom atmosphere has to be critical.

FM: It tends to be, though. I had an English teacher at Calvin who was a wonderful teacher when he read Shelley or Wordsworth. He had a kind of English accent. And gee, he didn't sound like anybody where I came from. When you're just a boy coming off the farm, or a boy coming out of the city working class, and you hear your prof say, "He had this in mind, or that was his purpose," you think to yourself, "Is it possible he knew all that before he began to write? I don't have that happen to me when I begin to write a short story, so I guess I can never be a novelist." It crushes you to hear all that stuff. But if you hadn't heard it, you wouldn't know that you couldn't do it, so you go ahead and do it. There's something about listening to profs who themselves will never write, who are a little envious probably, and who yet hide under the skirts of their genius: just like the disciples of Christ made him an overpowering world figure, they will make their favorite genius an overpowering person. That scares the hell out of your students: "I'll never be able to be that good."

In the beginning, you're like a little oak shoot, easily burned off, frozen off. An oak has to be a good twenty years old before it really will take hold and go, and it's the same with writers. It's like with an oak: if that little oak shoot could see the big oak, it'd say, "My God, I'll never get to be as big as that big oak sitting over there who knows how to resist storms and critical attention."

NB: Does teaching interfere with your writing?

FM: Yeh, it does. It takes a day away from my writing each week. Except in the summer. I would probably have had two more novels out by now; maybe even three. I will write them in the future. Luckily, the good Lord, or whatever, is going to give me many years of clarity and vigor, so I'll get in what I've intended to do.

I have wondered sometimes if that operation of being a boss—boss in quotes—of a class, doesn't make me possibly a little pontifical when I start writing and I worry a little bit about that.

When I drive to work in the morning, I turn my whole brain around to that day: how I'm going to handle that class and the people I'm probably going to see and the lunch I'm going to have. Then, when the class is over, as I drive home, I try to wash it all out so that the next morning I can go to work and forget the whole thing until the following Sunday afternoon. So far it's worked. But if I did any more of it, it would probably start pushing into the writing activity. You have only so much energy and so much *eye* (I) time. That's a pun, *e-y-e* and capital *I.*

Walter Clark regretted in some ways he had taught so much; he lost books to it. He only had four books printed. It's too bad he was pulled into the academic world; we lost a lot of wonderful books in Walter.

NB: We've probably gotten some good things from his students.

FM: That's true, yeh. But I don't know if they're going to get up to where Walter was. You got Walter...why take a chance on someone who might never become a Walter? It takes ten thousand good student writers to find one good Walter. You have new ones coming, but once you got a Walter, goddamn it, society should see to it that he has time and leisure to give us some books.

NB: Have you ever supported yourself doing anything else?

FM: I was a newspaper man before I went into teaching, and I worked in *Modern Medicine,* a medical magazine.

NB: Did those jobs interfere more or less with your writing than teaching?

FM: More. Newspapering was good for me for a while because I had to say things succinctly. But if you did it long enough, you wound up with non-metaphorical writing, and you also tended to load everything in the first two paragraphs rather than keep it for the climax. In medical writing you use a lot of polysyllabic words, which I always argue are nonfiction words. I throw them out. Einstein once made the remark that if you can't say something in simple terms that the average man can understand, you probably didn't have a clear thought in the first place. If you have to use heavy words to explain something, you probably don't understand it in the first place. The polysyllabic word is the hiding place of the uncertain brain.

NB: What do you get from teaching?

FM: Well, it paid bills; that's the left side of the brain talking. *(Laughter.)* Meeting fresh young minds, I have to learn how to be with them and how to handle them and understand them. There's a continual stretching of human tolerance and it enriches my ability to pick up new experiences that come willy-nilly at me.

NB: Why is writing the highest of the arts?

FM: I used to think music was. In the beginning I was affected more by a passage of music than I was by a passage in writing. Had I had somebody around me who knew music and could detect musical talent, I might have been a composer today instead of a writer. I probably write more as a composer than I do as a real writer. I can always tell, for example, when someone has cut one word out of my text. It's as if they've lost a note on me.

But now that I've written all these books, I've come to the thought that perhaps the art of writing is not only the oldest, it's the most enriching. Music, after all, is narrow. It's just sounds. You can get a musical sound that suggests, "I love you," but only after you've learned to think "I love you" in language. Writing gives the reader or the person who wants to enjoy something in the world of art the most reward because not only do they get something out of the prose and style and rhythm of it, but they get an enormous amount of life in it.

Interview with
Frederick Manfred—II

by Nancy Bunge

FM: As time has gone on, my male friends look at me with some disgust because of the way I'm always defending women and blowing them up into great stuff, probably because of who my mother was. As I look back now I can see that she was a very remarkable woman—probably very bright. Aunt Kathryn, my father's sister, was aesthetic and had a volume of poetry published when she was a young girl and that was on our parlor table, so even before I started school I knew that you could get printed; that left a *tremendous* impression on my mind. And I've slowly come to the realization that there are more good women around than there are men; not only physically, but mentally and spiritually.

That started off with my father who was supposedly an illiterate. One day he called me into the bedroom, my mother had died and he had six sons, no daughters, and we had trouble getting a woman to live with us for a while because it was hard to get help—women were busy with their own families. There were no hired girls to be found who would be old enough to handle the six kids. I was the oldest, eighteen, and then it went down to Henry at three. So Pa called me in one day and he says, "Pretty soon the pigs are going to come in and I want you to watch the sows. As the litters are born, I want you to mark the male pig, the man pig (as he put it) who is the first to get the titty and bump the others out until he has got his belly full. And you mark all the top male pigs of all the different litters that come in, and the top one of those tops—that's the one we trade with the guy in Edgerton." He was raising pure-bred Poland China hogs and both men had papers for them; they were worth a lot of money. And then Pa went on, "Suppose there are about 100 born. There will be 55 males and

45 gilts (gilts are the female pigs), but about 8 or 9 of the males will die within 4 or 5 days. Then later on 2 or 3 more will go, so it will wind up you have 45-45." So I thought it over and said, "Dad, I suppose you want me to watch who are the top gilts too – fair is fair." And he said, "No, you may lose one," he said, "but all the gilts are good stuff to breed. You don't have to worry about them – they're all good." I said, "Hey, that's hardly fair!" "No, I know," he said, "but that's the way God arranged it." So then I said to him, "Well, how about human beings?" And he said, with a laugh, "I ain't gonna say."

Later on I told this to Stark Hathaway, who invented the Minnesota Multiphasic Personality Inventory. And he started to laugh and slap his knee. I said, "What are you laughing about?" and he said, "There's a guy down in Indiana working on the same problem. He's Kinsey – you're going to hear from him pretty soon. That's what he has found too," he says, "That more good women are around than men. If you look around in the other species, the top alpha males get first chance with all the females and then later on when they're through, the other ones get a chance, but by that time the seed had been planted. That's how these species keep up. But if you let them all breed, it just goes downhill."

NB: Why aren't there more women novelists?

FM: Well, they get pulled into marriage and having children. One day I gave a talk about that in my writing class. I said, "Here you are, there are eight girls in the class here and four boys. You all write well and this is what's going to happen three or four years after you're out of college." To the boys: "Your family is going to say to you, 'My God, you are kind of a bum. All you do is weep around trying to write and you don't take a regular job and you don't get ready to have a family.' For you girls everything is going to be fine at first. . .your boyfriend – if you marry him, he'll be very happy about it. He's thinking to himself, 'Boy, if she has a bestseller then I can start my own business.' Then after three or four years, he's going to come home one night and say to you, 'Hey, I've had enough of this. I want my shirts ironed and I want babies.' And there go all the girls. So I don't know which one of you is ever going to become a writer." And there would be a terribly deep silence. I could just see them sitting there thinking how true that probably was. So it's a miracle if you get a writer out of those classes. And it's a miracle I had five published novelists those first three years! And they were stubborn men. Oh, one woman. That's right—she was very stubborn.

I think the women can probably write better novels than men too in the long run; they have a better sense of what a family means. They carry the babies; they nurse them into life. Maryanna my wife wasn't allowed to nurse her children, so she bottle-fed them. She was always tired. She also had tuberculosis, so I took over the ten, two and six o'clock feedings and then later on just two and six and I moved the two toward the six pretty fast. But I'd sit there at night and hold each child and watch those faces, put the bottle in their mouths you know—I was half woman.

The book called *Milk of Wolves*—remember that Fleur is killed (her brother kills her) and there Juhl is with this little baby. So what did Juhl do? He noticed that when he had the baby suck his man tit that the baby would quiet down. But, of course, there was no substance in there. So finally he crisscrossed his nipple with a knife and the baby sucked blood and pretty soon the blood had milk in it. You know where I got that?

NB: Where?

FM: Out of those Icelandic sagas. Then I got a hold of a couple of physiologists and they said, "Oh, yeah, that's possible." And then I remembered that when my daughter Freya was born, Maryanna had quite a time with Freya, so the doctor would come out and talk and visit with me; he noticed that I was always going like this (scratching) and he said, "Can I look at that for a minute?" So I opened up my shirt and one milk cell had awakened. He pinched it and a beebee of milk came out like a boil and there was milk in there. And he said that happens every now and then. A husband gets so involved with his wife having a baby that it awakens something, and he said that what your mind thinks can affect your physical body very much. You can almost do anything with it. I said, "You can't change me to have babies." "No," he said, "that's right." So I've been intrigued about the whole business of femininity for a long time. And, of course, I think, too, that every male has a female component lying there unused, but it can be awakened as time goes on.

NB: Bly seems to argue that producing art is connected with men getting in touch with that female component.

FM: Oh yes. That's right.

NB: Do you think that's . . .

FM: I think it's true.

NB: You do? Why?

FM: I'll change my mind a little bit. I've added to that—not changed. I have to be careful about that word "change." Because it isn't a total change. You veer a little bit. I thought that the women writers that came through, Virginia Woolf, Jane Austen, Willa Cather, that it was the seminal part of their minds that made the novel. But I have decided the other way around—that you should not say he's a seminal writer; you should say he's an ovarian writer. Because it's not semen, it's eggs. The egg goes into the womb and a sperm hits it, but an egg is the main thing. And then it becomes another creature. So it's probably a combination of being both seminal and ovarian.

NB: In the process of writing a novel, what's the equivalent of the egg?

FM: The germ of the book. The germ of the book is very similar to an ovum. It's something all sperm go to find. The ovum is very picky too: they've shown pictures where there are hundreds trying to get in and finally she lets one in that she decides she likes. And that's somewhat the way with a really good idea for a novel.

NB: When you have an idea for a novel, do you have a plot or a character?

FM: The plot grows up out of the idea. And the idea is always involved with a character.

NB: But you've said that a concept is the last thing a novelist wants to have in mind.

FM: No, because then it gets too artificial.

NB: It's an idea, but not a concept. So what is it?

FM: It's a problem usually. It begins as a problem. *The Golden Bowl*, my first book, first my attempt was to put everything in that happened to me in that hitchhiking tour

I described later in some detail in the autobiographical *The Wind Blows Free*. One thing that kept coming back to me was that hobo I ran into and finally a novel came out of that one hobo I only saw for about six hours. And that's what I mean: it was a problem with that boy. It bothered me. That's the ovum – and then you start filling in from your general knowledge and then it becomes a book.

It's more of an ovum process than it is a spermatazoa process. So I'm slowly changing my mind. I did write an essay a long time ago saying that women writers, if they're any good, probably have strong male sides to them.

NB: Clifford Maule shows up in *King of Spades* all of a sudden and he says that all men know that the eternal feminine is needed to draw men upward. I gather you don't agree with that much, you don't seem to be...

FM: Oh I think I do. I feel that.

NB: I thought he was a bad character.

FM: Yeh, he was. But bad characters can still project truths, you know. Yeh, he meant it in a bad way. I think he meant it.

NB: In the sense of repression. Maule argues that they should punish Ransom harshly because he had done this to a woman and woman represents high ideals.

FM: Yeh. That's right. I had almost forgot that. There's an interesting thing about a germ or an ovum idea. I, for a long time, have been interested in what two people make the best mates or the best friends – man and woman or between men. All my life I've been looking for the idea of a chum. When I was a little boy we'd go visiting somewhere and I'd ask, "Where are we going to go visit tonight?" "The Fabers." And I'd say, "Is there a little boy there I can play with that I'd like?" And so all my life I've been interested in that problem: what people like each other? And, of course, between male and female, what two people come the closest to almost the perfect overlap – not overlap, but lapping up together. Overlap means you are over the edge, but the lap together...and so I've been interested in the father-son, father-daughter, mother-son, and mother-daughter relationships, and so on.

And then one day I ran across this story in a local paper in Rock Rapids, Iowa that told of a Dr. So-and-so who says that if the Peeping Tom that has been bothering his house lately doesn't quit it, he's going to have to buy a gun. So then about a month later, there's another story – that the good doctor has been thinking of buying a gun. Then he has bought a gun – a word to the wise. And finally, one day, the front page: this monster first killed his wife and then killed his son and then killed himself. And I thought, "God, that must have been terrible." In other words, there was no Peeping Tom. The boy was between twelve and thirteen; he was just beginning puberty. So, instinctively, that father recognized that there really was a Peeping Tom. And I thought, "Wow! Suppose it happened that there was a rather young wife, suppose we make her thirteen cuz in those nearly womanless days if the woman was nubile, the men went after her. [She] has a baby at fourteen and then when the boy is seventeen, she'd be thirty-one. Because they wore a lot of pancake makeup and long dresses, without him knowing it, she could look young and he wearing a beard could look old. Suppose they didn't know that they once were related. What would happen? Would they instinctively know there was a profound attraction because he came out of her belly? You're watching to see what happens there. And then, of course, here comes little Erden Aldridge, the little girl who really should have been Ransom's true soul mate.

NB: Erden is raised by Indians and Fleur is an Indian and they both turn into religious figures by the time you're finished with them.

FM: (Loud Laughter.) Well, maybe so!

NB: A lot of the women in your books seem huge.

FM: Well, because I admire them. It's an interesting theory, by the way. Golly. What you are saying there?

NB: They seem mythic. Also, in the books you told me to read, women throw themselves at men all the time. Juhl has women throwing themselves at him all the way through the book. That's what his relationships consist of.

FM: Well, there are some men that happens to.

NB: And Flat Warclub...same thing. And Ransom also has this Indian-raised woman and then Katherine. There does seem to be that pattern.

FM: Well, when a woman finally gets down to business, then she's ahead of the man by a long ways. All he's really interested in is: "Oh, there's a nice female. I've got to get my seed in there." And then after the insemination, he goes over and crops grass as he collects his wits. And walks off. The woman is completely different. She doesn't think about the point right away, she thinks about some other things, kind of a big warm web. But when it's time to make the connection, then the woman is ahead of the man. And she also knows that she's got to hold him to get food from him and protection and so there's a bigger vision in her head than his.

NB: The women in the books I was just talking about don't seem to have any larger vision. They just float in and out of these relationships.

FM: Well, wait a minute. Flat Warclub, he wants to have a woman. So he says, "All right, I'll throw my life away provided I'm allowed to talk to these different girls." Well, when the word got around that he was free to talk to any girl in the tribe, there would be some girls who would volunteer for that. Not all of them, just three or four.

NB: You have the feeling that it was the whole tribe and one slits her wrists because she doesn't get to have sex with him. And Judith in *Scarlet Plume* just won't leave Scarlet Plume alone.

FM: Ha! But Judith was unhappy with her husband and didn't know anything about having orgasms and she's reduced almost to the lizard mind by hunger. And then the mammal mind starts coming back up in her, wakes up a little bit, and then pretty soon the neocortex starts to work. But before the neocortex can work, her lizard and mammal mind are already awake enough to rut there in that little hidden valley place. Because [Scarlet Plume] has a sacred mission to deliver her back to the white world, he doesn't want to put any seed into her. He finally says, "Well, if you had a husband, he would be my koda." And husbands once in a while did give each other their wives. That's the only reason he would accept her if she would consider him a koda to her husband. And, meanwhile, he's chased that antelope and got the meat, so he's awakened to the usual role of the male. Then there's that panther sitting out there waiting for him; that awakens a basic thing that goes on in human beings' lives. And I think deep down she has always wanted some relationship too with a man that would be wonderfully fulfilling for her and here's this man for her. Who has saved her! Kept her from dying. That makes it a little different. It isn't quite that she wanted to go to bed with the guys; something big goes on first before that occurs. Well, you raise an interesting question there. I suppose 50 or 100 years from now, if the books are read then – somebody is going to find that or perhaps they'll see it in here and they'll start investigating that and then they'll go off theorizing and go ZOOM –

NB: Might miss the point!

FM: They won't look at the whole. I've had women tell me that they feel wonderfully at home with me after a while. They know I won't attack them, that I'll be considerate. And I have a theory that's it's OK for the male to let the woman know, as he kind of snorts around and makes winning sounds, that he's very interested in her, but it should be up to the woman to say yes or no. My kind of man would find out first if she's willing; he wouldn't keep pushing and pushing until he gets his way.

NB: I see, so that's why the women do the initiating.

FM: Yes, that's why they finally say yes or no. They don't really make the first move. Males make really the first move with their snorting around, and then it's up to the female to say yes or no.

I'm going to read something to you I wrote just a few days ago. It's right on the subject of this mythic woman. It's called "Interior Commentator":

> I want to enjoy my sorrow by myself. Go away. Leave me alone. It hurts me enough as it is without having you throw me a bone. I'm too much a little boy or a puppy wagging my tail, eager to lick a face, for your lips to change that now, for me to grow up, prevail. Nor do I want to tell my interior voice, that deep part of me, my precious literate self, which sees things as they are, never lies, loves

flowers, loves lust, that longs for that final playful maiden elf, to shut up, to quit lusting for her.

There's your mythic woman. A playful maiden elf.

NB: Like Fleur and...

FM: They are that. So is Erden Aldridge.

NB: What is the lizard exactly? Is it getting back to primitive instincts?

FM: Yeh. Well, Robert Bly told me to go look at a book called *The Dying Self* by Charles M. Fair. I got that up there— but the guy speaks of the lizard mind. Those very primitive lizards—there is very little mammal in them; there's no milk. "Mammal" means momma or milk. And they're just sheer instinct. When an emergency comes, they either attack or retreat instantly. If you start thinking out what the problem is, you might lose out. But if your lizard *takes* over, it uses the neocortex and says, "Do this or retreat." In some people, that lizard has disappeared. It's probably still there, but way down inside. That's dangerous stuff to talk about around Christian people.

NB: You also said in an earlier interview that the man projects towers, builds bridges, while women don't have an instinct for that—they have an instinct to protect the home. But I guess you aren't really changing that, are you? You say that protecting and holding is the center of the novel.

FM: You know, it's interesting. We call the city "she." We never say "he" city—we never say "King City," we say "Queen City." But the men build them. Among primitive people the women construct little tepees and little huts; but when it came to the major things, then the men did it. They had more strength. Among the Indians the men did the writing—the pictographs on the back of buffalo after the buffalo had been dehaired. But women were wonderful in making art objects. The parfleches always had designs on them and the clothes had designs on them. The men didn't do that; women did that. So there's a strong artistic instinct in women that there isn't particularly in men.

NB: Somebody said to me that they thought that the female consciousness has always been central to the novel.

FM: I agree with that, I think. Yeh, they're interested in how the family operates.

NB: He also said the women have a more sophisticated psychological understanding than men do and also they are more able to articulate what they understand.

FM: Yes, that's right. I would agree with that. That's why I think that in some ways Karen Horney is deeper than Freud. But she was so pushed down by males in her profession that she didn't get a chance to really go, but she was a remarkable psychologist. And then Helene Deutsch, she was good too. But, you see, the trouble is that women have been so suppressed as far as doing recognizable things that they haven't even had a chance yet and that's why I urged my daughter Marya to go after the writing of symphonies and songs. Freya did go on to become a poet; she's a remarkable poet.

Marya wrote a book of poems, too, though she didn't try to publish them. She was ill and said, "Dad, there is no use living. I haven't done anything. Freya has done everything and Freddie has done this and I haven't done anything." So I went through all her letters to me. She used to visit my class and she'd ask if she could read a poem or two. I kept all those, so one day I went through all my files, I found them and I typed them up all neatly, didn't tell her about this, didn't change a word, and sent it to a publisher. He called me in two weeks and said, "You've got another eagle in your family." I said, "Well, we've got a problem here. I haven't told her yet that I've sent them to you." "Oh," he says. So I said, "Why don't you go ahead and print them and when you've got galleys, I'll bring them to her and say, 'He wants to know if this is the way you want it.'" And that's what I did. When it was published – and called *Original Sound* because she's a music sound girl – I brought the books to her. That evening the phone rings around twelve. "Say Dad, that book is important, isn't it?" she said. I said, "Yeh, it is, You're going to get good reviews." "OK, Dad," and she hung up. She did get good reviews. But she hasn't continued it. So maybe she is a music person. She was trying to do something for my class, really. Some of her published poems were buried in her letters to me. All you had to do was rearrange the prose lines in the letters a little bit and they broke into lines of poetry. So my mind has been enriched by my daughters and my wife and some girlfriends who I've had and my respect for women has gone up.

We're also overpopulated and we don't have to worry about having more kids to make the race survive, so women are going to have more and more freedom.

My theory is have the children early. Then when the woman is at about twenty-six or twenty-seven, the kids are in school and she's free from nine to three. All you need is two hours a day to write. Three hours at the most. You don't want to write any more than that because . . . well, then it's like you're a cross-country runner, you'll get too tired at the end. I always parcel it out four pages a day. Well, it depends on what the book wants to do — some books want to go five a day and some want to go three. But I generally go about four now. I can handle that. Sometimes I'm done in an hour and sometimes it takes six hours. But I always do four. Then when I get to the end of the page and if the sentence isn't finished, it stays there unfinished until the next day. And then I finish it. The idea is that the guy down in my basement knows I'm going to draw on him like a bank and he's gotta have that ready.

NB: I couldn't tell if in *Milk of Wolves* you liked Juhl or not. You said something about his being raised by his mother to be a king and he was arrogant in some ways. But, mainly, you seemed sympathetic.

FM: I was thinking about the alpha male. They tend to be arrogant. They tend to be bossy. There's a great story in Jane Goodall's book, *The Chimpanzees of Gambi*. There's one male who would love to be an alpha male, but the other males give him a hard time. One day he discovers that if you roll these big tin banana drums around, they make a lot of racket. So, he gets two of them and gets them to the top of the hill, right above where his bunch is sitting below in the bushes, and he starts rolling and kicking those things downhill, making a terrible racket, crashing through them. They fly in all directions and then he is the alpha male for six months. There's a lot of things sitting in that little scene. I'd go around town and say, "Oh, that's the Chamber of Commerce guy." The Chamber of Commerce guy gets tin cans and pushes them on through town and calls attention to his businesses downtown. They become the alpha male on Main Street. But that's an utterly great picture of how males think. To become the alpha male, to become the most recognized male.

NB: Juhl is an artist though.

FM: Of course, sure, he had that side to him, but still the alpha male would be a piece of being the artist. That would drive that a little bit.

NB: Oh, to be recognized.

FM: To be one of the top men. You know that's an interesting thing about that. My daughter Marya sitting there thinking about Freya's way ahead of her and she's nothing. I'd say, "It's all wrong to think that way, honey. If I went around sitting there fretting because Sinclair Lewis became famous, a Nobel writer, and John Dos Passos and Robert Penn Warren and all those guys, then I wouldn't write what I can do. So long ago jealousy was wiped out of me. I've also learned when I study, say, Meville, and even Hawthorne, but Melville more than anyone else, and then Cervantes, and all the men that I've really admired, they've really never worried about how good anybody else was. They were so absorbed in what they had found that they followed their own instincts and their own thinking and they didn't listen for models and they never worried whether they were following Shakespeare's tradition or who they were following. They'd worry about how they could get out what they had in their own head and not how good anybody else was. We're all brothers against darkness. Or sisters and brothers against darkness. So you, Marya, shouldn't be thinking at all about how good Freya is. You should be thinking about who you are and what you can do."

There's that tender aspect that males have if they become the top dog. That awakens in them. The whole complement of the hermaphroditic part of them.

NB: Succeeding is what makes it possible for them to be gentle?

FM: Yeh. Then we also have these guys that don't do that, Hitler and so on. And, of course, they get destroyed. But Pericles was a tender, warm man, He took most of his basic advice from Aspasia and he may have failed a bit because he wasn't hard enough. And all the artist leaders in our country we remember with great warmth, Lincoln and Jefferson. Both women and men can admire those fellows. There are some men who admire Hitler, or admire Napoleon, destroyers; but in the real men the whole being is awakened.

NB: It sounds as though you're saying that once they establish some strength, then they can allow this gentler side to be realized, or do you think that the fact that every side is active makes them leaders?

FM: Well, it's probably there ready to be developed, but they have to win first. They have to win. Sometimes they fight so long to win that they don't get a chance for their other side to come to the surface. Maybe that's what happens to a Hitler and so on, these so-called evil men that we talk about. To become a full human being is a very complicated business.

NB: I thought *Lord Grizzly* attacked a macho attitude. He tried to be tough and then wound up projecting all his own guilt on someone else.

FM: Yeh. So the feminine side of him, the forgiving side of him, woke up finally there. At the time I wrote it I wasn't aware of it. (Laughter.) But it's there, nevertheless. Profoundly, I was interested in that problem.

NB: You've said: "There's a quality about dreams that is hypnotic, I want that effect. I want the readers to think they are actually looking at a piece of real raw flesh accidentally walking into somebody's bedroom." Those two things seem contradictory in a sense, talking about trying to create a dreamlike thing that's hypnotic and wanting to expose someone to real flesh. But you've made other comments about wanting to get to what's really real. That sounds to me like the mythic level.

FM: Maybe what I'm putting down, though, is *really* real. And what the other guys are missing is what's real.

NB: That's what I meant, not real in the sense of realistic detail.

FM: That's right. Yeah. And then maybe I'm filling in stuff that the other guys never fill in. Women fill them in. You read Jane Austen and Willa Cather. . . .

Didn't happen in all the books, but when I started writing the trilogy, I thought deeply quite a long time, deeply, because

I worried about some things. First of all, I did want to use the fact that I was big and so on. Not uncouth, but not quite couth yet either. That reflected the American nation in the sense that we're the newest member of the western culture, and we're big and brawling and we still aren't really cultured yet in many ways as a nation, compared to say old France or old Germany or old Italy. Certainly not an old England, which has been a going culture since the days of Chaucer. So I thought, "I've got to be careful and not let that damn concept run the show here."

Then I thought, "I wonder what my real vision of Thurs in there is? What does he really look like?" I already had given him his silver forelock. Two friends had that; both terribly bright. That was gonna help me a little bit, but brooding over it, apparently it woke up the hallucinary part of my mind, and one morning as I was slowly waking up to day again, I saw him in my dream. There he was. I wasn't awake yet. I was still dreaming. But I was getting closer and closer to consciousness. There he was: he had a little narrower hips than I did, little broader shoulders. He had a broad brow and that silver lock was there and he didn't look like me, really; he looked like someone who might be distantly related to me. He was standing at the foot of my bed trying to mouth something which was maybe, "You haven't quite gotten this straight." As I woke up even more, I thought, "God, I'd like to have a good look at him," so I opened my eyes just a trace more and, yes, there he was in front of my bed. Then I worried, "Should I open my eyes up even further and have a better look or should I close them?" I made the mistake of opening them up; and then he just vanished—gone. Later on, I saw him walking towards me on the road. I was busy thinking about something else, but I was vaguely aware that there was somebody walking towards me. I looked up, and for a fleeting instant there he was. And then he vanished once more. And I thought, "If I tell this to my wife, she'll think I've gone crazy. And a psychologist, he'd be excited. Except Stark Hathaway, he'd understand. He always told me, 'Don't trust us. We make educated guesses and throw a polysyllabic at it. But you're an artist and you know. You know'." So . . . That's happened

a number of other times. I started this new book, *The Wrath
of Love;* it's an examination of love. At first I noticed that
I would write one page, six, one, two, one, as if the guys down
there in my basement, my subconscious, weren't quite ready
for me, and so I thought, "God, what's going on here?" And
one night I came out of a dream about two in the morning;
there in the dream was my character, Christian Nash, just the
way I pictured him in the book, and he was smiling at me
and shaking his head. So in the dream I asked him, "What's
the matter?" and he said, "You threw me in the wrong part
of the river." The river of life, see, flowing by. "Too far down,"
he said. So I think to myself, "Wow." Then I woke up and
he vanishes on me. So I gave that some thought. I quit writing
for three or four days, thinking it over all, walking and brooding
to myself, didn't dare talk to anybody about it; unless, of course,
if I might have had a nice lady at the end of my table who'd
understand. But I did move it back in time and it still wasn't
quite right. So I stopped once more and gave it further thought;
and thought, "Say, since this is about love, why don't I start
on Valentine's Day?" So I started in on that day and since
then I get four pages a day. This is true. Now, something magical
and important is going on there.

The Making of *Lord Grizzly*

Friends. It was in the summer of 1943, after I'd learned that my first novel, *The Golden Bowl,* was to be printed the next year, and I could relax a little knowing I'd be a published author some day, that I began to do further research on an idea that was eventually to become *This Is the Year.* I might remark at this point that when I lived on the farm I longed to get away from it. But later on, when I started to write about it, I discovered I had to go back and check things out because I'd forgotten them or hadn't paid any attention to them at the time. So I began to read farm manuals and old weekly newspapers dealing with Siouxland.

It occurred to me one day I should check out the WPA Writer's Project Guides—the various state guides that had been written by local state writers. I already owned the *Minnesota State Guide,* so I went to the University of Minnesota Library and got out the one on South Dakota. When I saw it was a lively book, I went out and bought my own copy. As I read through it, some ten pages a day, I suddenly stopped on page 210 a woodcut showing a mountain man being mauled by a bear. It instantly caught my eye. I read the legend beside it, and noted, among other things, that John G. Neihardt had written about the man and the grizzly. Not only had Hugh done a great thing in crawling back to safety after he was almost killed, but after he had figured out who had deserted him he chased them down, caught them, and then . . . let them go. I had read the Greeks by this time and it struck me that we too in our American past had had an Achilles. Hugh Glass was our Achilles. Nay, more. Where Achilles never forgave, Hugh Glass had forgiven his deserters. That was an act that put him above Achilles. In fact, Hugh Glass had performed his heroics while completely alone. Achilles always had a contingent of Greek warriors near by.

127

I went to the University Library again to have a peek at
John G. Neihardt's book, *The Cycle of the West;* particularly
the section entitled "The Song of Hugh Glass." I had the habit
in those days, before I took a book out, to page through it.
I wasn't going to carry all that heavy paper back home if I
wasn't going to use it. So I sat on a little hard bench and
examined it. I read a couple dozen pages, and then, reluctantly,
found myself not liking it too well. Neihardt had written his
account in imitation of Homer, and in English it didn't come
off too well.

But there was another reason why I stopped looking at
it. I'd lived in the country before the roads had been graveled
or paved. After a heavy rain my father always made it a point
to be the first down a rain-soaked road because, he said, if
someone had gone ahead of him in the mud, then he always
had to worry about the wriggling tracks already there. Pa said
he'd just as soon make his own wriggle first down the road.
I had the same thought. I didn't care to read Neihardt's account because then I'd have to worry what he did ahead of
me. I wanted to make my own wriggle down that muddy road
of the unknown. So I snapped *The Cycle of the West* shut
and handed it back.

The lady librarians at the University soon caught on I was
going to do something about the Hugh Glass story. They began
to find books for me. I don't know how many I read. More
than a hundred perhaps.

There were two books that in particular caught my eye.
One was *Life in the Old Far West* by George Frederick Ruxton.
Ruxton was a British boy who came to America and went on
a hunting expedition across the wild prairies into the Shining
Mountains. The other one was by Lewis Garrard of Cincinnati,
Ohio, who also wrote an autobiographical account of a trip west.
His book was *Wah-To-Yah: On the Taos Trail.* From those two
books I copied such passages of dialogue as I thought were
probably a correct recording of what was said by the mountain
men, some thirty pages in my notebook. Those two boys were
young, Ruxton was in his early twenties and Garrard was still
in his late teens, and I figured their memories would be the

freshest and the most accurate. They had probably given us the truest account of what the mountain men actually said.

I next checked out the guns of that time. It happened that below the hill where we lived in Bloomingtom, Minnesota, in a place called The Stagecoach, where we used to have barbecued ribs once in a while, was an extensive gun collection owned by an Ozzie Klavestad. Luckily Ozzie had on hand a replica of the gun used by Hugh Glass. Ozzie took me out to the woods in back, primed the old gun for me, and let me fire off a couple of shots, to get the feel of the kick it had, as well as get the smell of the old powder they used back in the 1820's.

I next decided I'd better have a look at the sites, so my wife Maryanna and I got into our old Ford and drove out to western South Dakota, to the town of Lemmon near the Grand River.

I should perhaps tell you a bit about the old Ford of ours. It'll help give you a picture of what I went through as a researcher as well as help set up the magnitude of Hugh's exploit. The old car had a short in it that no mechanic could ever find. At the most inopportune times the lights would go out. If one hit a chuckhole out went the headlights. Thus we always made it a point to drive it only in the day time. When we were crossing South Dakota to get to Lemmon, we had to hurry to find a motel before it got dark. Once, back in Bloomington where we lived, we decided we had to see a certain movie. We took a chance. Everything went fine on the way to the movie in Edina (near Minneapolis) but halfway home afterwards the lights went out. I pulled over in the dark, hoping we wouldn't land in the ditch. I found our flashlight. After some deliberation, we decided to drive home with that. So, holding the flashlight out of the left front window, we started to inch our way home. Well, it wasn't long before a state trooper pulled us over. "What's the problem here?" "I guess we have a short in the lights." "You know of course you could have been rammed in the rear." "I was watching for that in our rearview mirror. If a car came up too fast I was going to take the ditch." "Well, we better get you off the road. Look, I'll light you up from the rear all the way to your lane. All right, let's move it." All the while this was going on my wife Maryanna sat in stony silence. And it wasn't until we sold the car, and it was junked, that we found out the short was where the wire to the taillight went through the steel frame. Over the years the insulation on the wire had been worn off.

In Lemmon, South Dakota, we found a man named Art Svendby, owner of the local general merchandise store, who knew about the site of the mauling. Once I explained what I had in mind, he immediately took off work and drove us out to where the monument had been erected in memory of Hugh Glass. He showed us where local talk placed the mauling.

The next morning I drove out to the monument again and laid out a general plan of attack. I had two railroad maps with me which showed every square mile in South Dakota. I told my wife: "Now, I'm going to walk from this spot here to that spot there. Since there are no roads in this part of Dakota, you'll have to drive back to the main highway, go across to here, and then come down to here. I should be there in about three or four hours."

She slowly turned purple. Here was all this wild stuff in that fenceless country. We'd seen coyotes sitting on the hills. We'd seen antelope bounding through the draws. We'd also spotted dozens of rattlesnakes squashed by cars and trucks on the tar highways. "What if you don't show up there?"

"Well, wait at least until it's almost dark. If I don't show up by then, you better go get a room in Faith. And then tomorrow come back and look for me."

"What!"

"If you don't find me in two days, look for where you might spot some vultures circling in the sky. I'll be below them somewhere."

"Are you serious?"

"And if you don't spot circling vultures, and I still don't show up, then call the sheriff and have him get a posse."

By that time she knew I was teasing. "All right, Columbus, be seein' you."

I took off. I walked from near Lemmon on the Grand River, over the first height of land, past Thunder Butte, down to the next river, the Moreau, where Maryanna was waiting for me.

The next day she once again took the long way around, while I climbed the next hogback, past Rattlesnake Butte, down to where Cherry Creek poured into the Cheyenne River. There was an Indian agency at that confluence, and when I walked in Maryanna was waiting for me.

All the way over those two heights of land I took notes. I also had with me a gunnysack and some one hundred small waxed paper bags. Every time I saw something interesting, a flower, some grass, what a farmer would call a weed, I would clip it, mark it on the map, and put in in the waxed bag and then into the gunnysack. Why invent grasses or flowers when nature was far more inventive then I might be? Why not have it accurate so that when people read the book they would know that when I say Hugh saw this or that it was really there.

I thought too I should taste some of the things. So when I came upon an ant or a grasshopper, I pinched them in my fingers and tasted. I also spotted mice but them I didn't taste. I'd watched cats eat mice and knew how much they enjoyed them, so I figured that if I were Hugh and were hungry enough I'd probably bite in too—except maybe I'd first skin and disembowel it. Same way with gophers. Gophers wouldn't taste any different from squirrels, and I'd had squirrel meat pie at one time or another.

In the summer of 1823, Hugh Glass was a hunter for a trading party led by Major Andrew Henry. They were a part of a larger group out of St. Louis under General William A. Ashley. Hunters worked in pairs up ahead of the party. When they spotted deer or antelope or buffalo, they dropped them, skinned them and hung the meat up in trees along the river bank for the party to pick up as they came along. Hugh generally hunted up ahead with two young men, Jim Bridger and John Fitzgerald.

One day Hugh, in an ornery mood, went on alone. Grumbling to himself, pushing through a plum thicket, he came upon a she-grizzly with two cubs. Had she been alone she would probably have walked away from him. Grizzlies aren't all that pugnacious. They are curious but they're not wanton killers. Of course, with two cubs at her heels, she was instantly ready to protect her young. She attacked Hugh before he could get up his gun and fire. And it was too late for him to run. So he closed with her like a wrestler might, made it a point to get inside her reach. While she was clawing up his back, and gnawing at his head, he kept stabbing her repeatedly. Until finally both the she-grizzly and Hugh dropped to earth. Some accounts have it she broke one of his legs, tore his shoulder badly, even took one bite out of his butt.

When Major Henry's party caught up with Hugh, they found him unconsious but still alive. Every time he breathed a bubble of blood emerged out of one of the toothholes the grizzly had made in his throat. They stopped at the spot overnight.

The next morning, with Hugh still alive though breathing laboriously, Major Henry assigned Fitzgerald and Bridger to watch over him until he died, and then, finally dead, to bury him. Several days went by and still Hugh lived. They dug a grave for him. Meanwhile both Fitzgerald and Bridger were in fear of their own lives. The Arikara were on the warpath and should they find the two lads they were done. Sure that Hugh was going to die, they finally left him beside the open grave, took his possibles, guns, knife, flint, powder, so the Indians couldn't use them, and hurried off to catch up with Major Henry. They assured Major Henry that, yes, Hugh finally did die, and here were his possibles.

When Hugh at last came to, he figured out from the dead campfire that two men had been left to guard over him. From their special moccasins tracks he made out the two were Bridger and Fitzgerald, the very two he had taught how to be good hunters in the wilderness. Seeing the grave, discovering that they had taken his possibles, he slowly, numbly, worked himself up into a terrible rage. He swore vengeance. Those deserters! He was going to live and crawl back to Ft. Kiowa, and get those devils and kill them. To leave a man behind in the wilderness was one of the worst sins of the Old West. According to mountain men code, he had a right to kill them. And it was the swearing of that vengeance that saved him.

After all that walking, I next visited Will Robinson, director of the South Dakota Historical Society in Pierre. Robinson became intrigued in my project, though he held his head sideways a little as he spoke. He hoped that I wouldn't go about it the way Neihardt did. He said he had gone along with Neihardt to work out Hugh's trail, and once, as they were driving along, Neihardt suddenly asked him to stop driving. Robinson did. "Ah," Neihardt had whispered, "Hugh went along here. On hands and knees." Robinson asked, "How do you know?" "I can just feel him having been here." Robinson shook his head at me, and smiled deprecatingly. Robinson was a former Army officer and an amateur historian, and to him that was a ridiculous way of doing research.

Robinson did me several favors. First, he showed me on my map his idea of where Hugh had crawled. It was almost exactly the trail I'd worked out by walking it. Second, when I told him my wife and I had almost run out of money and weren't sure we had enough funds to buy gas to get home, he gave me a five-dollar bill. A loan. Which I repaid him the moment we got home. Third, he showed me a copy of a letter Hugh was reputed to have written to Johnnie Gardner's father to explain how Johnnie had been killed by the Rees.

That letter was most intriguing. After studying it a while I decided that Hugh probably hadn't written it; that he'd gotten a clerk at Ft. Kiowa to write it. The handwriting was that of a meticulous clerk. So was the language. When I wrote the book, though, I used the letter as I found it.

Home again in Bloomington, having seen the hills Hugh had had to crawl over, I decided to try crawling around on the hill we lived on. Our hill was almost exactly like the heights of the land Hugh had to surmount. I made a splint, or a slape as my father would call it ("slape" is a Frisian word), tied my leg in it, and on hands and knees began dragging the splinted leg through the tall grass up and down the hill. The perspective from that low point of view was astonishing. Eyes a foot off the ground I found it to be a new way of looking at life. I felt like Nebuchadnezzar of the Bible who had gone to live with the beasts of the field.

I next called on an old trapper living in my old home town of Doon, Iowa. Every fall and every spring he put out his traps to catch mink, fox, coyote, weasel. Talking to him, I learned he'd picked up the tricks of his trade from an early pioneer trapper named Old Dan who lived on the Big Rock River. And

that Old Dan in turn had learned how to set his traps from
the first mountain men in the area who were looking for beaver.
I found this all very thrilling.

Memory of a certain episode from boyhood days also helped.
I wanted a bicycle very much. My father said he didn't have
the money. I decided I'd do some trapping, catch a mink or
two, and then I'd have enough to buy a good bike. But no
matter how carefully I set the traps, using the instructions
that came with the shining steel jaws, I never caught a mink.
They were just too clever. Instead one morning, making the
rounds of my traps, I discovered I'd caught a skunk. The trap
had snapped hold of its rear leg, and when I came upon him
the shunk was calmly chewing off its leg to set itself free.
I felt terribly sorry for it. I was horrified. So I finally knelt
beside it to help it free of the steel jaws. The shunk didn't
understand my act of mercy; it still remembered what I'd done
to it in the first place. It let me have it full blast. From head
to foot. Luckily it didn't hit my eyes.

Well, a hundred yards from our farm yard, my parents
already knew I was coming. My father ran out and stopped
me by the machine shed. "That's far enough, son." It was around
Christmas time, and very cold, but he made me undress in
the machine shed. He brought me a basin of hot water, a brush,
and some harsh tar soup. "Now let's see how good you can
scrub yourself." My father built a little stick fire at the edge
of the grove and burned my clothes. When I couldn't damper
the smell in my hair, my father, screwing up his big nose, got
the clippers and cut off my hair, giving me a heinie haircut.
My mother brought me a fresh set of clothes. And my father
washed my four-buckle rubber boots with gasoline.

None of this helped much. I still stunk skunk. And that
night I had to sleep in the calf pen. All night long the cows
on the other side of the gutter, heads caught in stanchions,
tried to catch a glimpse of that strange stinking critter housed
in with them.

Next I had to learn something about the grizzly. I'd already
had one encounter with them in Yellowstone National Park in
the summer of 1934, when, just out of college, I'd hitchhiked
west to see the Shining Mountains. I'd caught a ride with an

old maid named Minerva Baxter and managed to talk her into stopping where the grizzlies were fed garbage. The garbage still hadn't been brought out but the grizzlies were already slowly drifting in from the forest. Several signs on the viewing platform warned guests not to go beyond a certain point. I spotted several huge grizzlies below us feeding on some berries. Without really thinking about what I was doing, I stepped down off the platform and approached the grizzlies. I got close enough to smell them. It was a wonderful wild unwashed-fur smell. All they did was just slowly swing their huge heads around and look over their silver shoulders at me, sniff at me, and then go back to their feeding.

About that time I became aware that a park ranger had stepped out onto the platform and was glaring down at me. He didn't dare yell at me for fear of stirring up the grizzlies. He had to shut up until I got out of there.

Very quietly, slowly, I backed away and then turned and stepped back up on to the safety of the platform. The ranger, furious, wild, gave me what-for. The devil. When he finished, I gave as my excuse the fact that I'd been raised around animals on the farm, that I'd never been afraid of them, and that the studs and bulls sensing that had left me be.

But that experience by itself wasn't quite enough, I felt. I learned that the Como Park Zoo in St. Paul had recently acquired a young male grizzly. I got permission to visit it before the crowds came in, during those hours when the help would be feeding the animals and cleaning up afterwards, from eight until twelve. For four hours every day I just sat there and watched the young grizzly. At first he was curious about me sitting there only eight feet away on the other side of powerful steel bars. He tried to sniff me. He tried to stare me down. He wriggled his hide over his massive shoulder at me. But finally after a few days he got bored with it all, and turned his back on me, at last even sliding under a bench as though to hide from my sight. Meanwhile I kept waiting for him to do something grizzly.

One day it happened. The guard came in with some fresh raw meat. Instantly the young grizzly moved from under the bench, surged up like a huge hairy amoeba, stood rampant at

the bars above me, sticking his snout as far as he could between two bars to get a better smell of the meat. That motion,
huge yet swift, rising over me, towering, was what I'd been
waiting to see. I now knew grizzly.

Just before I started writing the book I had a strange dream.
It was Hugh Glass, slightly bent with work and time, grizzly-
headed, knobby cracked red fingers, slowly sauntering away
from me, heading for his beaver traps in a cold running mountain stream. I slowly started to wake up. At that point I wasn't
sure it was a dream anymore, but possibly a real being in my
bedroom. I halted the waking up, let myself hang between waking and dreaming, hoping to keep up the scene in the dream
at the same time that I'd see a real live trapper mountain man.
I kept wavering back and forth between being in the dream
and then slowly out of it again. I got, though, a wonderful
view of Old Hugh. Then Maryanna sighed beside me and I
was awake. If Maryanna had known what I was seeing she
would probably have let out a shriek.

I was ready to write the book. It was early in 1953. We
were living out in the country south of Minneapolis on ten
acres we called Wrâlda. A little after seven every morning I'd
step across the backyard to my ten-by-fourteen cabin and begin
writing. I'd first check over what I'd written the day before,
correcting it some, picking up all the threads again; then I'd
read over those thirty pages of mountain men dialogue I'd copied
from Ruxton and Garrard, to get the feel of their day, to get
rhythm and cadence going in my head of that peculiar vernacular speech, even the odd syntax at work in it; and finally
I'd let the secretary of my subconscious start talking. Some
of that mountain man lingo even got into the exposition part of
the narrative.

As the various characters slowly emerged, besides that of
Old Hugh, I let them have their way. In my books everybody
has a right to his own paragraph. Even the author. I was careful
only to keep the colloquial talk from getting out of hand. I
get a little sick of the Brer Rabbit stories. Control is all.

I'd been a little worried about how I would handle Indians.
I wanted to present the real Indian; not the one Helen Hunt
Jackson gave us in *Ramona.* Their noble aspect as well as their

lice. As I went along I realized I wasn't doing too badly with my red friend. I was leaning heavily, I noticed, on three experiences with them.

In college I lived with a young man who'd been raised on the Navajo Reservation in New Mexico. Except for members of his family, he rarely saw white boys and girls. He was an excellent basketball player and had learned all his feints and dodges and shooting from the Navajos. He acted Indian, I felt at the time; it certainly was different from the way I'd been trained to handle myself. He often sat stonily silent in his chair staring at the wall in what I afterwards learned was the true Indian blues.

Later on I played basketball with a Yankton Sioux named Jimmy Wells. He was a forward and a great feeder. I was a center, and he knew just how to loft the ball up near the basket so I could dunk it. We roomed together; got to like each other very much. He told me many stories about his family. The way he handled himself gave me a vivid picture of the Indian man.

And when I was a boy we lived beside the old King of Trails (now Highway 75) which ran from Winnipeg to New Orleans. Every summer caravans of Indians came rolling by, coming down from Flandreau and Pipestone, on their way to Santee, Nebraska. My mother told me to quick jump over the fence and hide in the corn should I see them coming. Indians were known to kidnap little children, she said. I never did jump the fence. I just stood my ground in the ditch. They looked friendly enough to me. My mother's version reflected the time when Indian men would raid any enemy camp to steal a baby and give that baby to a sad mother who'd lost their child through sickness. The stolen child would help assuage her grief.

I must not forget to mention how I found the title, *Lord Grizzly*. Over those eight, nine years of note-taking, I'd called the project *Grizzly*. I knew I had to have that word in the title. But it needed more. Just before I began writing, I made two lists on the same sheet of paper, on the right hand side the word "grizzly" some twenty times and on the lefthand side various adjectives and nouns, such as, "king," "noble," "prince," "lord," "white," "wild," "count," and so on. Curiously enough, my eye didn't pause the first time I saw the two words, "lord" and "grizzly," together in the same line. It wasn't until later, happening to pick up the sheet of paper, that my eye instantly picked out *"Lord Grizzly."* I saw that it was perfect. The grizzly is the lord of the animal world on this continent. And Hugh Glass, after his heroic crawl, was the lord of all mountain men. Using that title as a bullseye helped me keep my eye on the main thrust of the story.

I finished the first draft by the middle of the summer of 1953. Glancing through it, I felt something was still missing. I needed more detail about the scenery. I climbed into our old Ford (with the lights still not fixed) and headed out towards Fort Berthold in North Dakota. I'd learned there were several very old Indians living on the grounds of the fort, an old Mandan and an Old Arikara. The Arikara's memory wasn't very good; it had faded. When I called on the aged Mandan, his wife came out of his log cabin to tell me that her husband didn't care to talk about the old days until just after the sun went down.

Walking back past the row of old weathered cabins, I spotted two Indian girls trying to get into the end cabin near the campgrounds turnaround. One was slim and very pretty, the other common looking. The pretty one was trying to get a key into the door but somehow couldn't quite get it to work. I stopped to watch. It was an old type large key and I knew that if one didn't get it exactly in deep enough, it wouldn't work. Finally I said, "Having a little trouble there?"

She smiled down at her hands. "I can't get in."

"Shall I try for you?"

She handed me the key.

I fit the key into the keyhole, found the right depth, and turned over the tumbler and opened the door for her.

She thanked me with the kind of delicacy I'd once seen at a elegant party on Mt. Curve in Minneapolis.

When the sun slid below the bronze horizon, I had my talk with the Mandan. It turned out he was a walking history book about the area, and not only knew Mandan history but also the Sioux and the Minataree and the Crow and the Hidatsa. The first ten minutes with him or so were touch and go, because

I caught him trying to pull my leg, as well as feed me stuff he thought a white man might want to hear. But when I told him it was probably all going into a book, for keeps, his attitude changed, even his glowing eyes became reflective, and he began to sound like an old Frisian skald.

It was almost eleven o'clock when he finally stopped talking, and he let me know he was sleepy and wanted to go to bed. I thanked him and headed for my room in the main house on the fort grounds.

I'd just barely crossed the big turnaround when an old Ford, one older than the one I drove, pulled up beside me. In it was the pretty Indian girl, alone, smiling demurely.

She asked, "Would you like to go to a dance with me up at New Town?" Fort Berthold would soon be submerged in backed up water from a new dam being built below, and most of the buildings on the old fort grounds were being moved to higher ground called New Town.

"You mean, Indian dancing?"

"Well, yes, that. And modern dancing too. You know, couples together."

I hesitated. She was so very lovely. Had I been single I wouldn't have hesitated even though I'd probably run into considerable hostility from Indian males. But I was in love with my wife, somewhat happily married, and finally, reluctantly, told her I couldn't go. "But thanks anyway."

"I'd like to drive you up there. I hear you want to learn about the Sioux Indians."

I smiled. "Your men friends will probably scalp me."

With that she laughed heartily, black eyes flashing in the reflected light from the dashboard. "You sure you don't want to go?"

"No. I'm sorry."

I never did find out her name, but that girl became the model for the girl named Leaf in my novel *Conquering Horse*. Henry James once made the remark that one only needed a quick glance at the changing of the guard in London to be able to describe much English history. That brief glance at that slender dusky beauty was enough for me to catch the general stance of the Indian woman.

The following day I drove west to the confluence of the Yellowstone and the Missouri rivers. I took copious notes. From there I drove still farther west to the confluence of the Little Big Horn and the Yellowstone rivers, site of Henry's Post. It was where Hugh Glass had caught up with young Jim Bridger, and after telling him to "Get up, I wouldn't kick a pup," let him go. I found a huge iron ring partway imbedded in a fat cottonwood where a hundred and thirty or so years before mountain men had tied up their boats.

I also ran into a funny anecdote about General Custer. Sacrilegious even. Following a long lane, I finally entered a tumbled down dump of a place: low log cabin, a corral, a wispy wheezing old dog who tried to bark at me but couldn't quite make it. Looking past the corral, I spotted a man hoeing in a plot of corn. I strolled out toward him. When I got close enough, his first words were, "What'd I do now?"

I laughed. "Nothing. I just want to ask some questions about this spot." On either side of us was the sound of low slapping water, the Yellowstone to the north of us, the Little Big Horn to the south of us. "Isn't this where Henry's Post was located?"

"Yeh, guess it was. So they say."

" 'They?' "

"Oh, some fussbudget professors come out here now and again and show their students where they *think* some kind of history took place. Puhh."

I'd noticed that there was one spot where the corn grew tall and deep green, while the rest of the field was scrawny and yellowish. "What happened there? An old manure pile butt?"

"Naw." He put a hand to his back and straightened up. He leaned on his hoe and stared with a smile at the tall spot of green corn. "That's where General Custer screwed the chief's daughter and spilled it on the ground. 'Cause he didn't want his wife to find out."

From there I drove the Old Ford over a height of land straight south into Wyoming. I followed a barely marked trail on a map. What I didn't know was that the road had been abandoned by both Montana and Wyoming. I had several close calls because of washouts which had narrowed the road to the point where on several occasions I had to fill in the holes with stones. Once the car almost tipped over on me. When I arrived at the bottom in Wyoming, I ran into an old cowboy sitting on an old nag of a horse. He shook his head at me and my old car, looking back up the trail I'd just come down, and said, "You mean to tell me you came over the top down that road?"

"Well, here I am."

"Nobody's been over that road in years in a car. Wagon maybe. But no car."

I smiled at myself. It was all part of getting the feel of the tough times Hugh might have gone through.

When I hit the Platte River, I headed east, taking mental pictures of the land as Hugh might have seen it. From the Platte I headed for the Badlands to have a glimpse of castle-like formations and delicate minarets. I had in mind having the fantastic scenery work on Hugh to get him ready for the act of forgiving.

I also drove down to Blair, Nebraska, where I'd heard people had found some artifacts of old Fort Atkinson. Kicking through an abandoned field, I found old glass, a broken cup, some gun shells, uniform buttons. As it turned out, I'd found the right place. The state of Nebraska is now in the process of rebuilding the old fort on that field.

I might remark that I had a reason for writing about the previous century, the nineteenth, instead of writing about my own century, the twentieth. After I'd written seven novels about my own times, I gradually became aware of an uneasy feeling that my work lacked the resonance of an olden time. When Dickens wrote his novels, there was always in the back of his head the knowledge that others had been there before him in England, making the land hallowed. For him his country was already celebrated in literature. Before Dickens, there was Wordsworth, before Wordsworth there was Milton, before Milton Shakespeare, before Shakespeare, Spenser, and before Spenser, *Beowulf.* I wanted echoes of an earlier American time in my novels. By writing about Hugh Glass and others, I'd be my own progenitor. I would father myself. Once I had determined that, a whole new concept of my role as writer sprang into my head. I'd create a long hallway of literary murals, from

1800 and on to the day I died, of life in Middle America. It would be a history, in fiction, of our country.

Some might wonder, in particular historians, just how reliable such a recounting might be. Historians can't tell us much beyond such facts as they find. They can speculate some, but it had better be done guardedly, with much qualification. The novelist, however, can fill in the gaps with speculation based on his or her general knowledge of human nature.

Suppose someone came to you and said, "I've got a month's vacation and I've always wanted to know more about the Victorian Age. Who should I read, Green and Trevelyan, or Dickens and Thackeray? if I don't have time to read both? Who'd give me the best and liveliest picture?" The answer is obvious.

Good theories of philosophy, good theories of politics, good theories of history, good theories of theology come and go, but good plays and good novels and good poems last forever.

When I was writing *Scarlet Plume,* a novel about the Sioux Uprising in Minnesota in 1862, I read General Henry Sibley's account of what happened when he took Indian prisoners, chained in wagons, out of Camp Release and rode past New Ulm. The German women of New Ulm, infuriated by what had happened to some of their husbands and sons, attacked the wagons with butcher knives. Something in the way they attacked the shackled Indian men made General Sibley blow his top. He was so angry he forced the German women to walk, not ride, on the way to Mankato. It was only when they neared Mankato that he let them walk back to New Ulm. After reviewing in my memory all such women I'd known, I finally decided that the women of New Ulm (it isn't important that they were German; they could have been of any nationality) tried to use their knives to emasculate the red braves. I'd run into many a strong-minded woman in my day. Faulkner spoke of farm mothers who stood in the doorways of their homes with their hands on their hips like generals.

Just to be sure, though, that I wasn't too far out of line, I mentioned what I had in mind for that episode in *Scarlet Plume* to Russell Fridley, director of the Minnesota Historical Society. He smiled a little, and nodded. Go ahead, use that, he said. We historians don't dare to speculate that that's what happened. We don't have any evidence. But if you use it, and get it published, then we can refer to your account in a footnote.

One more thing had to happen before I was ready to end *Lord Grizzly*. I'd never been asked to forgive someone of a grave crime against me. I wasn't sure I could write convincingly about Hugh forgiving Bridger and Fitzgerald. But then something happened to a relative of mine that gave me insight into the act of forgiving. It was as if the gods of the American West were arranging things for me to find. The relative had been falsely accused of molesting a young girl. It happened that another person in his community had a name exactly like his. The cops picked up the wrong man. The law hates to admit it makes mistakes and they harried him until his name was mud. Even his pastor was ready to have him read out of church. Finally, however, a wise judge got hold of the case, investigated it thoroughly, and recommended that the charge be dropped and that the State make an official apology. At that point his lawyer mentioned that before he accepted the apology he should think of suing the State for false arrest.

The relative sat in his swivel chair a while, smoking his pipe, looking out the window. At last he said, with a drawn smile, "Naw, I think I'll let 'm go. They made an honest mistake."

I was sitting across the table from him when it happened. What he said was not lost on me. I was ready to finish *Lord Grizzly*.

The Little Spirits, or Deons

The last several years I've found myself intrigued in the world of quantum mechanics. The findings of Einstein, Bohr, Schrödinger, Dirac, and Bell indicate that the more we explore the makeup of the atom, the less mass or substance we find. By remarkably accurate speculation we find that the atom is made up of neutrons, protons, and electrons. That those three can be further divided into small particles, quarks and leptons. That the quarks and leptons once more can be divided into pre-quarks and pre-leptons. That these in turn can be distinguished as to whether they are colored or colorless. It is as if way down in there the final building block of the universe is going to turn out to be something that resembles "little spirits." (Cf. Plato's "Ideas.") If one piles up enough of these "little spirits" a shadow shows up. If one piles up enough shadows "colors" show up. And so on until we once again are back at "recognizing" the existence of the atom. I call these little spirits "deons." ("Deon" comes from the two words, "deon," meaning in Greek "godlike," and deontas," meaning in Latin "that which without it there is n‚thing.")

It struck me one day that I'd heard the sum and substance of this years earlier when becoming acquainted with the Yankton Sioux, the Oglalla Sioux, the Hidatsa, the Mandan, and the Arikara. The American Plains Indian believed that "the spirit world" inhabited all things: stones, leaves, grass, insects, four-footeds, two-footeds, earth, and stars. If one listened carefully enough one could get messages from them all. They were all "wakan," part of the great spirit Wakantanka. When *Conquering Horse* and *Scarlet Plume* listened to "the little spirits" they found "the right road."

It seems there is some evidence that the deons communicate with each other. The deons are alive in a very strange way and they are able to relate to each other instanteously, even

144

over vast distances. When we conceive of them as being connected across all space we can speak of them as being parts of God.

The Indians have always known this. They got this knowledge by way of their religion.

November, 1984
The Institute of Indian Studies
University of South Dakota

Old Voices in My Writings

First, I'd like to read you something from Homer; it isn't going to be very long. This is my fourth time through Homer. The first time was in college; I read Chapman's Homer and then later on I got hold of T.E. Lawrence's *Odyssey* and a man named Chapman for his *Iliad.* Then I read Lattimore's translation. And now I am busy with this translation that Robert Penn Warren recommended to me in a letter. He and his wife were reading it. His wife slowly went blind. Her name is Eleanor Clark, a very fine writer in her own right, novelist and historian, a recorder, and he was reading his friend's translation for her, Robert Fitzgerald's. I find that that's by far the best. It's the most lively, most poetic; I think also by far the best translation. It has somewhat of a modern American flavor to it. It isn't jazzy or vernacular but it's still very lively.

The other night I was reading in it (I try to read about five, six pages a day—I don't want to get too much honey in me at one time 'cause then my teeth hurt) but in any case I read four or five pages and I happened on this passage, and I thought, well, I'm going to start the thing off today with this.

Odysseus has been picked up by King Alcinous's daughter, and given clothes, and then bathed by the maidens. They had a marvelous custom in those days—if they found a man on their shore and he was in bad shape and they decided he was okay, they brought him inside and had the maidens give the man a bath. I'm all for that. I've been thinking I ought to get lost on one of those islands of Greece myself someday and maybe they will still have that old custom.

Alkinoos, king and admiration of men,
how beautiful this is, to hear a minstrel
gifted as yours: a god he might be, singing!
There is no boon in life more sweet, I say,

146

than when a summer joy holds all the realm,
and banqueters sit listening to a harper
in a great hall, by rows of tables heaped
with bread and roast meat, while a steward goes
to dip up wine and brim your cups again.
Here is the flower of life, it seems to me.

I feel the same way. When I'm at the end of a day's work—
four hours at the desk and then two or three hours in the
yard somewhere—and I have a few minutes to myself and can
look out over the countryside—that feeling is the great life.

I don't know quite where this talk is going to go. I've got
some little signposts here (points at notes) and if I get lost
I'll look them up, but what I'm going after today are voices.
They're hard enough to nail down in any case because some
of them are ghostly. It's a little bit like if you were quartering
after a quarry of some kind. As a hunter you know there's
some kind of an animal out there that you want but you're
not sure what it is. You've seen the grass move and you've
seen the leaves move on the trees. You might be chasing a
fox that later on turns out to be a wolf, and when you get
a little closer it might turn out to be a jackrabbit. When you
get still closer it might turn out to be a swamp ghost. And
even a little closer still it might turn out to be a handful of
fireflies. But somewhere along the line we'll find it.

The first voices that enter you before you know about it
are those when you receive milk from your mother's breast when
you're a day or two old. You don't remember them now but
all that cooing and soft murmurings that your mother uses;
she babies you and holds you and feeds you. Without any question that gets into you very early on. Those are the very first
sounds you ever hear. They probably set you for life as to
what you'll accept later on. It comes in with the mother's milk;
it comes in with something that comes from Ma.

It's interesting to note that the words we like to hear, and
the names we like to use, often have the letter "M" in it, because
it's associated with "Mama" and "Memma," meaning milk; and
that the words which mean something that isn't good, "bah,"
"bah-bah," are associated with Pa.

There was once a time, a long long time ago, when fathers were enemies of their children. This is still true in the animal kingdom. The female in the animal kingdom doesn't trust the male until the young are fairly well along. It doesn't take long before that little mind there starts dividing all sounds up into two big portions – the "Ma" sounds and the "Pa" sounds. You'll notice, too, that names that you remember with warmth are names that are kind and warm, that have "M" sounds or "N" sounds in them; and the names you remember with aversion are those with bad sounds in them, "P's," "H's," "D's," "F's," "B's."

I happened to be born first in my family so I didn't hear any brothers and sisters around me, but I've often thought about my brother Henry, who was sixth to come along, what an odd world he grew up in. First he heard his mother's "Ma" sounds, later on he heard his father's "bah" sounds, and then he had those five older brothers squabbling and fighting ahead of him. When that little mind began to pick up meanings, what an incredible world he must have thought it was with all these terrible giants around, all ahead of him; that he had to fend his way amongst them. How to handle them, how to survive, how to not to be submerged, how not to be buried under all that. His mind is filled with different voices than my mind. The voices I heard, generally speaking, were clear and most of them all right. But the voices he heard were voices that he had to contend with. So I became a writer and he became a lawyer.

I would like to see a paper some day done on that subject, see where lawyers come from in the family – are they often the youngest? I suppose if a father is a lawyer that his oldest son will become a lawyer, but lawyers who come from families where there were no lawyers before, it would be interesting to see which part of the family they come from – the youngest, the oldest, or the middle ones. Because obviously my brother Henry did have to contend with four sharp hawks and one chicken. (One of my brothers was a tender-hearted gentle fellow who wouldn't hurt a fly. My mother often said she had given birth to five hawks and one chicken. And I could see why she would say that. Not because we were mean to each other, but because five of us were just quicker to get what we wanted to have at the supper table.)

Then there are relatives to contend with. If you have a lot of relations (to use a Siouxland term) as I have, I have some four hundred of them – two hundred on one side and two hundred on the other – they obviously, especially if you're the oldest, they've all got to see you when you're the firstborn. I have no memory of it anymore, but I can easily imagine all these fat-faced aunts leaning over me and saying, "Oh, he's cute," and so on; and then stepping away four or five steps and saying, "You know, he's kind of an ugly mutt. Doesn't look like either the father or the mother. Doesn't even take after the grandparents." All these things. But I'm sure my little mind was already picking up, if not the words, the sense of some kind of opinion being established around me, a climate of opinions through which I would later on have to find my way.

Then, since my people were churchgoers – we didn't have babysitters – the baby was brought into the church, and if the baby cried then it was given titty. And so obviously for those first years I had to sit and listen to the preacher without even knowing if I wanted to or not, and that sound of a preacher's doleful voice, going every week – let's see, twice Sunday that's 104 times a year – it had to have some effect on me, and that voice I'm sure has landed somewhere down in my subconscious too. And sits down in there, waiting for some day when it can spring out and find a vehicle, a character, through which it can talk.

Then there are the teachers. I was lucky. Of all the teachers I had I do not know of one I did not like. I might have been a teacher's pet, because if they kept books in front of me they had no trouble with me. If there wasn't something to read, then of course I would get into trouble. I'd dip pigtails into the inkwell ahead of me, and so on. But if there were books around, then they never had any real trouble with me. Teachers had a powerful influence on me.

My Aunt Katheryn, for example, had me very early on. She was a little more strict than my mother. There was some resentment in me about it. One day one of the boys caught a mouse and put it into a Bull Durham sack. He asked me

if I would let that thing out when the organ was being played
by Aunt Katheryn when we were going to sing the *Star Span-
gled Banner*. I was happy to do this. Of course I really got
it from her afterwards. Not from my father and mother. My
mother didn't say much; she just gave me a reproving look.
But Aunt Katheryn was mad at me for about six months while
Dad laughed about it for about six months. He thought that
was a great joke.

Then soon there are other sounds that enter you. I'm going
after sounds too because sounds later on will find figures and
frames in which to live. There are blizzards, there are tornadoes,
and then there are gentle soft breezes. (Like today, a little soft
breeze, a little cool, a great thing to feel across your face.)
When you're very young, all these leave a very prominent impression on you, always have something to say to you. Then
there's rain, all different kinds of rain, including hail.

Then there's land. If you are born on a farm as I was and
spend most of your early life on relatively flat land, slightly
rolling, you learn it intimately. When I found my first May
flowers, I brought them to my mother. She thought it was
very nice of me, but told me that within two hours, no matter
what she did, put them in water, they would die; and that
the best thing for me, if I really loved flowers, was to leave
them where I found them. Don't pick them. And of course later
on I did learn in a botany class that if you're a wild plant
lover, you must love them and leave them. You don't take them
home.

Then the trees. Trees speak to you too. There was an article
recently in some scientific magazine stating that if one tree
gets attacked by a bug in a forest, it sends out a note of alarm
by way of smells. The trees nearby pick it up, and then they
too turn out an acid that resists bugs. There is a form of communication going on of some kind between trees. There are
those who argue that trees and plants hear talk about them,
that they are affected by that talk. That's a whole world we're
just now exploring.

As a very little boy I was somewhat of an Indian in a
sense that I felt that all things were talking to me. That's
why it was relatively easy for me to write *Conquering Horse*,

in which I said that stones and various things talk, and even move a little. We had a big grove on one farm, I remember, and my mother used to wonder what in the world I was doing in it, because I would go over to a tree, put my arms around it and my ear against it and listen, and go down along all the trees, up and down in the grove, to check their sounds. I still do that today. Each tree has a different sound. What you hear, if the wind's blowing, are the various fibers rustling against each other, the bark rustling against the cambium, and of course the leaves, and here and there if there's a branch about to break off — you can almost hear it about to break. But each tree has a sound of its own. It is a form of music.

Sometimes I'm sorry that I didn't go into music because I'm affected mightily by sound, and I'm quite aware that when I write that the first law is really how does it sound in my ear. It is as much a musical composition as it is a literary composition. So I'm very easily offended when someone wants to take a paragraph or a word or two out of the text. Copy editors go too much by the sense of it and don't hear the sounds in it. It would be as if you took out four notes from a Beethoven sonata. He would rightaway notice those four notes were missing and of course I notice it too if you start taking words out.

I had a test run on that one time. My publisher forgot to send the setting manuscript along with the galleys, so I called in and said to send it out. Meanwhile, I had my own copy. Just for the fun of it, I read two pages into the galleys and found that in almost every other paragraph some little change had been made that was not in the original. When the setting manuscript finally came by mail, sure enough, I found I had picked up every change they'd made. It didn't ring right on my clavichord when I tried to play it back.

Then there are other voices. Perhaps I should give you a couple illustrations of what I mean and I hope you don't think I'm a little whacky. But for some time I'd been bothered by the fact that my five Buckskin Man Tales were with four different publishing houses. They had all gone out of print. I learned that there was a possible chance that I could get the New American Library to reissue them all in a uniform edition. But how was I to get those properties back? The agent

was reluctant to arrange it for me. That was the first time
I learned in my naive way that the agent really represents
the publishers more than he does the writer. Because I don't
have the money; the publisher has the money. So the agent
is going to represent the publisher slightly more than he does
me. I was wondering what I should really do about this. One
morning I was writing up on Blue Mound. All of a sudden
I heard, as distinctly as if a person were standing behind me,
a voice saying: "Go to New York!" I remember jerking erect
and looking around to see if someone had quietly come up the
stairwell. But there was no face sticking up over the edge. So
I got up and went over and looked down the stairwell. Nothing
there either. I even went down the stairs to see if I could catch
someone walking away. Nobody. I found nobody home. Everybody was gone. But I very clearly heard that voice.

Well, I decided that somewhere in the back of my head,
or in my subconscious, that genie that puts things together,
had decided that I should go to New York and visit these four
different publishers and see if I couldn't get those contracts
reverted back to me. So I promptly called the airport, ordered
the airplane tickets, and packed. As I was leaving the yard,
Maryanna my wife came home, and said, "Where are you going?" I said, "I'm going to New York." "Well," she said, "you
didn't mention it this morning." I said, "No, I didn't. I didn't
know about it until just a moment ago." I didn't know if I
should explain to her that I heard a voice in the stairwell.
She's a very brilliant woman and superior critic, but there were
things I often did that puzzled her. The best way was not
to say anything until it was all over with. The trip was
successful.

Again, one day the phone rings. I picked it up. It was
Freya in California, my oldest daughter, a poet. I said, "Hello."
"Dad!" "Yeh, what's the matter?" "Dad, I just heard a voice!"
I knew she was having some problems with the people she
was living with there. Very quickly I said, "Good! Now I know
you're one of us." "Ohh," she said, "Dad, am I glad to hear
that." I said, "What kind of a voice did you hear?" She explained to me. I said, "My dear, that's the animal or secret
part of you, your lizard or Old Eve, who really knows what

the lizards of your hosts are really thinking about you. They wish you'd leave. You're being polite, and they're being polite, and you're not telling each other what you are really thinking, but down below you both really know what you're really thinking and that's where that voice is coming from. So I'd listen to it and get out of there." And that's exactly what she did.

Now to move over to the books I always wanted to write. My first writings were mostly poems; little bursts of things that came to me and I wrote them down. Usually the first four or five lives were pretty good and then they sort of tailed off. But as I got used to catching these little bursts that would come flying up in my mind, I learned after a while how to be very gentle and pull them out, like you might pull an angleworm out of the earth. Don't pull them out too fast. There's usually a lot more down there, and after while you do come up with the whole poem. In the beginning you're too impatient. But you've got to be patient.

I used to worry about how in the world do I fill as much as twenty pages for a short story let alone for say two hundred pages for a book. How do I add one sentence after another and make them sound meaningful? It took me a long time to figure that out. I don't know how many short stories I didn't write, fifty or more, that weren't very good. I burned most of those. In almost every case I was imitating somebody. I'd be reading a lot of Hemingway and then what I wrote would sound like a pale Hemingway. Or I'd read a lot of Steinbeck and it would sound like a pale Steinbeck. And John Dos Passos.

One Saturday night it happened. A friend I knew was interested in the fact that I wanted to be a writer. He'd wanted to be one too and had one book published. His name was James Shields and the book was *Just Plain Larnin'.* It's his only novel. It deals with a teacher who's told to teach just the 3-R's— readin', ritin', 'rithmetic—no other stuff in that tobacco town. He finally had to give it up because there was no money in writing. But he was really hopped up about me becoming a writer. He invited me over to a party. He said there'd be some really nice people over, most of them social workers loaded with stories I might like to hear. The only trouble was I worked til about 12 o'clock (on the *Minneapolis Journal* as a reporter). He said the party usually lasted til one or two in the morning.

After I got through work I checked it out. Sure enough the lights were still on in his house. I went in, not by the front door but the kitchen way. I was terribly shy in those days and I had trouble talking to more than four or five people in one room. Two or three I could handle, but four or five was too many. I remember a couple standing in the kitchen chatting, smiling. They were married, but they weren't married to each other. I went into the living room and I snuck in behind a plush chair and sat on the floor. Pretty soon the host, Jim Shields, noticed me. "Oh, Fred, there you are. Did you get yourself a beer?" "No." "Why don't you get yourself one?" So I went into the kitchen again and there I found these two smooching. I apologized, got myself a beer, went back down. Finally Jim said, "I want you to tell the story, Fred, about South Dakota when you hitchhiked through there in 1934." I didn't want to. But he kept after me. He said, "It's a very good story." I didn't want to tell him I was a terribly poor storyteller, even with just a close friend. I always gave the point away or forgot the ending.

But this story...of course having hitchhiked through here in 1934...I had $11 in my pocket when I started out and came home with $8...I lived on $3 and a few pennies for two weeks. It was so vivid in my mind that I couldn't, you know, have trouble with that story. It was all sitting there in my head. I told it.

When I finished, I noticed, to my surprise, everybody was listening intently. There was a silence. Well, on the way home it hit me that I'd finally found my voice. The way I had told it was the way I should write it. Not be imitating Hemingway or Steinbeck or anybody else. This is the way I should write it. Instead of going to bed—I was very tired—I had worked all day from seven until twelve at the newspaper. I sat up all night and all day Sunday and wrote the whole thing I'd told that night, some sixty to seventy pages worth. Then I went to bed.

Next Monday I went to work. Monday night I came home. After a pork-and-bean supper and some weiners—I was baching – I had a little nap. Then I pulled out this manuscript and read it. When I finished reading it I knew suddenly that I'd become a good writer. It was all sittin' in there. It was rough and ragged, but there was an impact and an emotion and a sound in there that was true.

It is interesting to note that as time went on, I wrote six more drafts of that story. As I went on, I kept peeling off stuff, concentrating more and more on one thing – and that was the hobo I ran into. I saw him just briefly. Part of an afternoon and an evening and part of a night. If you want to have the whole story, read it in the book called *The Wind Blows Free* which the Center for Western Studies published. I concentrated on that hobo and that became *The Golden Bowl.* That's not me, that's this fellow I ran into. He really hit me hard. He had lost his family in Oklahoma, he had lost his girlfriend, and she had lost her people, to dust pneumonia they called it then.

Well, you see I didn't know too much about him and to make a story out of him I had to fill in a lot. All I saw really was the front side of him. If you conceive of yourself and of ourselves as all of us being flesh-prisms with many facets, and a light in each of these flesh prisms (demonstrating) when these two flesh prisms face each other, the light from this prism will light up only the facets facing it on this prism. The same thing the other way. But this light will never light up the facets on the back side of that prism – the backside of the moon of each person. So to fill in a rounded character you then fall back on your general knowledge of humanity. You fill in the back side of his moon and it becomes a rounded whole. I remembered this boy's voice, and some of his manners, but I filled in all the rest around that voice from my general knowledge of people and from the experience of my people who hung on and survived the dust bowl.

Dinkytown

It was in April of 1937 when I first began living in Dinkytown. I'd just gotten a job with the old *Minneaplis Journal* as a reporter and checked into a boarding house at 628 14th Avenue Southeast. My brother Floyd, freshman at the University of Minnesota, had found the room for me. He lived across the street; I didn't have a car so each morning I caught the Como Harriet streetcar to work a block north of 15th Avenue. The lawns had just barely turned green and the lilacs in the backyards were cropping out with thick brown buds and the crocuses on the sunny side of the garages rustled soft purples.

The job as reporter provided me with my first real full-time salary. Before that, from 1934, when I graduated from Calvin College in Grand Rapids, Michigan, until that April I took on a variety of part-time work: dollywhopper in Grand Rapids warehouse; roustabout in a Passaic, New Jersey, rubber factory; reporter for a weekly in Paterson, New Jersey; basketball player; farmhand; filling station attendant in Perkins, Iowa; house-to-house salesman in South Dakota. I cared for none of those jobs; took them only to survive through the Great Depression.

It was thrilling to know I was a reporter for a nationally recognized newspaper. I was quick to use the *Journal's* stationary to let my various friends and classmates know that at last I'd arrived and could finally consider myself a full-time citizen *who was working*.

On my day off, Thursday, when I wasn't typing what eventually became my first novel, *The Golden Bowl*, I often sauntered south down the street to visit the various stores near the corner of 14th Avenue and 4th Street: five-and dime, ice cream palace, Walgreen's Drugstore, the Minnesota Bookstore, Perine's Bookstore, and several hole-in-wall groceries, Chinese laundry, radio repair shop, dry cleaners, a ladies style shop, Varsity Theatre, book-and-stationary shop.

Late in the afternoon that corner swarmed with students and occasional professors and housewives. Times were very tough then, yet most students wore good conventional clothes, sober colors for the men gray and blue, somewhat more lively colors for the ladies yellow and green, with the housewives almost always wearing a shawl pulled tight over their hair only their faces showing. Quips and laughter could be heard all afternoon long. Since everybody was just about in the same plight, almost broke, everybody bore up with a tough-titty smile. We were all in the same foundering boat so we might just as well smile as curse.

Thursday evenings I often went to a movie at the Varsity. I somehow always managed to scrape up a quarter for the show. I was quite shy, and didn't date, so the movie was a welcome way to spend an evening. I often looked at the girls, and wondered when I'd finally get up enough nerve to ask one of the prettier ones, coeds, if I could take them out. It is interesting to remember that in the two years I lived on that side of the University of Minnesota campus I didn't once run into my future wife, Maryanna Shorba. She lived within a block of where I lived, from 1936 until 1939. In 1939 she became ill and had to go to the Glen Lake Sanatorium in Oak Terrace (near Hopkins). When I finally did meet her in the same sanatorium for tuberculosis (I became ill in April of 1940) I thought her a beautiful woman and I've always been sure that had I seen her earlier in Dinkytown I would have surely sought her out.

My housemates at 628 were two students going to the University farm campus, Zebe Lumb and Ralph Craft from Webster, South Dakota. Both were studious at the same time that they loved good stories. When they'd be done studying, they often came to my room to talk about the old days back on the farm.

There was one story I told they loved. But it didn't happen on the farm. It happened to me on my way to work at the *Journal.* Early one morning I walked over to Cooke Hall, the athletic building on the campus, to interview freshman football coach Dallas Ward. Ward had helped me get a job on the *Journal* by way of my brother Floyd. Finished with the interview,

I boarded an Oak Harriet streetcar on 15th and 4th that was headed for downtown. A bunch of students stepped aboard with me. The streetcar was already full and there weren't any seats left, so I and the students had to stand pressed together in back. After a while, one of the men students threw me a significant look, first in my eye and then down to the front of my trousers. I wondered what he'd found wrong with me and so after a bit I felt my fly. Sure enough I'd forgotten to zip it up. Zippers had just come into style then and it was hard to remember to zip up when one had always been used to buttoning up. As unobstrustively as I could, I slowly pulled the zipper up.

Everything was fine until we got to where the Oak Harriet car crossed Central Avenue. There was some rustling motion amongst the students standing snug against me, including one lovely girl who'd found herself pressed tight against my thigh. When the others in front of her stepped down to catch the Central Avenue car, she moved to do the same – only to discover she was tied to me. She had on one of those stylish camel-hair skirts. And in zipping up my zipper, my zipper had caught some of those long camel hairs. She tugged one way; I tugged the other way. It didn't take but a moment for everyone in the streetcar, including the conductor in back, to see our dilemma, and wild laughter broke out. Lord, did I turn red. But not as red as the girl. Because it looked like we had been having intercourse standing up. Finally, I suggested to the girl student that we should walk off the streetcar in lockstep, as though we were in step to slow dance music with her back to me. A woman in a nearby ladies dress shop saw our problem once we were on the sidewalk and she came out with a tiny scissors and snipped us apart.

After that first summer in Dinkytown, my brother Floyd and I decided we should live in the same house. We found a large room – it was once a living room – at 522 12th Avenue Southeast, with a Mrs. Pappas. Her son was a cartoonist for the sports department at the *Minneapolis Star*. She had two very lovely daughters, who she guarded as closely as a Spanish duenna might, to the point where the girls were growing up goosey and silly, certainly not the kind of young women to awaken me as a man. A better candidate as a lover was a niece of Mrs. Pappas, Romelle, who came to live with her late in the fall. Romelle soon got a job with a beauty parlor in Dinkytown. But before I could get up enough nerve to ask her for a date, one of the boys boarding upstairs, a fellow named Benny, seduced her. Disillusioned, that was the end of that for me.

The next spring I decided, after I'd built up somewhat of a wardrobe, to buy myself a car. I finally settled on a blue second-hand Dodge. My brother and I began to take rides out in the country of a Sunday. Slowly I became acquainted with both the city and the country.

Sometimes I attended the Second Ward meetings of the Farmer-Labor Party held in an empty store across the street from the Varsity Theatre. Listening to the arguments between the radicals and the old-line liberals, between the Reds and the University crowd, livened up many an evening, and taught me something about our society as well as the political climate of the time. There I met several lovely ladies who weren't adverse to having me take them home in my rumbling old blue Dodge. Two of them were delighted to learn that I lived nearby and that most evenings my brother was busy at work (as a way of paying his way through college.)

One day Benny and a roommate of his brought home a long two-by-ten plank. They snuck it into the house when Mrs. Pappas was out. It wasn't long before we found out why. Our red house was only some eight feet away from the house next door to the north and that house was full of coeds. Benny and his friend, after a signal from two of the girls that all was clear on their side, would place the plank across the gap, from their windowsill to the other windowsill, and pay the other house a visit without having to go through the front door. Benny and his friend never told us what went on there, but from their self-satisfied smirks we know that the Seventh Commandment was being broken regularly.

One night the landlady next door living below the two coeds heard what she thought was some suspicious noises directly over her bedroom. She was a huge tall woman with square shoulders and long powerful arms. She burst in on Benny and his friend as they were coupling with two of her female boarders. She let out a roar, pulled the plank over to her side, gave Benny and his buddy each a tremendous kick in the butt, and banished the two girls. Then she sailed over and made a complaint to Mrs. Pappas that she, an abandoned wife, was running a house of ill repute, full of vipers and fornicators and despoilers of virgins, and that she was going to report her to the housing authorities at the University of Minnesota.

It was at 522 12th Avenue Southeast that I wrote the second and third drafts of my first novel, as well as the first draft of what eventually became my novel, *This Is the Year*. It was also at that address that I got my first boxful of rejections on both the first novel, *The Golden Bowl*, as well as on *This Is the Year*. The rejections hurt, especially when I began to get long letters from editors telling me that, while they enjoyed reading the manuscripts, they felt the books weren't quite right for their lists. I took long walks to help handle the hurts. I'd walk down to the Mississippi River and follow it from the Tenth Avenue bridge all the way to the Franklin Avenue bridge.

It was while living at 522 that I did finally get an opinion that made up for all the rejections. I'd heard that Meridel Le Sueur the novelist and strong-minded leftwinger held a writing class in a bar in downtown Minneapolis. So one evening I sauntered over to see what sort of class it was, to get a line on her. If I liked her maybe I might ask her to have a look at the manuscript of my first novel. Meridel, I was told, had a national reputation.

It turned out to be a joy to watch her run that class. One of her students would read a couple of pages and then Meridel would first try to get comments from the other students listening in and only after they'd given their opinions would she then, in a mild voice, offer her criticisms. Her comments were always apt, and she had a tendency to stress the strong or good points of the manuscript, and not to say much about what didn't impress her. Her comments were upbeat. The struggling writers needed to be encouraged by positive comment; not discouraged by negative criticisms.

When the group broke up, she called over to me. She asked my name, what I was doing, the like. When she learned I had a finished manuscript at home and that I hadn't known quite what to do next, she suggested I bring it around to her house. I did.

About two weeks later I had a call from her. Could I meet her for lunch at the Stockholm Cafe on Washington Avenue? I said I could. The Stockholm was where lumberjacks and railroad workers hung out.

We both had a beer and a hamburger. She had the manuscript of *The Golden Bowl* with her and placed it to one side of our booth. But she didn't look at it as we talked, but instead questioned me closely about my political views, did I have a girl, what had my life on the farm been like, what was my job like as a reporter. Meanwhile, I kept wondering what in the world she really thought of the manuscript. I was afraid that she didn't like it and that that was why we didn't begin with it. Finally, when it was almost time to go, she picked up the manuscript, and in her warm earth-mother voice, said, "I read your book about the Dust Bowl. It is already better than John Steinbeck's *Of Mice and Men*. It does need more work, but let me give you some advice. Never take instruction on how to improve it from some other writer or from some self-appointed critic. You're one of those writers who should be allowed to work out your own style and your way of treating your subject matter. Learn to be your own best critic. That's the last thing you'll learn as a writer but I can see already that you're bright enough to become that. If you listen to others, you'll be thrown off your course. Your stuff isn't surface material that with a little tinkering here or there can then made publishable. You write out of something deep within you, and only you will know when you're voicing that deep-within-you truly. What would an outsider, no matter how good a critic she or he might be, know how you really feel about life, how you magically get these things up out of you? And don't worry, you're a good one, and you're going to get better—provided you work at being your own best critic."

Well! I nearly exploded. I tried not to let my feelings show, and thanked her quietly, and then we each went our way. From that point on I knew I would eventually be published—on my own terms. That happened in 1938, one year before Steinbeck's *The Grapes of Wrath* came out.

Late in August of 1938, Mrs. Pappas decided to move across the corner, to 1119 Sixth Street Southeast. Two of the boys upstairs, brothers, Milton and Clifford Maxwell, decided to move with her; as did my brother Floyd and I. Floyd and I took the two rooms facing the street and the Maxwells took the two rooms in back. We had more room and we liked it that Mrs. Pappas seemed more relaxed at the new address. That tight little red house at 522 had got on her nerves.

During those days in 1938, I met through Arthur Naftalin, who was taking journalism at the University, various members of the Jacobin Club: Fred Rarig, Eric Sevareid (then known as Arnie), Sherman Dryer, Richard Scammon, Lee Loevenger, about a dozen of them. Eric also worked with me for a time at the *Journal*. The Jacobins questioned everything and in general tended to be quite liberal. They were much influenced by the debonair and brilliant Professor Benjamin Lippincott of the Political Science Department. He attended some of their meetings. (Benjamin Lippincott's wife, Gertrude, was a well-known dancer; and when those two put on a party it was something to write home about.) The Jacobins questioned everything and in general tended to be quite liberal. Their sharpest inquiry was directed at both extremes, the conservative and the communist. From them I learned to have a kindly feeling for Norman Thomas the Socialist.

There were several bookstores in Dinkytown at the time. The biggest and the best was the Minnesota Bookstore where students could buy textbooks and where the general public could buy trade books. Bobby Clark was a clerk there and she and I became good friends. Her husband, John Clark, taught Chaucer in the English Department. The other bookstores featured second-hand and rare books. Julius Butwin ran such a store next to the Crane Stationery, and it was from him I got Skeat's *Etymological Dictionary of the English Language*, a book that helped me discover the importance of my Frisian-Saxon ancestry, helped me understand how come I could read Chaucer with some ease.

Late in 1938, my brother Floyd and I, with our buddies Milton and Clifford Maxwell, moved to 711 Washington Avenue, S. E., which of course took us across to the other side of the campus. Later on, in 1939, we moved to 609 Ontario Street Southeast, and still later to 507 Oak Street Southeast. While living at those places I still visited Dinkytown many times, to buy books, to go to the Varsity Theatre, to go to Farmer-Labor meetings, etc.

Our gang broke up early in 1940. Floyd left to have a tryout with the Eau Claire Baseball Team, then a minor league farm of the Minneapolis Millers. Floyd had overpowering "smoke," and once, while in high school, lost a 1-0 game to the great Bob Feller in an Iowa district tournament. Floyd struck out more men than did Bob Feller. Milton Maxwell got married and got a job as an accountant. Clifford Maxwell also got married and took a job with the YMCA. I wound up at 314 Walnut Street Southeast.

Early in 1939, I was fired from the *Minneapolis Journal.* (Eric Sevareid was fired by the same man the year before.) The *Journal* was in the process of being sold, and the management was cutting back on the help, and the rule was, "last hired first fired." There was also in the firing the hint that I'd been a bit too active in helping establish the Newspaper Guild in the Twin Cities. I lived on Workman's Compensation for a while, was a busboy at a teahouse on Washington Avenue, walked the streets looking for work (of any kind!), and wrote when I had the heart for it.

And in April of 1940, while walking home to my room at 314 Walnut Southeast, I fell down on the sidewalk with severe cramps in my chest. It developed I had pleurisy as well as tuberculosis. I was sent from the Lymanhurst Clinic straight to the Glen Lake Sanatorium.

Two years later, when I was allowed to leave the sanatorium, I first took up residence for a few months at a halfway house at 1827 Portland Avenue South, and then in the fall of 1942, I lived with Maryanna Shorba and her mother Mrs. Mary Shorba in a house east of Van Cleve Park, at 1016 18th Avenue, S. E. Maryanna and I were married on Hallwe'en, 1942, at the Little Brown Church in the Vale, Nashua, Iowa.

In the spring of 1943 the phone rang late one evening. Maryanna and I had already gone to bed. We'd learned that the only way we were going to stay ahead of our arrested tuberculosis was to get plenty of sleep, along with of course good food. The phone kept ringing, so I crept downstairs and answered it. It was Arthur Naftalin. He said he and his friend Kirk Fitzpatrick was over at Hubert Humphrey's house.

"Oh," I said, "I know him." I used to visit Hubert when he worked in Brown's Drugstore on Washington Avenue. Earlier one night I'd met Hubert while visiting Zebe Lumb and Ralph Craft. Zebe and Ralph and I were laughing when suddenly the door opened and a lean dark head poked in. Zebe introduced Hubert. We liked each other immediately.

"So Hubert said," Art went on. "Can you come over? Hubert is thinking of running for mayor of Minneapolis and we'd like to get your advice. You were once a newsman and you know the leaders of the CIO."

I left a sleepy bride and went over. The four of us talked until early in the morning. By the time I left to go home, it was decided Hubert should throw his hat in the ring.

In August of 1943, Maryanna and I (and her mother) moved to 1814 Fourth Street Southeast. So she and I were Dinkytowners again.

Across our block, living on University Avenue, was Joseph Warren Beach, critic, poet, and head of the English Department at the University of Minnesota. His wife was novelist Dagmar Doneghy Beach. We shared a garage in the center of the block. At Beach's house we soon met a lot of interesting creative minds: novelist and critic James Gray (who wrote the first article ever about me as a coming writer, in 1939), William Van O'Connor, Allen Tate, Carl Sandburg, and many a lesser literary light. Through my wife Maryanna I met her classmates Russell Roth, Max Shulman, Dan Brennan, Thomas Heggen, Bud Nye, and Norman Katkov. It was also while we lived at 1814 that I wrote my very first piece of writing to be published nationally, "Report From Minnesota," in *The New Republic*, CIX (October 11, 1943). In it I discussed Harold Stassen and Hubert Humphrey. I predicted that brainy Stassen was too cold a man to make it nationally in politics, while Humphrey might become president. Humphrey had warmth and brilliance.

During the winter of 1943-44, Robert Penn Warren called me one day. He'd read my article in *The New Republic*, he said, and would like to talk with me about Minnesota politics. He was writing a novel about southern politics. I said it would be all right. He suggested we first take a walk and then retire to his home on Logan Street where we'd have a hot-buttered rum. The rum would lubricate my tongue. He was a little concerned that what he wanted to learn from me might also be useful to me someday, that I might want to use it myself for a novel. I said I'd be happy to unload what I knew about Minnesota politics, that he could take what he wanted, because later on, should I write about it, I'd take a different tack anyway. Later on I discovered he was writing the final draft of *All the Kings Men* at the time.

We took at least a dozen walks, around Lake Harriet, Lake Calhoun, once even along the Mississippi River at my suggestion, from Dinkytown to the Franklin Avenue bridge. He wanted to know about the latter, "How's the footin' there?" and at first I had trouble catching the word "footin,'" he spoke in such a soft Guthrie, Kentucky drawl.

During our talks he'd casually drop remarks about various critics and authors, people I'd never heard of before: Kenneth Burke, John Crowe Ramson, Cleanth Brooks, Allen Tate (later on, as mentioned above, I met Tate). I promptly went out and bought their work.

We also used to meet downtown Minneapolis at Charlie's, with Russell Roth and Dan Brennan. Those three eventually got around to talking about William Faulkner. I had tried to read Faulkner and couldn't get into him. I felt that at least two-fifths of his work was written by the old Jack Daniels. Finally, not to be left out of their delighted talk, their laughter about Old Bill, I asked Red Warren one time as we headed for home after such a luncheon, what book of Faulkner's should I read to get started with him. "Get Cowley's *Portable Faulkner*." So that same afternoon, January 27, 1949, I headed for Powers Bookstore and bought a copy. That same summer I asked Julius Butwin, rare book dealer on 4th Street, to search for Faulkner first editions. He got me at least a half-dozen of Faulkner's early work. That fall Faulkner was awarded the Nobel Prize for Literature.

One day in the early Fifties, I happened to wander over to Walgreen's Drugstore to get some cough drops. There, sitting on a stool, having a soft drink, was James Wright, poet. We'd met several times at parties in the area, at Morgan Blum's house, at our house. I was surprised to see he was crying. I said nothing at first, and ordered a soft drink to keep him company.

Finally I had to ask him. "What's up, Jim?"

"Oh," he said, "I've got to go over to the University Hospital and have some more of those electric shock treatments."

"What! What for, for godsakes?"

"Oh, to help me get rid of that part of me that wants to write poetry. My wife just wants me to be a teacher, no more. Bring home the paycheck like any other workman father. Forget about writing poems. There's supposed to be something wrong with me that I still dream of becoming a famous poet. I guess I'm too stubborn to give it up."

I was outraged. Those goddamned average chickens he was associated with! I said nothing more to him. But the moment I left the drugstore, I sailed over to the University Hospital and looked up a friend I knew there, a clinical psychologist. I'd had dinner one night at the home of this psychologist friend and had noticed that in his basement he had the most complete collection of Little Magazines I'd ever seen. I figured he would be inclined to listen to me. I told him what I'd just heard at Walgren's Drugstore. He too was outraged. "Lord, and I know who's responsible. He hates creative artists. I'll look into it right away." Jim's electric schock treatments were abruptly stopped. In the long run, no one wife or no one husband is worth one good poem.

At about the same time, I met several more writers: Saul Bellow, Mark Harris, Mark Schorer, and the above-mentioned Allen Tate. Bellow I didn't much care for. I thought him petulant and somewhat arrogant beyond his means. Mark Harris made me think of an alert ground squirrel sitting at the opening of his hole and wondering how he might outwit the neighbor's dog. Mark Schorer gave me the impression that he was desperately currying the favor of the New Critics, that as a critic he longed to be safe in the arms of a genius. In my experience he was not a very good scholar. For his biography of Lewis he accepted Malcolm Cowley's report on Sinclair Lewis's funeral; instead of accepting mine. Cowley got his knowledge of it from me. Cowley was hard-of-hearing and got it all mixed up. Besides, Cowley's report was second-hand; mine was first-hand. Allen Tate also had an arrogance about him, but in his case I liked it. He knew his stuff. What he had was what I call a permissable arrogance.

Of that whole bunch, the most remarkable men were Robert Penn Warren and Eric Sevareid. Warren was truly "a gentle man," full of wisdom, wonderfully gifted as a poet and as a thinker, and a trusted friend. And Eric had class, and in him we lost a great novelist when he decided to become a mere nightly commentator for CBS instead.

I still drive up to the University from my Luverne home once in a while and I always stop and park in Dinkytown. I love getting a malted at Bridgeman's, I like dropping in on Larry Dingman's Dinkytown Antiquarian Book Store, and I sometimes go walking up those streets I once haunted as a hungry terribly ambitious young man. And in those first early days a virgin.

Tom

The late publisher Alan Swallow of Denver told me about a poet he was going to publish and how high he was on him. When Alan mentioned the title, *Letters to an Imaginary Friend*, I was instantly captivated. Any child with any kind of imagination always has an "imaginary friend" to whom he or she confides all. Flesh friends often turn traitor on one, but never one's imaginary friend.

When Alan finally did publish Thomas McGrath's *Letters*, he sent me a complimentary copy of Part I. I had some trouble getting into it at first; it was so very different from what I expected an epic poem to be. It was all very interesting but the long poem didn't fit any form I knew. Gradually though on rereading it the epic took me over. All the wisecracks and the idioms of the day that I'd heard on the farm and in the warehouse in my youth had been lovingly crocheted into swinging lines. I hadn't known that such talk, when woven by a musician of words, could set up a legitimate poetic cadence of its own, as good as the cadences of Whitman and Wordsworth.

Sometime later Robert Bly invited me to visit him on his farm near Madison, Minnesota, some ninety miles north of my Blue Mounds home on the old King's Trail (now Highway 75). Robert had several old shacks on his farmyard in which he housed visitors. I slept in what was once an old chicken coop. And it was at Robert Bly's home that I met Thomas McGrath. Tom had come down from Moorhead with his young wife Eugenia. Also there was the poet James Wright who came out from Minneapolis.

The four of us were about as different as four people could be: Robert, the smiling articulate poet politician; James, the poet with a fabulous memory and vaulting imagination; Thomas, the poet with a quiet smile and measuring eyes. And myself, a novelist.

It didn't take us long to fall into long talks, each taking his turn, while the others listened with glimmer-eyed respect. We talked about our boyhood: Tom telling of how it was in North Dakota, Jim telling of how it was in Ohio, Robert telling of life on the farm in Minnesota, and myself of how it was in Siouxland (Iowa). There were tales of threshing, and riding horseback, of fishing and drinking beer, of baseball and horsing around on Sunday.

Sometimes Jim would break out in an orgy of quoting poems that fit what we were talking about: from Yeats, Dante, Whitman, Neruda, Trakl, Rilke. Then Tom would come up with his favorites. And then Robert.

The air would become electrified: full of magnetism. We forgot we were hungry, or had bathroom needs, or that the pebbles in the yard were hot where we walked barefoot, or that a storm was coming up in the west, dragging its black bottom along the ground and brushing its cumulus head against the moon and the stars.

Once on a very hot day we decided to go swimming in Lac Qui Parle Lake. We took a boat out to an island in the middle of the lake and then, naked, jumped into the lukewarm water. The lake wasn't very deep, only up to the hips for Tom and Robert and Jim, and just barely above my high knees. We played like boys again, shooting water at each other with a hand half-cupped and the heel of the palm just catching the surface. When we looked up from our water battle, we discovered that a boat had drifted into view around the side of the island. In the boat was a husband and wife fishing. The boys laughed when they saw how I had to skootch down to hide my shame. I had to kneel around in the water until the boat drifted out of sight. All the while the husband and wife fished nearby I prayed that a Moby Dick might show up and that their hooks might catch him and then that he'd drag them out of sight.

Soon Carol, Robert's wife, came out from the far shore with a picnic lunch. She discreetly approached our island in such a way that she wouldn't see us, and hallooed when she hit the island, and left the lunch and tea on a big boulder, than oared herself back. We climbed out of the water and sat, each on a huge rock, and indulged ourselves in dried-beef sandwiches.

When the sun sank, and cool air descended from the darkening blue sky above, soothing our white skin, we dressed and climbed into our own boat and rowed home.

Through it all I became quite aware that sitting in that skull of McGrath was a watcher, a coiner of well-wrought lines, and a self-made philosopher.

I saw Tom several times after that: at Bly's home; up in Moorhead where I went to read; in Minneapolis and St. Paul at parties.

When Tom's Part II of *Letters* came out, I was convinced we were seeing the birth of a remarkable American epic. There wasn't another like it. It made T.S. Eliot's *The Wasteland* look like a pale poorly mixed half-baked pancake. In that Part II, I found all kinds of good grist for Tom's mill, all well-ground, and caught up in a matrix of sweet flowing syrup and wild honey.

The story of Jenny the country girl who opened the silk gate for the hero of the poem and led him through marvelous and terrible thighs to an ancient and aweful world is unforgettable. The Jenny story made all of Wordsworth's little poems about country girls seem like saltless ginger cookies. Jenny carrying ears of corn in her apron against her belly, ears taken from an enchanted field, still walks in beauty in my imagination, where she shall never die.

One evening the phone rang in my home on the Blue Mounds. It was Tom.

"Fred? I just agreed to write the *Conquering Horse* screen-paly for Mike Cimino."

Then the phone went dead. Tom didn't wait for me to make comment of any kind, or exclaim, or wonder how come.

When I asked director Michael Cimino about the matter, he explained to me that Tom was known as a very good screenwriter in Hollywood. Mike thought that Tom was more apt to catch what I'd been up to in my novel *Conquering Horse* than anyone else. Like me Tom was from Siouxland and would know the true feel of the place. Later, when Mike sent me the screenplay I saw rightaway that Mike had been wise in his choice. It's still the best screenplay I've ever read. Mike has paid us both but he still hasn't made the movie. (Mike has since made *Lightfoot and Thunderbolt, The Deer Hunter,* and *Heaven's Gate*.) Hollywood has a way of ruining good novels, but if Mike finally does make the movie, based on Tom's screenplay, it will be a good movie. A classic even.

Several years ago, the poet Philip Dacey found some money and invited writers from the area, mostly from Minnesota, to the campus of the State University at Marshall, Minnesota. Some sixty poets and novelists showed up for a week. There was good talk, some fine readings, several good panels. One day Robert Bly was holding forth, and after a half hour got aboard a wild horse and began riding roughshod over us all with his provocative theories and strong opinions. Great stuff, though some of it got to be a bit thick. Tom and I were sitting together, wondering where Robert would fly next and where he would finally land.

Finally Tom had enough. Robert happened to touch on one of Tom's territories with his sharp hooves, and Tom stood up, and said in his quiet voice, "Oh, come on now, Robert, that's not true. And you know it." Robert hesitated; smiled; and said, "Well, maybe I'm wrong. But how would you put it?" Tom waved a hand at Robert, smiled, and sat down, as if to say, "It's your show. But be careful what you say around me." Everyone in the audience laughed. They liked Robert's fire, and they liked the way Tom tried to cool him down. Both were loved for what they were.

Robert has several times been heard to remark that he wished Tom would let him edit and cut *Letters*. But Tom has only smiled and has waved him off. Robert likes to cut; Tom likes to sprout many leaves and petals.

On still another evening the phone rang. It was Tom. After I'd said, "Hello," Tom said, "Fred, I'm alone again. Eugenia has left me," and hung up. He gave me no chance to commiserate with him, or offer him healing words, or inquire how it had happened.

The week of October 8th, 1977, turned out to be a good one for Thomas McGrath. He was given the Distinguished Achievement Award by the members of the Western Literature Association at their annual meeting in Sioux Falls, South Dakota. It happened that I was asked to make the presentation and Tom accepted in his usual modest manner. At that same gathering Robert Bly gave the banquet address.

The three of us hadn't seen each other in a while. After the ceremonies, there was a party in Arthur Huseboe's rooms in the downtown Holiday Inn. While everyone was standing around with a glass in hand, talking, telling stories, Tom McGrath, Robert Bly, and I rested on a kingsize bed. We didn't hear a word said by the celebrants. Heads together, legs sticking out over the edges of the bed, we were commiserating with each other, about how come all three of us, pretty good fellows really, had trouble keeping our wives happy. We liked our wives, loved them, but somehow our marriages were going sour. None of us said anything mean about our wives. All three of us wondered if somehow we were at fault; and if we were at fault, what was the fault.

Not one of the scholarly heads above us, sipping from a glass, paid any attention to the quiet scene on that big roomy bed. No one noticed the grave brows, the slow shaking heads, the slowly articulated doubts, the wrinkled grimaces. I've never forgotten how those three Siouxland fellows, while resting their elbows on the bed and their heads in the hands, had bared their souls about their sad domestic life.

Roundwind, 1984

Calvin College in the
Early Thirties

Five of us arrived on the campus of Calvin College early in September, 1930. We were from Siouxland: Edward Bierma and Chris Gesink from Sioux Center, Iowa; John DeBie from Hawarden, Iowa; Johan TeVelde from Hull, Iowa; and I from Doon, Iowa. We met at a filling station in Perkins Corner.

My father took one look at the old Ford sedan that Bierma was driving and promptly suggested I come back home with him and instead drive my own nineteen dollar 1919 Ford touring car to Calvin. Bierma had bought his old jalopy at a junkyard for a dollar; had tinkered it up enough to make it run; and had bought a dozen used tires and patched up rubber innertubes for another dollar.

But I was game to go. I'd stayed home two years after graduating from Western Academy at Hull (a marvelous prep school, by the way, with such teachers as Garrett Heyns and Garritt Roelofs) and was hungry for learning. My mother had died the year before and I didn't get along too well with my stepmother. My stepmother didn't want me to go; as the oldest boy she thought I'd make a sort of tough foreman for my younger brothers on our half-section of land and so make life easy for her and her three girls. She didn't like it that I always had my head in a book, or played baseball, or "secretly" wrote stories up in the haymow of our barn. In fact, Dad snuck fifty dollars in the palm of my hand as we shook hands good-bye. I felt a crinkle of paper and was careful to close my fist; and then later on, alone, examined what had been tickling my palm.

Bierma's old Ford, which was nicknamed Susie, was a sight to see. Its black paint had faded to a vague gray from all those years of rusting in a junkyard. Its radiator cap was a

173

corncob. And Bierma, to make room for five passengers inside, had tied the dozen tires and the suitcases on top of the curved roof, so that Susie resembled more an overloaded camel than a car.

Before we arrived at Calvin, a number of wild things happened to Susie. She lost her low gear before we hit Dubuque (the weathered braided lining simply shredded to wisps) so that to get up the bluffs on the Illinois side of the Mississippi River we had to back up to the top; she was stopped in downtown Chicago by a cop who couldn't believe what he was seeing and who then ordered her out of town before she ran over any lakefront shoppers; she lost her reverse in Holland, Michigan, from too much use as a brake; and she roared through west Grand Rapids in the only gear she had left, high, going through stoplights, cops waving arms, and clusters of running pedestrians. Susie made it to the campus all right, but just as Bierma wheeled her up into the parking lot next to the Dorm, she died, and the four of us had to jump out and push her the last dozen yards. Then Bierma leaped out with a piece of 2"x4" to block the rear wheel.

We were supposed to pay Bierma five dollars each for the trip, and we'd been hoping that since we'd all worked so hard to make it, he'd reduce the fare. But no, he demanded the full five dollars. Bierma was a pre-law junior and was already practicing the hard-nosed tricks of his trade at that early date. A year later, in the same Susie slightly reconditioned, with just about the same run of luck, Henry DeMots was a passenger. When we arrived beside the Dorm, and it was Henry's turn to pay his fare, he mused outloud with a little smile, "You know, Bierma, the White steamship line in New York lets young college students work their way across the Atlantic Ocean to London . . . . I'm wondering if you wouldn't consider the same sort of arrangement here. From my point of view, I worked my way across middle America. I changed six tires, I pushed the car uphill seven times, I drove Susie two hundred miles, I provided humor most of the way, and three times I got under Susie to tighten up her petcock. What do you say?" Well, Bierma laughed at the humor but continued to hold out his hand for the five dollars.

Within a few days it was time to enroll. It happened that kindly Chris Gesink, pre-seminarian, took a liking to me, and helped me make out my class schedule, making sure I took nothing but prerequisites available, "so as to get them out of the way early, Fred, and you can then take up electives later on." I had just enough money left to pay tuition. Books and board and room were going to be a problem, but there President R. B. Kuiper stepped in. He decided he liked me and he arranged for a well-to-do relative of my father to help me out.

The first few days in the Dorm were, from my farmboy point of view, exotic. My roommate for a few days was a fellow from Chicago named Adam Ooms. He was a sophomore and as a sophomore he was out to get revenge for the hazing he'd received as a freshman. The sophomores of the previous year had been unmerciful with him. He reported my every move to sophomore Red Huiner. Huiner was so hard-chinned I was sure he had once worked for Al Capone in Chicago. One evening Huiner and Dutch Waalkes and a bunch of jeering sophomores trapped me coming out of the new Hekman Library. I escaped that time by climbing up an electric light pole, then worked my way like a chimp along a support cable to a tree, from where I jumped on the porch roof of the nearest house. A fellow freshman let me inside.

The next night as DeBie, John W. Huizenga, and I were returning from listening to Billy Sunday give one of his rousing evangelical revival meetings in downtown Grand Rapids, we were trapped by some twenty sophomores again led by Huiner. At the time my first impulse was to fight. You don't lightly tackle someone from Doon, Iowa. Doon had the reputation of producing ruffians. There'd been a murder on a nearby farm; the butchers from Sioux City used to come out on a weekend special train and hold a picnic in a pasture near the Big Rock River, which included taking along card sharks, white doves (prostitutes), boxers, wrestlers, and a dance band; and it was rumored that most members of the Doon Christian Reformed Church were outcasts from Orange City and Sioux Center and Hull, even as far away as Pella, Iowa. (Later on, as a janitor in the Dorm, I overheard Peter Eldersveld tell John Hamburg Schaal he'd never accept a "call" from that pesthole known as

Doon.) But my mother, who knew that on a bet arranged by my father I'd once lifted the rear wheel of a three-box wagon full of shelled corn and had set it down (the said full wagon weighing 4,000 pounds), had warned me never to let my temper get the best of me. So I didn't fight back even though I knew that with a couple of swipes of my hand I could have annihilated the entire sophomore class, a sort of Christian Goliath come out of Siouxland. The result was we were all too soon bound with ropes, carried to the unfinished attic of the new Seminary Building, had our backs splashed with red barn paint, and then tied to 2"x6" uprights. We managed to wriggle lose; then spent several hours in the Dorm shower room scraping off the paint.

I can still see poor Huizenga wincing as I rubbed and rubbed his slender back with rough towels to get that red paint off. Huizenga and I had met earlier that summer of 1930 at my father's uncle's farm, Andrew Feikema, where he'd gone with his cousin Peter Kortenhoven to see Kortenhoven's aunt Mrs. Feikema. Huizenga and I became fast friends immediately.

I asked for and got a new roommate, and wound up living first with TeVelde and later on with Don Houseman.

In my junior year I lived alone downstairs opposite Mrs. DeBoer's door to her apartment. She was our housemother. About her I must tell one incident. I happened to check on some noise cut in the lobby at two one morning, when who should I see emerge from Mrs. DeBoer's rooms but good old campus janitor Mr. Norden. He saw me; blinked; and went on his tired way. The next day he visited me in my room. DeBie and I had been given jobs as janitors in the dorm and he'd often complained about our work. But after the night of his visit to Mrs. DeBoer's rooms he couldn't have been nicer. For myself, I wasn't too shocked, since I came from Doon. In fact, my opinion of Doon improved because of that incident. Exposure to the variety of life in Doon had made me a wiser man. Doon was a great place to come from.

Later on, Mr. Norden shared some campus secrets with me. He had bad knees and often asked me to check on things in Old Main at night. Among other things told me that if I went down to the huge main furnace in Old Main during class hours, and if I opened the little "luikjes" (trapdoors) in the heat ducts near the furnace, I could overhear what went on in the various rooms upstairs. He pointed out that the most interesting ducts to listen in on were those of the faculty room and Dean Johanna Timmer's office. One could get the lowdown on faculty politics in the former and listen in on girl student confessions in the latter. The most interesting confrontation turned out to be the time Miss Timmer tried to get Clairbel Freyling to confess she'd broken one of the Commandments with her boyfriend. Clairbel told her where she could go, with her blessing.

A couple of weeks after I arrived on the campus, basketball Coach William Cornelisse and his assistant Venhuizen spotted me playing pickup baseball with John J. Timmerman, Henry Stob, and others. They promptly "impressed" me into joining the freshman basketball squad, much as the British navy captains "impressed" captured American sailors into joining the British Royal Navy before the Revolutionary War. When I objected that I'd never played basketball in high school, they overruled that on the grounds that 1) I had good hands and was used to a round object, and 2) I was six-eight and so could get the tip-off and a lot of rebounds. (Over the next five years I added another inch in height.) To this day I still have the sneaking suspicion that Coach Cornellisse went to President Kuiper to get him to write Reverend Betten for more money.

Everything seemed to go along smoothly—until right after Christmas vacation. I'd gone home to visit my family in Doon for two weeks and had a glorious time with my five brothers, cob fights in the barn, skating on the Big Rock River, storytelling, etc. And then the axe fell. Miss Timmer, my freshman English teacher, handed back the last of my first semester papers, and as I looked through them for her marks and her corrections, I could see she was going to flunk me. Finally on page five of my term paper, I spotted the following in red ink: "Dear Mr. Feikema: I am very much disappointed with your papers. They have no literary worth at all. They are blotted with grammatical and rhetorical blunders. Often you even forget to put your name at the head of your themes. Can you not do better? There is no need of my finishing this paper. Too many mistakes have already occurred to warrant a passing mark."

Well, the fur flew after that. I got up from my chair and decided to go back home. I'd had enough of college and city life. I started to pack. I was about done when Bierma happened to step in. When he found out what was up, he took me by the arm and then walked me over to Wealthy Street and bought me several glazed doughnuts and a cup of coffee. Wisely he said very little, until we were almost back at the dorm. Then he took my arm again, and said, "Listen, Fred. You've got the brains to make it. And more. Don't let that dried up old maid throw you. I'll help you with your themes and papers the second semester." Upper classman Sam Steen also took a hand in the matter. "Stick around, kid. You've got more on the ball than most of us."

At about the same time Coach Cornellisse went into action. What? His future basketball star flunked? He sailed into President Kuiper's office to see what could be done to keep me on the campus. After much soul-searching, and remembering that until then Calvin didn't have a very good record in basketball, it was decided that Miss Timmer should give me a conditional mark for the first semester, with the proviso that if I did very well in her class the second semester, she could average out the two marks for both semesters.

Bierma's coaching wasn't of much help. He liked to use long legal polysyllabic sentences. It only confused me the more. So I hit on my own strategy. Miss Timmer's class was the first one in the morning at eight. I had a free hour right after her class. I made it a point to listen carefully to the way she spoke, her phrasing, her gestures, her lip movement, absorbing not the sense but the manner, and then hurried back to my room. Mimicking her, I quickly wrote the assignment for her next class. Sometimes I even first toed around in my room imitating her flat-heeled stride for a few minutes and then sat down to write. The ability to ape someone was always strong in me.

Miss Timmer was almost beside herself at my remarkable recovery and at the swiftness with which I'd learned to write the perfect English sentence. Result: I was given passing grades for both semesters; and went on to glory.

It was during the second semester of my freshman year that I became aware of class distinctions on the campus, not one of money but one of talent. In those days John J. Timmerman, Henry Zylstra, Leroy Vogel, Don Stuurman, the Frankena brothers, Henry Stob, Peter De Vries, were considered the heavyweights when it came to gray matter. Some of them even walked with their heads inclined to one side a little, so ponderous was their thinking. And if you had any brains at all, you aspired to join the Plato Club with Professor Harry Jellema as faculty sponsor. It was an all-male club. Of course the bright women on the campus responded by forming an illegal sorority which they called the KKQ Club. Some dormitory wit soon dubbed them the Knock Kneed Queens.

Some years later those who I sat with at the same table in the dorm dining room were dubbed the Brains Trust. The other tablemates were Huizenga, Johan TeVelde, and John DeBie. The reason? We subscribed to *The New York Times* and *The New Republic*, and often discussed world problems as well as strange social issues – alien to the pre-sem foresome who sat at the next table.

When my first poem was published in *The Chimes*, I took a lot of razzing. The poem was read outloud during dinner at noon hour with what was meant to be in the high poetic manner. Lines were sometimes quoted at me as I swept the hallway as part of my janitor job, or as I shot baskets during basketball practice down in the gym. What? A yokel from Doon, Iowa, the biggest hulk ever seen on the Calvin campus, presumed to write hallowed poetry? I only smiled. I remembered the kindly looks of Timmerman, and Zylstra, and Stuurman, and Sam Steen. And most of all I remembered the encouragement of John W. Huizenga.

One night four of us managed to scrounge up enough money to see the movie *All Quiet on the Western Front*. It was the first movie I'd ever seen and I was bowled over by it. When it was finished, we got up and started to move up the aisle for the front door. Still in a sooze over it, I didn't see what my three buddies had spotted – that Professor Henry Van Zyl was standing under the glowing marquee outside. My three buddies promptly ducked out through an exit on the alley. When

I finally saw what they'd spotted, it was already too late. I stuck out too far over the crowd. I stepped directly up to Dr. Van Zyl and said, "Good-evening, Professor. Have you seen this movie? You haven't? Well, let me recommend it. Has to do with the horrors of war and why we shouldn't ever fight again. Very educational. I urge you to see the second show." Dr. Van Zyl didn't blink an eyelash; said only, "Thank you, Mr. Feikema. I shall think about it." Afterwards I wasn't called on the carpet. But the other three rapscallions were. Dr. Van Zyl had placed another spotter near the alley exit.

The Chicago bunch had an apartment near the Wealthy Theatre, and one night, after I had gone to see a movie alone, *Roberta*, I dropped in on them, and discovered they were playing strip poker. By the time I arrived some of their guests were down to their beeveedees. Every time one of the Chicago boys won a hand, he'd take the clothing that had been bet and toss it over his shoulder into the laundry shoot, and say, "The hell with it." I was invited to sit down and join the fleecing, but I'd spotted that they were playing with a marked deck. Among those being ruped was a pre-seminarian and two co-eds.

Calvin always had its lovely talented women. In those days it was generally agreed by the dorm savants that Clairbel Freyling, the Gezon ladies Ruth and Helen, and the Reitsema sisters Marion and Mildred and Helen were Muses related to the Graces of ancient Greek mythology. If any one from the dorm dated one of them, he was subjected to unmerciful teasing. When I finally got up enough nerve to ask Helen if I could see her home after church one Sunday night, I was given the business. Bierma permitted me to drive his old Susie the one-door Ford and I parked it a block from the LaGrave Avenue Church. After the service, I met Helen on the front steps and with some pride told her I had a car for the night. I led her to Susie. I had to explain to Helen that the driver had to get in first because of the one-door arrangement and for her to enter last and close the door. When I stepped on the starter, I knew disaster had struck. It wouldn't start at first; and when it finally did, it popped so irregularly that the old creature shook like a horse trying to get rid of a plague of botflies. I finally got it warmed up enough to pull away from the curb.

I started down the street with Helen's eyes as big as new silver dollars, and my face red and my hands shaking. Then, at the intersection at Jefferson, it quit, blocking the traffic both ways. I had to crawl past Helen to get out. I cranked and cranked, until I had blisters in my right hand, but old Susie wouldn't start. Finally, with Helen at the steering wheel, I pushed it across the intersection and parked it along the curb. But Helen was a game one. As we started walking home, a considerable distance, she said, "All week I'd been looking for adventure, for something exciting to happen, and here at last it's come."

The evening continued to be one of disaster. When I arrived at Helen's house on Virginia Street, her mother served us hot chocolate milk with a marshmallow floating on top. When I went for my first sip I promptly got the melted marshmallow stuck on the end of my nose. A few minutes later there was a knock on the door. It turned out that "my friends from Iowa" had come to my rescue. It was Bierma and DeBie wearing their workclothes. Out front was Bierma's other vehicle, an old truck with which he hauled ashes for people who had coal furnaces. When Helen's mother answered the door she had to have spotted what was chalked on the side of the truck: "Get your ashes hauled cheap. Call 85222." On the way back to the dorm, I explained that Susie had conked out on me. They nodded, laughing, and told me they'd rearranged the wiring to the sparkplugs. I almost didn't forgive them. But after a while I too had to laugh; and I have often laughed about it since.

When I was a junior I was fortunate enough to have one of my literary "gems" published in *The Chimes* reprinted in a national college miscellany. It caught the eye of Peter De Vries, by then living and writing in Chicago. One day as I was studying, there was a knock on the door. I looked around and there stood Pete, dressed up like a lord: immaculate gray hat tipped to one side, light gray suit pressed to knife-edge, spotless gray spats, and a cane. He slowly inspected my room: to see if my bed was well-made, looked at the few pictures on the wall, peered down to see if my floor was swept and if there were no dustballs under the bed, even ran a gloved finger over the windowsill for dust. Then he turned and headed for the door, whirling his cane dextrously. Just as he was about to step out, he said over his shoulder, "Keep writing. You'll do." He never cracked a smile. Nor did I.

Some years after I'd graduated from Calvin, I began to appreciate the classical training I'd had at Calvin. I discovered in chatting with graduates from Harvard, Yale and Princeton at The Players in New York that I knew as much, if not more, about the classics, about history, about logic, than they did.

There is no question that going to Calvin sets a person apart. I give you one incident to show what I mean. I learned one day while working as a reporter for the *Minneapolis Journal* that poet Paul Engle was to lecture at the University of Minnesota. I got permission from the city editor to cover the event. After Engle's talk, I followed some students into a reception room where he'd agreed to answer questions.

When a silence fell, I wondered outloud if I could ask a question.

"Go ahead," Engle said.

I did ask the question. It involved his philosophic attitude towards poetry.

He jerked erect and looked at me penetratingly. "You aren't by any chance a graduate of Calvin College?"

"I am. Why do you ask?"

"Because of the way you framed your question. Don Stuurman used to go after me like that. Give you fellows one inch, the original premise, and we're licked."

Don Stuurman was the first and only Rhodes Scholar Calvin ever had and he was at Oxford with Paul Engle.

Frederick Manfred, Outsize Man and Writer

by Robert W. Smith

It has always been my belief that if one wishes to speak
with truth in the brain one must speak with love in the heart.
— Manfred

Frederick Manfred has been writing fifty years and now
has behind him twenty-five novels and volumes of short stories,
essays, and poetry. Some are towering contemporary epics of
the American land and its people, fed by rich personal experience
and recollection, and others, like the five novels of his unique
Buckskin Man Series on the settling of the West, are derived
from rigorous research as well as imaginative force. His best
work looms over most contemporary fiction. *This Is the Year*
(1947) and *The Chokecherry Tree* (1948), depicting the human
struggle to exist in a harsh place and time, evoke rural reality
on a par with Ruth Suckow, O. E. Rölvaag, and John Steinbeck.
Lord Grizzly is our finest mountain-man novel, *Conquering Horse*
one of our best Indian novels, and *Riders of Judgment* is high
on the list of cowboy novels. Through a mastery fusion of reality, myth, and romanticism, Manfred has made ephemeral aspects
of our Western experience into enduring literature.

Born Frederick Feikema in northwest Iowa of Frisian-Saxon
stock from north Holland and northwest Germany Manfred (he
changed his name in 1952) was raised with five brothers on
a farm. After graduating from Calvin College in Grand Rapids,
Michigan, in 1934, he roamed Depression America working at
a variety of jobs, seeing, storing impressions, and scribbling.
Settling in Minneapolis, he became a newspaperman, but, after
a close call with tuberculosis, chucked it for full-time writing.
His first book, *The Golden Bowl*, was published in 1944; and
he's been pounding away at his dream ever since.

183

Meeting Manfred, one throws out previous categories and assumptions. All bets are off. Here is a masterless man. A presence without pomposity, a six-foot-nine-inch tower who seems taller, a laughing blue-eyed suchness looking twenty years shy of his seventy-four, he goes barefooted in and out of his stone house on a windy October afternoon. The house near Luverne in southwestern Minnesota he shares with son Frederick, Jr., thirty-two, a playwright, and Marya, thirty-seven, a poet (the oldest child Freya, also a poet, is married with two children living in Bloomington, Minnesota). It stands on a small hill and looks across a couple of miles to Blue Mounds State Park. Manfred previously owned a house on the Blue Mounds until the state claimed it in 1975, and, after a conversation-filled repast, he drove me over to feel the tug of it. From his former house there (now a State Interpretive Center) one can see thirty miles into South Dakota and Iowa—part of the area he calls Siouxland and which has been the locale of much of his fiction. Then we drove into the quiet, nearly crimeless town of Luverne with its quaint houses where no one locks car doors, and past the library: "I'd set my hat for the librarian but she's got a fellow, and I don't want to break into that." Then home again into easy chairs, where, watched by a photograph of his grandma and grandpa ("She had the height, he had the strength"), we began to talk.

Robert W. Smith: Your books have brought you critical plaudits and close encounters with the Pulitzer and Nobel prizes, but, too good to be commercial, only a modest financial return. Do you have any regrets?

Frederick Manfred: None whatsoever. I'm lucky to be here. I spent 1940-42 in a tuberculosis sanatorium (see *Boy Almighty* 1945) where at one point I saw the stark word "Terminal" in my file. So everything since has been a gift, starting with meeting my wife, Maryanna, there; having three wonderful and talented children; writing books I wanted to write; and making many great friends. So, you see, no one can hurt me. In the light of all this, I don't regret anything that has happened to me.

Smith: When you recall yourself as a six-year-old, where did your eyes reach on the kitchen table? Raised on a farm, you must have learned to ride a horse early on. And learned also of the ways and wonder of sex?

Manfred: At six I was tall for my age and could not only see but reach the sugar bowl in the middle of the table. And I rode early. Astride Tip, a bronc, I herded cattle along country roads and in wastelands along riverbottoms. No one is bashful for long in a barnyard. We saw animal sex around us all the time. And talk was frank in the barn where the men were. But in the house, we learned decorum in such matters as sex, manners, and respect for one's elders.

Smith: I've read that when you or your brothers got into a fight at school, unlike most parents, your folks wanted to know who started the fight, and had you boys thought of the other guy first, yourselves second? Did you pass this trait on to your three children: And did writing, that merciless master, prevent you from sharing time with them as they grew?

Manfred: Yes, I tried to pass that trait on. I saw my children daily because I worked at home just as a farmer is home all day. I played with them, read to them, hugged them. Like my father, I'm a toucher. This can get you into trouble sometimes, especially if you run into someone who was reared in a chilly home with cold parents. Maryanna and I didn't have to discipline our children much, feeling that if we set the right example and they came to love us, they'd emulate us (I haven't written that book yet). They saw that we regarded and treated books as holy things. When Freya, the oldest, was little, she pulled out a book from the bottom shelf and began to color in it. It turned out to be an inconsequential book so I let her do it. Later on when she asked me to read her a story I picked out that same book and pretended I couldn't read it. When she asked why, I said, "Somebody's colored in it and now I can't read it." That did it.

Smith: Which persons in your life have you most admired?

Manfred: *Prime Fathers: Personal Portraits,* my book of reminiscences of some of my favorites, will emerge shortly. But the list is longer and would have to contain, after my father, Feike Feikes Feikema VI, and my former wife Maryanna Shorba, my philosophy teacher in Calvin College, Dr. W. Harry Jellema (see *The Primitive*), my high school history teacher,

Garret Roelofs (see *Green Earth*), Hubert Humphrey, Sinclair Lewis, John Dos Passos, Robert Penn Warren, Caroline Marshall, Robert Bly, Thomas McGrath, Alan Swallow, Vardis Fisher, Frank Waters, Walter Clark, Herbert Krause, Marlon Brando, and Korczak Ziolkowski.

Smith: Ziolkowski?

Manfred: Yes, the greatest sculptor since Praxiteles, a consummate craftsman and an enormously learned man. He is now carving a mountain into the likeness of Crazy Horse riding a horse. I overheard him respond to a question about what creation by man would be around 1,000 years from now, with *"Lord Grizzly* by Manfred," surprising in that one would have expected he would have given pride of place to his own Crazy Horse Mountain monument.

Smith: You mentioned Hubert Humphrey.

Manfred: Yes, I met Hubert in 1938 when I was a reporter for the *Minneapolis Journal* and worked for him in his abortive bid for the mayor's job in 1943. He was bright and volatile and honest and it was easy to see the enormous political promise in him. Two years later he became mayor and soon was a national force. We remained close — during a lean period following publication of my first book we borrowed diapers from Muriel who was between babies — though we saw less of them after they went off to Washington. Though close friends, I was never able to sell Hubert on listening sometimes rather than talking and on resigning the Vice-Presidency over the despicable Vietnam War. But politics isn't for me. Reagan is personable but his Reaganomics pitched to the rich won't work. What would work is "Tenthing and tithing" — returning a tenth of one's income back to the source and paying a 10% federal sales tax on everything except food. This take-off on Henry George's single tax idea would for once prevent the rich from escaping taxes.

Smith: And from an early age you've been friendly with the great writers.

Manfred: I've always been an omnivorous reader. I loved the classics, reading Aeschylus, Aristophanes, Sophocles, Euripides, Homer, Plato, Virgil, Dante, Cervantes, Goethe, Chaucer (in the original), Spenser, and Shakespeare. And later greats like Tolstoy, Pushkin, Chekhov, Balzac, Fielding, Smollett, Thackeray, Dickens, and Conrad. And I read them complete in each instance. Though I occasionally dip into modern writers, I don't read them complete, so I can make no real assessment of them. I do read Robert Penn Warren complete and consider him our one true man of letters: a superb poet, a challenging novelist, a fine critic, and a very good teacher. There is no one his equal on the scene today.

Smith: Family, friends, books, and life then coalesced in you, outing in an urge to write. You began with *The Golden Bowl* (1944), a grey and grim story of Depression America, followed with *Boy Almighty* (1945), derived from your nearly fatal stay in a TB sanitarium, and *Year*, a brilliant evocation of an American farmer, Pier Frixen, battling nature while trying to stay tender enough to sustain his family. Frixen, unable to write but a horse of a worker, stubbornly stupid on accepting new farming methods and on the sexual needs of his wife, but withal a pretty wise clodhopper ("... nature is an onery bitch," "Wal, to tell y'u the truth, I'm eating a little too little to live and a little too much to die"). In 1948 *Chokecherry* came out to general applause. But your next three novels, conflated as *Wanderlust* in 1962, didn't get readers, and your career didn't move until *Lord Grizzly*, when it skyrocketed. The succeeding four novels of the Buckskin Man Series were uniformly, if differently, excellent, but sales were neither large nor sustained. Since then, your books have sold indifferently. Why this unevenness of acceptance, do you suppose?

Manfred: I think each succeeding book has been better than the last, but apparently critics and the public don't agree. But that doesn't bother me: I keep plugging away. A writer doesn't worry about outdoing himself. He merely throws his best pitch hoping to strike out that cleanup hitter Jack Death. Sophocles wrote *Oedipus at Colonus* in his nineties to prevent his son from having him declared incompetent. If that old boy could do that in the winter of his life I can still get wood on the ball in my autumn.

Smith: I'm told that every morning you go outside, look out across Siouxland in a silent meditation, and then stride out back to your writing shack awash with books, photos, and charts you are using for your current work. There you sit down and start pounding your old Remington 17. Have you always typed your first drafts and do you set a wordage goal for yourself each day?

Manfred: I wrote *Lord Grizzly* (1954) in longhand first and then typed up the final draft. I returned to the Remington with *The Manly-Hearted Woman* (1975). With *Of Lizards and Angels: A Saga of Siouxland* I'm going for four pages a day. I usually let the idea set the pace and after a few weeks it finds it. Sometimes I'm through by ten a.m., sometimes by noon. I always try to get the four pages in no matter what. That way my subconscious well learns the hard way that it must come up with so much water a day.

Smith: Much of your work has a musical quality. Is this a consious thing; is it forced?

Manfred: It's there but not forced. When I write I hear music all the time and much of my writing is often written to musical cadences. If you don't hear the cadences, you're missing me. Part of this derives from a musical theory course and piano lessons I took in my middle thirties when I found I had perfect pitch. The musical training got sidetracked by life, but I believe my writing has always been the better for it.

Smith: Confucius said that happiness is neither higher nor lower than a man—it is the same height. In your case, then, happiness is six-foot-nine-inches high, and you glory in it. Pier Frixen in *Year* muses, "What a life. There's so little happiness in the world a man might just as well make up his mind to be happy without it." And Elof in *Chokecherry*, wearing shoes several sizes too big, tries to make Effie in the back seat but gets his foot caught under the driver's seat and can't get leverage, and when the guy driving gets to her house and she scurries in Elof tells him, "Get off that front seat once!" And on and on, the punctuating, pervading humor. This quality has to stand as one of your hallmarks.

Manfred: Yes, humor has played a large role in my life. It springs from what I call "warm irony." If you look carefully there's a little smile on every page I write. Much like Chaucer, my literary hero. I think of him as my favorite uncle. I like Shakespeare and Sophocles and Cervantes too, of course, but

I feel closest to Chaucer. I love telling stories with a warm Chaucerian/Rabelaisian turn. In fact, in *Of Lizards and Angels* I'm going to have what I call Stoop Talk, when in the evening after chores the family gathers on the cool side of the house, and slowly everybody pitches in with his story of the day. But I also remain as naive as I am wise....

Smith: What part does poetry play in your life?

Manfred: A very important part. A volume of my poems, *Winter Count*, was published in 1966, and another, *Winter Count II*, will be issued shortly. Both of my daughters are poets; even discounting my bias, good ones. Poetry comes unbidden to me. When I hear the first lines in my head, while walking, reading, musing, I discover, when I give it a pull, that a whole poem follows, almost always done.

Smith: Besides your new books on poetry and reminiscences, you have a novel, *Flowers of Desire*, making the publishing rounds. But your big one, your capstone book, is walking around with you or sitting with you every morning in the shack. Could you say a bit about it?

Manfred: Sure. *Of Lizards and Angels* is the story of the Freylings, a family of ten, starting in the 1880s when Tunis and Clara meet in their twenties. They farm and live and over time the family explodes outward like a true nuclear family, one child becoming a missionary, another an editor, a lawyer, a soldier's wife, and so on. It will go into the 1970s. I don't know what book in literature it will resemble, but I don't worry about that. It will reflect the endless rolling prairies of Siouxland, and is exciting fun to write. I hope it will be the same for readers when it comes out a few years from now.

Smith: Critics have been mixed on the bulk of your work, those in the east generally being cooler than those in other parts of the country. How do you view critics?

Manfred: The Irish poet Brendan Behan remarked once that a critic was like a eunuch in a harem: he knows how to do it because he often sees it done — but can't do it himself. Lest that sounds mean-spirited, let me say critics are necessary, and the good ones, the conscientious ones, quite valuable. The four critics who command my respect, Aristotle, Kenneth Burke, Edmund Wilson, and Robert Penn Warren, I read and reread.

I've looked at other critics but I find they can't help me much. Most deal with books as categories. However, some books — mine among them — are not category writing, but books of singular art that require new critical approaches to handle them. So I can't be angry at critics for misreading or neglecting my work. I'm willing to wait — even until I'm dead. I propose to live until I'm 100 years old; perhaps by that time they'll catch up. In my case, I plan to outlive the critical sonsabitches in the Eastern literary establishment, who are able, because of the concentration of publishers in New York City, to dictate that quality writing comes only from their region and from patches in the South. When I learn that an unfavorable review is coming my way — there's always someone willing to send you an unfavorable review — I file it away unread but may read it later on when it's been balanced by good reviews. I don't want to get angry at anyone, especially a reviewer whom I might meet and like later. So I stay cool. The book is out so I can't use some of the reviewer's advice even if I wanted to. And I'm not sure I'd want to. Who wants to read a book by Faulkner conceived by Edmund Wilson? If you want Wilson, read him; if you want Faulkner, read him.

    Smith: Some critics have attacked you for what they regard as occasional prolixity and diffuseness, a lack of restraint. Isn't restraint art?

    Manfred: Not necessarily. What about *Don Quixote, Moby Dick, Les Miserables*? Like Shakespeare I sometimes let myself be drawn off the path of a predetermined plot for a visit into some flower-filled dell or to a whorehouse. The logical side of one's mind — the left — is not the creative. Real art comes from the right side where the intuitive freewheeling impulses jump up. The art is in the jumps. By the time I send a work to the publisher I've filed it down and smoothed it out until it plays perfect on my clavichord. Though often I feel I may have taken off too much fat, a book shouldn't be like a vase. Sure, there is an informing and a controlling going on in a good writer's work, but it should seem effortless, like life itself, a new life, seemingly chaotic, so that even the reader, when done, realizes he has lived in a new way through the prose.

    Smith: How do you see the future of books in our society?

Manfred: Just once I'd like to see a book advertised as an exclusive right, not one given to everyone. As an aristocratic privilege that one has to earn. I mean *aristocrat* in the sense of value. For mankind to survive, let alone improve, we must aspire to something better.

Smith: I'm afraid our merchandisers will never try such a novel idea, not when bombast and back-scratching reviewers work better; not while bad writing drives out good and the sterility of television cuts into reading habits.

Manfred: Television actually is a boon for the common man who rarely reads books anyhow. It amuses and entertains him. And, if anything, has helped book sales. The recent production of even such ordinary books as *Roots* is a move in the right direction. Public Television has already been doing this. Good readers, even if they watch TV, eventually find themselves going back to the source. Not that I'm much of a TV viewer. I doze during newscasts, watch some football, the Cubs, and the quality plays on Public Television.

Smith: Yet there are atrocious books of ephemera, violence, sex, and besetting neurosis selling by the bushels. Does this bother you?

Manfred: Nope, Michener, L'Amour, and such commercial writers do provide reading for people who, if all they could read was real literature, would read nothing at all.

Smith: How does an artist balance his responsibility to his art with that to his family and to the life around him? T. S. Eliot believed in the Republican cause in Spain in the 1930's but stayed aloof from politics just as Saul Bellow and some others do nowadays.

Manfred: If one is truly an artist, that comes first. There are always too few of us. Voltaire admonished writers to survive a revolution and write about it. Too often, a change of governments is only a changing of the guards. When I can, when I've finished my four-hour stint at the typewriter, I'll do my best to help (1) prevent nuclear wars since such wars now mean the death of all human life, (2) protest, either vocally or by letter, injustices done to the poor, unlettered, and underprivileged, (3) ensure we all, rich or poor, bright or dumb, have equal right to vote, and (4) protect the right of privacy in one's own home.

Smith: Buddha believed that the twin evils of our existence were anger and fear. To which we could add the search for power and the zest for adventure. Have these ever troubled you?

Manfred: Some anger is very good and often helps to establish justice and cleanse the mind. I hate bullies and it is often therapeutic to get angry with them. Fear can also be beneficial if it can be overcome or controlled. I don't care much for power except as I can use it in my writing. As for adventure, I confess I like diving into unknown situations; taking a chance when I don't know what's coming next.

Smith: You do considerable teaching and public speaking. Do you attempt to project an image, to posture, or are you just yourself without trying to figure out how you're coming across?

Manfred: I try never to think of myself of how I might appear in public. I give many talks but never like it. I have to steel myself to do it. When you speak you become a sort of actor, and afterwards I always feel a little ashamed of myself. That's why I wish I never had to face a class or an audience again, but could just sit here at my desk of judgment, take my walks, split wood, grow a fine garden, laugh with my children, make love to a dear woman, eat healthy foods, and smile at the fire in my fireplace. I simply try to follow what I find in my three brains – neo-cortex, mammal, and lizard – without really trying to figure out how I'm coming across.

Smith: It's obvious that you love the eternal feminine, but probably agree with the old French line, "The most beautiful woman can't give you any more than she's got." Would you comment on this and on feminism and homosexuality?

Manfred: One of my favorite subjects. I respond to feminine beauty, but generally I look past it. Beauty vanishes after the second or third child. If there isn't a brain there, or a person, you're up a tree with a scold. As for feminism, it is true that women have a helluva time in this male-dominated world and should fight for equal rights and equal time and equal reward. But I think women are making a mistake in competing with men using male techniques. They are different and should recognize the difference and make it their strength. First of all, women are generally superior to men on almost every count.

They live longer and are sounder humans than men. More females make good breeding stock than men. Look at other mammals: for every ten good females there is usually only one good male. Moreover, women think with their whole being and not just the neo-cortex or rational side. They work more from the right side of the brain, thus are more on target and *right!* But females should compete as females, full-blown women, free as men, rather than as some sort of male hybrid. I feel sorry for the homosexual, but will delight in his or her work if there is light in it. We can never have enough light!

Smith: Many writers seem unable to meet the muse without the help of alcohol and tobacco. Were these ever a problem for you?

Manfred: I never cared for alcohol. Dad served us homebrew during threshing season but did it just as we began the evening meal, each a little according to age and size. That way it was a food for us. None of us six boys became drunkardo. I did smoke for a couple years after college but when I got tuber-culosis my wonderful doctor, Sumner Cohen, took a new carton of Lucky Strikes from my bedtable and threw it into the wastebasket.

Smith: Rangy and powerful, you've always been attracted to athletics, though you apparently lacked the time to develop them professionally.

Manfred: I never cared much for basketball and didn't even play it in high school. I learned from scratch in college but didn't peak until two years later when one night playing in-dependent ball I scored fifty-seven points. Baseball, though, was my true love. As a teenager, I had a helluva fast ball and big curve, could hit a long ball and my eyes were so good — still are, I still don't use glasses — that I seldom struck out. Boxing I never cared for, but after learning a great deal from a college classmate, a Golden Glove champion, I was talked into getting into the ring in Mora, Minnesota, on July 4, 1939, with six-foot-six-inch Tor Johnson, who I learned later had been a sparring partner for Joe Louis (if I'd known before, I would never have agreed). I was taller but he had fifty pounds on me. It was agreed that we would "show," go through the motions without trying to hurt each other. But he suckered me in the side coming out of the first clench with a punch that nearly tore me apart. Miffed, I feinted with a left hook, then threw a short right cross that caught him square and he dropped like a tree. But that was the extent of my boxing which, as I say, I never liked. I quit while I was ahead.

Smith: What regime, if any, do you follow now to stay fit?

Manfred: I used to run a daily mile but when my right knee gave out from the effects of too much heavy lifting and basketball as a youth, I fell back to brisk walking which I find not only physically mending but also *solvitur ambulando* ("You can sort it out by walking"), helpful mentally. This I combine with some bullworker isometrics every day to keep my muscles in trim. "Use it or lose it" is a motto that applies equally to muscles, brains, and sex. And writing.

Smith: Have you gotten conservative with age?

Manfred: Not a bit. Probably I'm more liberal in most matters. These days I'm willing to take greater chances and my mind comes up with more daring ideas. There is no such thing as time, for example. Everything is Now. You can point at something in space, but not in Time. So, even Einstein was wrong on that one.

Smith: Remembering the past and looking forward, are you happy?

Manfred: Happy, yes, but since Maryanna and I were divorced eight years ago I miss a wife and helpmate, someone with a career of her own but who is willing to share what she learns with what I learn. But I like going to bed at night knowing that in the morning I'll find something new in my typewriter or pen. Looking forward to breakfast and work. I take walks. I smile at my children and love them up as I do my twin grandsons, Nicholas and Rowan, when I see them. I like gardening, splitting wood, and building a fire. I like my stone house which I designed and helped build. I find myself smiling all the time despite some family sorrows. But I do miss a woman. Trouble is, I'm too picky. After having known a great woman as my mother, a fine woman in my wife, and a soul of goodness in her mother, the new one is going to have to be special. And, more importantly, I've got to have the magic. Romantic love.

Smith: If you had but one minute to live and were given the privilege of making a final statement, what would it be?

Manfred: I'd say, "It was all marvelous, I don't regret a minute of it. Even the pain and hunger, the almost broken head and the broken heart, were sweet to have. It was life; not death. And all moments of life are very precious."

Visit with Marlon Brando

Twice I had a fellowship of three months each at the Huntington Hartford Foundation in Pacific Palisades, California.

What had once been a stud farm in Rustic Canyon, a canyon lying between two ridges in the Santa Monica Mountains, had been converted into an art colony by Huntington Hartford. There were sixteen studios, some scattered down along the stream in the bottoms and some up along the sides of the ridges. At the widest part of the bottoms, a community house, an elegant white barn with a tack room, a large swimming pool, and housing for the help straddled a trickling stream.

In 1963, I worked in a studio in the bottoms at the south end, and in 1964 I worked in a lovely studio designed by Frank Lloyd Wright high up along the east side of the canyon. I called the Wright studio The Bird: it was set out over the valley on stilt-like legs, and when one sat out on its wide redwood veranda the veranda had the feel of wings under one. It was while I was living in The Bird that I had a chance to meet the actor Marlon Brando.

One day one of the fellows at the Foundation remarked that he'd visited an interesting bookstore in downtown Pacific Palisades called Brando's Book Bin. He said it was run by Jocelyn Brando, sister of Marlon Brando. I had already discovered on my own that Frank Gruber, writer of popular westerns, owned a bookstore downtown, run by his wife, but I hadn't seen any other bookstore. I decided to go have a look for myself. I had been wanting to meet Marlon Brando, somehow; I thought he's make a good Hugh Glass should someone ever decide to make a movie out of my novel *Lord Grizzly*.

I wasn't the only one who thought Brando would make a good Hugh Glass. Over dinner at Dominick's with William Froug, Walter Brown Newman, and Lester Linsk, Brando's name was brought up a number of times as the one actor who could put *Lord Grizzly* over as a movie. At the time Froug was an executive producer at CBS in Los Angeles, Newman was a well-known screen writer, and Linsk was an agent. Brando was the one to handle those long stretches of acting alone on the screen. Foug had long wanted to produce *Lord Grizzly* and Newman even longer wanted to write the script for it. Linsk wondered if maybe Brando wouldn't be too expensive; Brando was charging outrageously high fees for acting in even ordinary humdrum movies. Also, Brando had a reputation for being difficult. He reported late for work; sometimes didn't show up at all. He often demanded changes in the script while the shooting was going on. His pictures were rarely made on time and almost always ran far over the budget. He was a difficult man to deal with.

Froug persisted. Brando had been overheard to say that he'd like nothing better than to for once confound his critics.

Newman brought up some old stories about Brando: how Brando had wrecked the budget of *Mutiny on the Bounty* with his arbitrary tactics; how he'd spent an outrageous amount of time and money directing and acting in *One-Eyed Jacks*.

Froug smiled, and shook his head. "I think Fred here is the one guy who could talk Brando into it. Fred has a way with people, winning and ingratiating, at the same time that he's a solid old salt. If Fred could only get to see him, we'd be in like Flynn."

With all that in mind, I cranked up my old yellow monster, a two-door Buick, and drove up the winding road out of Rustic Canyon, took Amalfi down to Sunset Boulevard, and then Sunset into downtown Pacific Palisades. It was a Saturday, and clear for California, and many little foreign cars were snorting up and down the boulevard. Most of the cars had their tops down, and both driver and passenger, burned a deep tan, flew along with their hair wild in the wind. There was something other-worldly, romantic, about Sunset Boulevard. The homes on either side of the street were beautiful, the wind coming off the ocean had the smell of primal salt in it, flowers were blooming pink and blue and gold, the girls were all starlets with shoulder length hair and flowing dresses, and everybody had the look on their faces that they'd either come into some big money or they'd just been named royalty of some magic far-off kingdom.

I parked in the Hughes Grocery parking lot and walked west down Sunset, past Gruber's bookstore, past a restaurant. At a filling station on a corner I asked a handsome blond attendant if he knew where Brando's Book Bin was.

"Sure thing. Just a half block down that street. It's partway up an arcade. You can't miss it."

I found it easily. It was on the east side of the arcade, amongst some flower and dress and pottery shops. It was a small nook of a place, with only a few volumes, most of them art books and very expensive. It was neat, and quite posh, and aimed for the rich trade. Two women were in it, one of about forty, with a touch of gray in her blond hair, a squarish face, lovely kind blue eyes, and the other younger, also blond, vaguely ill-at-ease, modern.

I browsed a while first, looking for the fiction table.

Presently the older woman, sitting on a stool by the cash register, got to her feet and came over. "Can I help you?"

"Oh, I'm just looking around a little. I can't resist bookstores."

"That we like to hear," she said.

After a bit we fell into talk about an Indian picture book.

As we talked, a slow look of recognition opened her full face. "You're an author, aren't you?"

I allowed I was.

"I thought I recognized your face."

So I introduced myself and she introduced herself as Jocelyn Brando and her assistant as Sandra McVicker.

She wore glasses which she kept pushing against her brows by touching the bridge with her forefinger. She also kept brushing her hair back, sometimes even flipping it back with a throw of her head. She had the manner of a loving sister. No flirt. Just a solid fine warm-looking woman. I told her I was staying at the Huntington Hartford Foundation, that the previous spring I'd finished a novel there called *Scarlet Plume* which was scheduled to come out that fall, 1964; that I'd also written the first draft of yet another short novel there, *The*

Man Who Looked Like the Prince of Wales, scheduled for 1965; and had just begun a third one, *King of Spades*.

She told me she'd just gotten an assignment to act in a new motion picture, and would be out on location for several weeks.

I saw her several times before she left and got to like her. She always made me feel at ease. Unlike some others I'd met in Hollywood she didn't have the air of a gal on the make. Nor was she vain about being an actress. She didn't wear a succession of masks to fit the occasion, but was one solid straight person, the same person, every time I saw her.

When she came back from her work on location, we continued our talks. I bought some books from her.

One day she told me she was going to hold a sherry hour, and would I please attend. She wanted her patrons to think the Book Bin was the "in" place, where even authors liked to drop around and browse a while. Several Hollywood gossip columnists and a few local authors showed up. Marlon Brando didn't. I did.

Some time later she invited me over for dinner in her home on East Rustic Road in Santa Monica Canyon. She was divorced and lived with her young son. She'd wanted me to meet her son. She said he didn't get to see enough of grown men. The boy was very handsome, likable. He asked me endless questions about my country, Siouxland, and what kind of boyhood did I have, and how old were my children, and did I ever go horsebacking and still play baseball.

Jocelyn talked about her family, about her love for her brother Bud (her nickname for Marlon), about how hard they'd had to struggle to get started as actors. She told about their early life back in the Midwest, about her mother and her aging father. I was struck by the names her father and mother had given their children: Jocelyn and Marlon. There was a hint in the names of an unusual taste, suggesting that Jocelyn and Marlon came by their quests honestly.

One Sunday I invited her over to my The Bird studio, along with James and Carole Moloney, Jerry Romanoff and Maddalena Mauro (niece of Mussolini, from Italy). I got Jocelyn and took along her barbecue grill. We had a great time roasting sausages

on the wings of the veranda of The Bird. Jim, who'd once been
in the movie business as an agent, and who'd once represented
me, couldn't resist speculating outloud how marvelous it would
be if we could get Marlon to play the role of Hugh Glass in
Lord Grizzly. I flinched at the time and quickly changed the
subject. Jocelyn only smiled. Slender volatile Jim was an in-
veterate promoter, and went on at great length about how to
put together a picture. Jocelyn still only smiled. Later that
night I brought her home along with her barbecue grill. We
said goodnight. I didn't have the heart to bring up the *Lord
Grizzly* thing. She'd become a friend. In no sense did I want
her to think I was using her to get to Marlon Brando.

Froug and Linsk and I had another meeting at Froug's
home over a dinner. Froug wanted to know if I'd gotten to
know Jocelyn well enough to push in to see Marlon.

"I know her too well now."

"What's this? Don't be a fool."

Linsk gave me his ancient Egyptian smile. He had heard
it many many times.

The rest of the evening, in a sometimes subtle, sometimes
brusque way, I was pushed to go after Jocelyn. It was all done
urbanely, very civilized, the claws hidden, and damned hard
to resist.

Froug reminded me of the awful debt I had hanging over
my house back in Siouxland. (The truth was I was in danger
of losing my home. Royalties had been few and far between
and I hated to charge for talks, let alone give them.)

The next morning, May 13th, I got a letter from home
giving me a more devastating detail about our current financial
plight. We owed money everywhere: grocer, garage man, filling
station, were late on the mortgage payement, etc. It was time
I overcame my scruples.

That afternoon, after a nap and a nightmare, I drove down
to the Book Bin.

Jocelyn greeted me with a warm smile. She was sitting
on a stool beside the cash register. She was alone in her little
store. Her young blond assistant Sandra had suddenly and
mysteriously left her.

I pushed past the smile. "Jocelyn, there's nothing I hate more than to 'work' somebody. Just the same, I'd like to throw an idea at you, see what you think."

"Yes."

"Remember Jim Moloney talking about your brother making a great Hugh Glass?"

"Yes."

"Well, my agent Lester Linsk and Bill Froug a producer at CBS have been after me to ask you to introduce me to Marlon." I was trembling I so hated to ask her.

She slowly nodded and shifted on her stool. "I've thought of that."

"You've read *Lord Grizzly*?"

"Last week. And Bud would make a great Hugh."

"Is there any chance he might?"

"Trouble is, right now Bud isn't home."

"Out making a picture?"

"No. He's in the hospital. To remove a fatty tissue tumor. And several little warts in his scalp."

"Sorry to hear that."

"In the process his doctor discovered Bud also had a small duodenal ulcer."

I shook my head commiseratingly.

"Oh, he's going to be all right."

"Then you two keep in touch."

"Every day. He often calls me at night just as he's about to go to sleep."

I marveled that brother and sister could still be that close after all those years out of the nest.

"Bud tells me all his troubles. Sometimes he goes on and on. And I listen. And that comforts him. Sometimes he goes to sleep talking to me. His voice slowly drifts off, his breathing changes, and then I know he's fallen asleep."

"Well, if he's in the hospital, the whole idea is off. I'm going home on the 15th, day after tomorrow, and will have missed him."

The next day, a Thursday, the 14th, I rested most of the day in The Bird. I wanted to enjoy the studio for its own sake. I sunbathed on the wings. I read the newspapers and the mail.

I napped. I wanted to have a least one day in which I could loaf in luxury in that paradise.

Late in the afternoon, I began to pack. I hated to leave the Foundation. I'd made some good friends on that second tour. Among others, I got to like Max Eastman. One day I even took Max over to see Henry Miller (who lived in Pacific Palisades) and I watched with delight as those two old giants talked freely and with great candor about their careers and their loves. Also, I'd gotten a fine start on a new book *King of Spades*.

It was going to take some will power to face my griefs back home.

The doorbell rang.

I went out and found a note stuck in the door. It was from the secretary of the Foundation:

> "Fred —
>   Just had a call from Jocelyn Brando saying she's set up a date for you to see her brother at five p.m.
> Betty Izant"

I glanced at my watch. It was already five to five. Lord.

I dressed in several swift jumps. I decided I'd better call Jocelyn first to tell her I'd only just then got her note, that I was sure to be late for the appointment, and would she call her brother to tell him I'd be late. I rolled my yellow monster down to the Community House to make the call.

Jocelyn sighed with relief when she heard my voice. "I was worried maybe my message would get to you too late. But you go on up there. Bud still isn't back from the doctor's, but he's expecting you to be there when he gets there."

"From the doctor's? Then he's been home from the hospital?"

"Yes. He went home last night. And then this afternoon went back to his doctor about something else."

"I see." I hesitated, then wondered, aloud, "You're coming by to take me up in your little car?"

"No. You're to go alone."

"Okay." I preferred that, actually.

She gave me his address, and in case I got lost his unlisted telephone number.

I was going to miss my last dinner at the Foundation, always a treat.

I drove up Rustic Canyon, then down Monaco Drive, took a left on Sunset Boulevard, another left up the San Diego Freeway, and finally a right onto Mulholland Drive. The traffic on the San Diego Freeway at that hour was thick, but on Mulholland it was like taking a country road. Mulholland cuts along the top of the north side of the Santa Monica Mountains.

I found his address without trouble and rolled past some brown mailboxes up to a gate. I leaned out of my yellow monster and punched a button in a stone wall. It was the same sort of button the fellows at the Foundation had to push in order to enter the grounds there.

A woman's voice, grated by the intercom mechanism, asked, "Who is it?"

I gave my name.

The wings of the heavy black gate parted and I drove through. The gate closed behind me.

I followed a winding drive up and around to the back of a single-level house. The house appeared to have been designed by a Japanese architect. It had floor-to-ceiling windows and was fitted around and into the rocks at the top of one of the peaks of the Santa Monica Mountains. Looking north and down, I saw the vast San Fernando Valley spread below.

There were several cars in the parking area, foreign as well as domestic. I pulled up beside them.

Just as I stepped out of my yellow Buick, a pretty dusky girl came running out of the door. "Mr. Manfred?"

"Yes?"

"I'm sorry to have to tell you but it seems Mr. Brando can't see you after all."

"What seems to be the trouble?"

"His doctor has just informed him he may have the mumps."

"Then Mr. Brando is back from the doctor's?"

"Yes. He got home just ahead of you. I'm sorry."

I was disappointed. Among other things, I'd delayed starting for home just to see Brando. The Foundation was pretty strict about any one staying beyond the time agreed on, even for one day. I'd have to cajol Dr. John Vincent, head of the Huntington Hartford Foundation, with some of my better Siouxland blandishments.

The young girl gave me a commiserating smile. "I'm sorry."

"Actually, you know, the kids at home have had the mumps all around me. Besides, I've got three children and my wife thinks that's enough. So if I should happen to get the mumps, I'm still ahead of the game."

She laughed.

I reached into my car and picked up a paperback copy of *Lord Grizzly.* "Would you give this to Mr. Brando?"

"Surely."

"I'll write in it a little to make it worth something to him." I scribbled in a few lines and signed my name. I stood beside the Buick and used its top as a table. I was aware as I wrote in the paperback that other eyes were on me. Someone in the house was watching me.

I was about to hand the signed book to the dusky girl, when another girl stepped out of the house, also lovely. She came toward me with her sunned blonde head cocked to one side, sensitive eyes crinkled with curiosity, lips touched with a private smile.

I looked at her, eyebrows up.

"I'm Alice, Mr. Brando's secretary. If you've really had the mumps, you can come in. If you wish."

Ah. Someone had been watching me. Mr. Brando himself He'd overheard me; had probably laughed to himself when he heard me say that my wife thought three kids was enough. "Good."

I followed Alice into the house, then around through a hallway in back, and finally into a large bedroom. It was my kind of bedroom, very roomy with tall windows, the walls lined with books, and with a huge king-sized bed.

Brando was in bed with an ice pack held to his neck and, save for jockey briefs, lying naked. He was quite tanned and his skin was in vivid contrast to the white sheets. He greeted me warily. "Hi."

I was a bit wary myself. I was bearding a Hollywood lion in his own den. "Hi."

He shifted the ice pack to the other side of his tanned neck.

"Well," I said, "despite all, here I am."

"Yes." He looked me up and down. His dark-dotted grey-blue eyes opened a little at my height. Jocelyn had probably told him I was a big man but what he saw still surprised him. His eyes warmed up and a little smile moved at the edges of his full lips. "Well." Then, still holding the ice pack to his swollen glands, he sat up and reached out across the foot of the bed to shake hands. "Sit down. Take a chair. There."

I pulled up a chair to the bed. I sat smiling. I had the signed copy of *Grizzly* in my hand and slowly slid it out of sight into a side pocket of my jacket.

There were two great dogs, Saint Bernards, lying on the rug. After a moment of listening to my voice, they decided I was all right, and came shagging over, resting their massive muzzles on my high knee and wanting to be petted. I love dogs, and after a few strokes over their heads, and a scratch or two deep into the nape of the wide necks, we were friends.

Brando noted with pleasure the way his two big dogs and I took to each other. He warmed up even more. He smiled privately to himself about something. "Did you have trouble finding this place?"

"Not with Jocelyn's directions at hand, no."

Just then the phone rang, as if on cue. It was Jocelyn, checking to see if I'd arrived. With a laugh, a brother's laugh, he told her he had me in his bedroom and that we were already old friends. He listened to something she had to say, then said, "Everything's fine. Thanks for sending him over. Bye."

To myself I thought: "Now wasn't that thoughtful of her."

Brando had a tender look for his sister. "That Jocelyn, what a great gal. Really. She was the first wave of our family to hit the beachheads here in Hollywood and she took all the first flak and shelling. It's always easier for the second and third wave. Jocelyn opened the door here for me. And she's had to suffer for it. Running into all kinds of bastards. Now it's my turn to run interference for her. A wonderful sister. I couldn't have asked for a better."

I noted as he talked that he spoke clearly, with none of that mumbling I'd observed in the movies *Cat On a Hot Tin Roof* and *Waterfront*. When relaxed, his accent was in fact midwestern.

Alice came in with her arcane smile. She carried a pill in a shot glass along with a tumbler of water.

"Thanks," Brando said. He let go of his ice pack for a moment and threw the pill onto his tongue and then swallowed the pill with some water.

I stood up. "I hope I'm not running into your dinner time, Marlon."

Alice spoke for him. "Mr. Brando's already had dinner."

Brando reset the ice pack against his swollen neck. "Sit down," he said to me. He rubbed his stomach with his free hand. "Got to cut down on my weight." He smiled lazily at Alice. "Alice is my watch dog, to make sure I don't get too fat."

"Yes," she said, "and to make sure you also lose some weight." Smiling to herself, Alice left.

I had noted little rolls of fat pudging over his tight jockey briefs. He had the kind of physique that ran to fat. He'd have to watch it all his life.

Presently the phone beside his bed rang again. He grimaced. Apparently Alice had decided it was another important call. He picked up the black phone. "Yes," he said gruffly.

It turned out to be a woman who'd sent him a script. He'd read it, he said, but it wasn't for him. The woman persisted. At first he tried to push her off with some Brando blandishments. When that didn't work, he turned rough, and hung up.

I cocked my head at him, smiling, trying to show that I was sorry I had to overhear that conversation.

He shook his head. He snarled in a pleasant way. "Women are such a puzzle. Such a torment. God."

I waited. I was kind of glad to hear him speak frankly, with a gush of feeling. I had no sense he was talking out of a mask. Most actors are nobodies without a script in hand. Rarely do they have an original thought of their own; but they are marvelously entertaining when filling out a script written or created by someone else. The public often thinks it's the

actor who's great, and pays him inordinate attention, and over-
whelms him with praise and money, when the real engines of
a society are the original minds, those who write the plays,
the poems, the symphonies. Before me in Marlon Brando I was
seeing an actor who also had in him the motions of a vital
person. He seemed self-animated and wasn't lost without a script.

"Take that poor gal I married who pretended she was from
India. She was probably sick to begin with and I didn't spot
it right away. Now she and I are fighting over custody of my
son. Or, her laywers and I are. Damn those laywers out here
in Hollywood." His grey-blue eyes fired up; the black dots in
them deepened. "Well! she's not going to get him and raise
him to hate me. He's my son! I want to raise him my way
of being a man. And have him love me. When I get custody
of him, I'm going to put him out on my island in the South
Pacific. That's the place to raise him. Away from all this mess
here in America. Especially here on the Coast."

I nodded my head in commiseration.

He went on to have some sharp things to say about the
sex revolution. "If a girl screws by the time she's fourteen,
she's probably not going to turn out very good."

"Yeh. With the pill available, a lot of them will feel free
to do it."

He nodded. And shook his head sadly. "They'll all be doing
it soon. There is something to be said for the old fear of getting
pregnant."

"What about the other side of that coin though? If a boy
screws by the time he's fourteen, what about him?"

"Well, yeh, fair is fair. I guess you've got to say that's
no good either. Though a boy has a bigger problem than a
girl. He has to develop courage and daring. Get it up."

"But a girl has to develop it on her side too. Her way is
to get wet."

A very strange look passed over his face. It was a deep
inner private thought. I wondered what it could be. Was he
wondering, maybe, as to how far I'd gotten with his sister
Jocelyn? Well, he needn't worry.

"You have a gal, now that you've broken up with that
princess from India?" I asked.

"Out in the South Pacific."

"I've had some rough goes with women myself. Mostly my fault though."

His expressive eyes opened in surprise. "Your fault? How so?"

"I'm too trusting. I'm a romantic. I believe in noble love. I tend to make too much of women."

"You still married?"

"Yes."

"Any children?"

I got out my billfold and pulled out several pictures of my children, Freya, Marya, Frederick, Jr.

He looked at the pictures one by one. "Good looking kids. You're lucky."

"My wife is good-looking." I next showed him a picture of my wife, Maryanna, taken at about the time she and I met. In the picture she was dressed in white slacks and resting on a low-hanging limb of a tree.

Brando's eyes opened. "Hey, no wonder you're a romantic, believe in noble love. That's my kind of woman." He held the picture a while, studying it, soaking it up. It was as if he was trying to become the person in the picture. "Too bad you two aren't always happy."

"Yes."

"How long has this been going on?"

"Too long."

"How can you stay married and both be unhappy?"

"Well, as you see in that picture there, she's beautiful. Also, I can explain most things she does in terms of a very unhappy childhood. Bad father. So on."

"That's a point."

"Also, I love the children."

He handed all the pictures back to me. He made some remarks about how perceptive children were about parents who weren't getting along. "Kids often know before the parents that things are going to pot."

"Like a family dog will know if a stranger coming on the yard is going to be a friend or a foe."

"Sharper even than that. Kids right away know if a snake's crawled into the nest."

I thought that pretty good. There was a little smile on his lips indicating that the snake he was thinking of was the same one I was thinking of.

"It's harder on the kids to be in such a nest than if their parents would just straight go out and get a divorce. Then the kids'd know for sure just how things stood. They've got to know and know for sure.

I remarked further that kids were a little like the blacks, Negroes, in our society, extraordinarily perceptive about whether or not a white was friendly.

"Right."

We talked about the Negro in America for a while.

He sympathized with their marches; understood their burnings. He'd been reading black literature and pointed to a book lying beside him on the bed, James Baldwin's latest. Noticing a wrinkle creeping up around my eyes, he said, "Oh, Jimmy isn't just interested in men. He has women too."

"There was a black gal at the Foundation this spring," I said. "A painter. She loved him. There was an air about her that no one, but no one, was going to get near her. Touch her. She belonged to Jimmy and that was it. So maybe you're right."

Brando said, "What counts, really, is what he has to say. The rest is his private business. And Jimmy has been a great power for good."

"I agree."

"Now that we've got the black man on the move, we've got to get the red man going. It's the red man's turn." He shifted the ice pack. "Now, there's a people who really got screwed by the white man. The red man owned this country in the first place. And we shoved them out. Shot, raped, killed, burned them out. Betrayed them at every turn. Lied to them. Made treaties with them that were worthless."

"As my father would say, weren't worth the paper they were written on."

"Right." Brando put his ice pack to one side and hopped out of bed to show me his Indian books.

I got to my feet too.

Standing beside me Brando barely came to my shoulder. It made him back away a step. A smile opened his eyes very wide. His face didn't seem to change expression so much as did his grey-blue eyes. The eyes receded and opened full of warm appreciation. When he smiled that way, hot but controlled, fully risen within, he was marvelous to behold. It was sincere; it was no actor's mask quickly put on to fit the occasion. It made one think of him as a warm brilliant man. "Christ, what a big devil you really are. Man."

I stood a little sheepish for being so tall. I said, "Well, yeh, I guess they piled it pretty high in my case."

"Hey, be proud of it." He pulled out some books and showed me some passages.

It was my first chance to look at all the books close up and I was surprised to see the range of subjects: anthropology, archaeology, ethnology. It was better than my own library. Almost all the books had little slips of paper in them as book markers. Brando was a reader.

There were also several books about the mountain man. Here at last was the perfect opening to talk about the greatest mountain man hero of them all, Hugh Glass. But, for the life of me, I just didn't have the heart to take advantage of it. I was a poor hunter. I was better at being a bard recounting another hunter's kill.

The phone rang. Again it was a call Alice decided he should answer. He crawled back in bed, pushed the ice pack against his swollen neck, picked up the black phone. The call was from the agent.

I went back to my chair and sat down again.

When he'd finished with the agent, he went back at it. "We've just simply got to get those Indians going. Somehow. Get them to declare their rights. What is justly theirs."

The phone kept ringing. I'd often sat in an office talking with a man or a woman only to have a lively chain of thought interrupted by a goddam jangling phone, another person butting in without so much as an introduction or an apology, and I hated the ringing phone even more just then. He should have told Alice to hold all calls until I'd left.

I got up several times during those calls as if to leave, but each time he waved me down and covered the receiver with the palm of his hand to tell me it wouldn't be but a minute.

When the phone rang for about the tenth time, I finally couldn't help but remark on it. I said I had people bother me too at times with their pesty telephone calls, but nothing like that. "That's terrible, Marlon. Holy balls, man, it'd drive me nuts."

He liked my rough language.

"Really. That's brutal."

He started to tell me about his future projects. I was tempted to ask him why he let himself be talked into doing mediocre movies, even some that were pretty bad.

It was as if he read my mind. "Sometimes I take on projects I hate. But I've got a lot of people to support, you know. A small nation, almost. I've got that island out in the South Pacific. Then I'm fighting that 'princess from India.' I've got all this help here to pay wages to. My father to keep going. And then there's my sister Jocelyn. A lot of people. So to pay all the bills I've sometimes got to take on jobs just for the money that's in it."

"You help Jocelyn too? Financially?

"Of course. You don't think for a minute that her bookstore makes enough for her to live on, do you?"

I had wondered about that. The times I've been in her store I had rarely seen customers.

"I can't let her sit at home doing nothing between acting jobs. Of which there are all too few for her. You have to be young to be in demand. There aren't many roles for middle-aged women. So I set her up in a book shop. With the hope it might go someday."

I remarked I'd gone to a sherry thing she'd held sometime ago. I'd gone there at her special request. She wanted to be able to say in her ads that live authors would be on hand.

"She told me about that. And it was good of you to show up. But there weren't many real patrons there, were there?"

"No. I got the feeling most people just showed up hoping to see real celebrities. So they could have their pictures taken with them."

"Yeh." He almost snarled. "Vip chasers."

I liked what I was hearing.

He went back to the Indians. "I want to use the power of the movies, the visual power that's in film, to put the message across about them. Help them all I can. In between the money-making movies, I also want to make a movie someday about Wounded Knee."

I almost smiled. Here I'd just finished writing a novel about the Sioux Uprising of 1862 in Minnesota. *Scarlet Plume.* I ventured to tell him a little about it.

He listened. He shifted the ice pack from side of his swollen neck to the other.

I was hoping he'd ask me to send him galleys.

Instead he said, "Well, it's good that you're writing that kind of book about them. But I'm not too interested in the old history about Indians. What went on back there." Again he put aside his ice pack and hopped out of bed and strode to his bookshelves and pulled out a book.

Of course I recognized it instantly. It was my own *Conquering Horse*, published a few years earlier. "This is a wonderful story. Sounds all true to me. Helped me understand the Indian. But what I want is a contemporary story about the Indian. Today's Indian. About what's happening to him today. To make a movie about this kind of Indian history"—he shook the book up and down—"won't help much. It'll just be an interesting tale. It won't get people worked up. It won't help to get the red man to marching. What I want to do is make a movie that will so outrage the red man he'll get out his warclub and start marching. Today. Now. And will so outrage some of the whites that they too will join him in getting him justice. Today!" He spoke with passion. His tanned face reddened. His grey-blue eyes burned magnetically.

I understood then why people went to see Brando's movies. He was a magnetic man. A real power. A king and a father and a priest.

He went back to bed and his ice pack.

I resumed my chair at the foot of the bed. "That's all very well that you want to make such a movie, Marlon. But I just wonder if you can get the red man to marching as easily as the black man. You're dealing with a different breed of cat."

"You think so?"

"Oh yes. The red man's sense of pride is different."

"How so?"

"Well, he's inclined to be more stoic. He has a kind of iron gravity that the black man doesn't have. The black man is much more volatile. His emotions are closer to the surface. While the red man is more reserved. Place has a lot to do with that."

His eyes steadied on me, thinking.

"The two don't think much of each other, you know. And that should tell you something."

He thought to himself some more.

I decided to bring up the *Lord Grizzly* matter after all. The paperback copy I'd autographed for him on the roof of my car burned in my pocket. I told him about William Froug, who was thinking of quitting his job as executive director of CBS so he could produce *Lord Grizzly*. I told him about Walter Brown Newman, a fine script writer, who for many years had wanted to do the screenplay. I told him about Lester Linsk, my agent, who wanted to put the package together. I said all three wanted him, Marlon Brando, to play the role of Hugh Glass. I went into some detail about our plans. I told him the gist of the novel; then outlined what we planned to do in the movie. About having hants in it to make it go during that part where Hugh is all alone on the screen. I told him about young Sammy Goldwyn's interest in it. About Robert Mitchum's remark when Sammy asked him to take on the role of Hugh Glass: "Who do I act against?" I went into somewhat of a passion myself, saying that I'd told Sammy Goldwyn, in his home on Tigertail Road, that it'd been tougher for me to make that story of Hugh's crawl interesting for some hundred and seventy pages in writing, than it was going to be for some director to make it vivid in picture.

He shook his head. "Jocelyn talked to me about *Lord Grizzly*. But I decided it was not for me." His eyes fired up. "If I'm going to do anything at all in that vein, it's going to be on a modern Indian problem. About their wretched life on the reservations. Like I said before I want to do something for them here and now. To help them immediately. Today. If I

can only get them to marching . . . at least. Somebody like
me, who's got some influence, has got to step in and help them."

He was so emphatic about it, I let my shoulders down,
and I dropped all further thought of Marlon Brando doing Old
Hugh Glass. I wanted to get up and leave right then and there,
since I'd long ago used up my welcome. I glanced at my watch.
It was going on eight. Outside it was already darkening on
his side of the Santa Monica Mountains. But I hesitated. To
get up just then wouldn't have been proper either. It would
look too blatantly as though I'd come solely to talk about *Lord
Grizzly*.

A silence fell between us.

I did decide one thing though. Since I'd already inscribed
a copy of *Lord Grizzly*, I thought I might just as well give
it to him. I took the paperback out of my pocket and handed
it to him.

He turned it over in his hands without really looking at
it, then placed it to one side of him on the bed.

"You'll look at it? Jocelyn told me specially to bring you
a copy. She got it for me in her store."

"I'll give it a whirl. But no promises."

The big dogs kept milling around the room. There was also
a small dog, a female, of a breed I didn't know, and it hopped
up on his bed and tried to lick his face. With a smile Brando
held it off. Brando said, "Then you've met the modern Indian,
I see."

"Oh yes." I told him about my visits to the reservations
to do "research" for my Indian books. I told him Indians often
came to visit me. Some of them, to show their appreciation
for what I'd written about them, brought me presents. "Once,
when I was working in my cabin, I heard a sudden single
drumbeat outside my door. Boom! I got up from my chair for
a look, and there was Otto Thunder and some red friends of
his, all dressed up in dancing regalia. They were kneeling in
the grass around a big drum under one of my big oak trees.
The moment they spotted me, they began to sing. They beat
the drum hypnotically. In the middle of the song I heard my
name pronounced. When they finished, Otto got to his feet
and turned to me and said, 'That song was for Fred Manfred,

our friend.' Then Otto motioned for the others to get to their feet and they all headed for their battered old car. I ran after them. 'Hey, wait a minute. I'd like to thank you for that. How about coming into the house with me for a cup of coffee or something?' Otto and his bunch gave me a funny look, as if that was completely out of the question, that they hadn't come to trade favors, only to sing me a song and then go home."

Marlon loved the story.

I told him some yuwipi tales, in which little spirits appear in a darkened tepee, tormenting those guilty of social errors. I told him about an incident a friend of mine, Fred Blessing, had witnessed in which a medicine man caused a little wooden effigy to dance on a mound of dirt by just sheer sweated will power.

Brando said he believed such things. No doubt of it.

I told him about the time up at Red Lake, Minnesota, at an Indian celebration of the white man's Fourth of July, I had been invited to help beat the big drum with some drummers and singers. I'd told the head man, an old chief, I wasn't sure it was proper for a white man to participate. Yet I wanted to show respect for the Indian ways, so what should I do. The old chief said, "Take the stick and just tap lightly along the edge of the drum. In token."

Brando became excited all over again. "I've just got to see that country. And I'm going to see it too."

"I'd be glad to take you around."

He considered the idea. "Well, if we two do go, we've got to go incognito at first. I want to wander around, just looking, before the reporters spot me and follow me around."

"Well, we can go as Bud Brand and Fred Mann."

He laughed. "As a boy I was known as Bud. Or Buddy. That's where Jocelyn gets it. But now"—he snorted to himself—"now of course I'm known as Marlon."

I had some more pictures in my billfold, of my home in Bloomington, Minnesota, high on a bluff, as well as a few of Siouxland, and I showed them to him. He looked at them all with interest. To point out some of the special features, I had to get closer to him, and I soon found myself sitting on a corner of his huge bed. I noted that his little female dog had

curled herself up on the copy of *Lord Grizzly* I'd just given
him, rumpling the cover. Smiling, I took the paperback out
from under her. "It must be a good book if a dog takes to
making a mattress out of it."

Again there was that gleaming luminous smile, showing
he was having a jolly time, unexpectedly so. He stroked his
stomach and with his thumb and finger lifted up a bit of the
flab pudging over the top of his briefs. "God, I'm getting fat.
I've just simply got to lose some weight."

"How about running it off?"

"I'm doing that. I sometimes trot ten miles a day."

"That'll help. But the best exercise is to push yourself away
from the table."

"You run?"

"At the Foundation I run a mile and a half a day. Hard.
Part of it up the side of that canyon there."

"That's pretty steep. At least a four percent grade. Climbing that is almost as much as running ten miles."

"That's what I fugured."

He asked, "Are you happy?"

"Mostly, yes. I'm doing what I like to do. Write the books
I find in my head. And I'm still young and have all the best
yet ahead."

"How old are you?"

"Fifty-two."

"Naw. Not fifty-two?"

"Yes."

"How do you keep so young?"

"Get plenty of sleep. Don't drink. Don't smoke. Mostly
though it's an attitude of mind. Not to mention some heredity."

Again he rubbed his tanned stomach. "I've got to get rid
of this."

"I mean to keep on improving until I reach ninety. By then
I should be writing at the top of my bent. Writing my great
book. Or probably I should say, my best book."

Once more that marvelous inward gleam appeared in his
luminous grey-blue eyes.

"If the Greek civilization could produce a Sophocles who
in his nineties could write the wonderful *Oedipus at Colonus,*

which some critics consider his greatest work, why, then maybe
our American cicilization can come up with a writer who can
write a fine novel or a fine rume at ninety."

"That's the spirit!"

It was time to go. I'd fallen into a bragging mood, a mood
I never liked to see in others. Also, we were at the peak of
having a good time. Leave when one was hot. I got to my feet.

"Must you go?"

"I've still got some books to pack. I was really going to
leave late this afternoon. Get a start towards Reno, Nevada,
where I want to visit with Walter Van Tilburg Clark. And then
after Walter, head for home. But then Jocelyn's call came."

"I see."

"Now I'll have to call ahead to say I'm going to be delayed
a day."

He hopped out of bed. "I'll walk you to the door."

"See here," I said. "You're not supposed to be doing that.
Your doc won't like it. I can find my own way out."

"Aw, heck, I'm boss here. Come on." He waved a hand and
led the way.

As he walked slightly ahead of me, I noted his fine muscular
stride. "You'd make a fine quarterback, Marlon."

He stopped to show a big scar over his knee, the result
of a football injury.

We came out on the paving where my car stood.

"Well," I said, "there she is, my beloved yellow monster.
I bought her for two hundred twenty-five dollars and she's taken
me everywhere."

Again the narrowed gleaming smile.

We shook hands, heartily, warmly.

I got into the car, started it up.

"You know your way out of here? Through the gate?"

"Yep." I backed up.

"Good-bye." He waved his hand. "And I'll give it a whirl
like I promised."

"Good." I waved back and headed down the curving drive.

A few minutes later, as I wheeled off Mulholland onto the
San Diego Freeway, I wondered if, upon returning to his room,

he'd picked up *Lord Grizzly* and had found the inscription I'd written in it. The inscription was as follows:

> *To Marlon Brando—*
> *Let us be kodah* to one another.*
> *A companyero,*
> *Frederick Manfred*

> **"Blood friend"*

Before I went to bed that night I typed up some notes on my visit to Brando while the event was still fresh in my mind.

The next morning I made two telephone calls from the Foundation.

First to Jocelyn, to thank her for arranging the visit with her brother.

She then told me how she'd gotten the interview. She'd said to Marlon, "Bud, I don't often ask favors of you, seeing as how you've already done so much for me. Or ask you to meet someone. But I've met a man you really should meet. It would be too bad if you didn't. Bud said, 'It sounds like you really like this fellow.' 'Yes, I do. You really want to meet him.' 'Well, all right, tell him to come at five this afternoon.' 'Good, because there is one fellow I'm sure you're going to get along with. There may be a little business talk between the two of you, but what I want is for you to meet him on his own ground, in his field, and in his own right. You two are bound to like each other, and you'll like each other apart from the business talk.' 'You really like this fellow, I can see that.' "

I thanked her again.

She went on to say that she'd talked to Bud right after my visit the night before and he'd said, "I'm glad you sent him over. I enjoyed the hell out of it. I must go see Fred in his Siouxland."

(A month later I called Jocelyn from my home in the country near Luverne, Minnesota. She told me that Bud hadn't had the mumps after all, in case I was worrying. It was only a low grade infection in his lymph glands.)

I next called my wife Maryanna to tell her I would be home a day later than I planned.

"Where are you now?"

"Still at the Foundation. I'm leaving in a few minutes."

"How come you didn't leave yesterday afternoon?"

I told her about the call from Jocelyn Brando and then the subsequent visit with Bud Brando in his home up on Mulholland.

"You were in Marlon Brando's house?"

"Yes."

There was a pause. "Wait till I tell Freya. She loves him so."

"Tell her I'll give her all the details when I get home."

Another pause. "Where do you get that?"

"What do you mean?"

"You know, the confidence to just go in and visit such a celebrity."

"Why not? He's just an actor, for godsakes."

"Yes, but he's famous."

"Shucks, Maryanna, it would be different if he were an original. You know, a Faulkner or a Beethoven. Though even then, that wouldn't phase me much. There isn't that much difference between a Dizzy Dean and a Bob Feller."

"Just the same."

"Listen, Brando at best is just an interpreter. A Vladimir Horowitz to a Charles Ives."

"Och, you always like to make those comparisons."

"They're apt though. Charles Ives as a maker is a first-rate artist, and at best Vladimir Horowitz as an interpreter, a renderer, is a second-rate artist. You've got to have those originals first before you can have concerts. Somebody's got to make the wheel before you can have a Ben-Hur driving a chariot."

Maryanna laughed. "But we're still happy to have the Vladimirs."

"Besides, a real artist would never let himself be talked into 'walking through' some of those awful movies he's made."

"That's because he's more practical-minded than you are. Not such a dreamer as to think he should only do something if it's the right thing to do. For art's sake and not for money."

"Nevertheless, because he does junk once in a while tells you something about him fundamentally. He isn't really tough and hard as an artist. And I'm not talking about any kind of final glory either. I'm talking about pride in workmanship. I don't give a rip for glory. What really counts is how you feel after you've done a good job at something."

"Then you're starting for home this morning?"

"Right."

"The garden is waiting for you to plant it."

July, 1979

The Siouxlander

What's a Siouxlander?

Well, it's a people living mostly in the Big Sioux River valley drainage basin and its environs. The area takes in the eastern half of South Dakota, the southwestern corner of Minnesota, the northwestern part of Iowa, and the northeastern section of Nebraska.

People in Siouxland rarely ever mention the states involved. When two women in Doon, Iowa, gossip over the telephone, and one of them says, "Oh, say, I'm gonna be gone all day tomorrow." "Where you goin'?" "Sioux Falls." Or, the woman might say, Worthington, or Norfolk, or Sioux City, but she'll never mention the states involved. That some cartographers a century or more ago, not knowing very much about the Indian territory, made some arbitrary geographical boundaries for almost imaginary states means little or nothing to us today.

Even the young don't ever worry about the Mann Act (1910) which imposes a severe penalty for interstate traffic in girls. A young man in Worthington, Minnesota, can date a girl from Sioux Falls, South Dakota, and take her to rock concert in Sioux City, Iowa, and that night on the way back get lost in a blizzard and take a wrong turn and wind up in Norfolk, Nebraska, where he'll stay overnight with her. The two of them may very well each sleep in a twin bed and never touch each other, but in any case won't worry that the boy might be arrested by an over-zealous U.S. Marshall for having transported a girl from one state to another and having slept in the same room with her. In fact, having grown up in Siouxland, I never heard of the Mann Act until I went to Calvin College in Grand Rapids, Michigan, where a young man I knew was charged for having broken the Mann Act law.

There are many reasons why we never mention the four states involved when we travel around in Siouxland. First, it's natural for Siouxlanders to prune out of their talk all unnecessary and already understood terminology. We even prune poly-syllabics whenever possible, for example, "caterpillar tractor" becomes "cat," "vibrations" becomes "vibes," "interstate highway" becomes "I 90," etc. So why should we keep mentioning any one of the four states involved? To use them just takes that much longer to get to the point.

Secondly, the people living in Siouxland are all pretty much alike. Most of them are protestants. Most of their ancestors emigrated from Northern Europe and the British Isles. And as time has gone on, after five generations, it has become dif-ficult for any one of us to claim that he is of pure German or Norwegian or Frisian or Dutch or English descent. Watch the wedding announcements in the various newspapers in the area, either weekly or daily, and you'll see the young with Norwegian names marrying the young with Frisian names, the young with Dutch names marrying the young with German names. I knew of one fellow with a Norwegian name who had only one-sixteenth Norwegian blood left in him. We have become over the generations pretty much a purebred people with what I'd like to call Siouxland blood in us. And five generations from now our family names will even have become reshaped and honed so that they'll all look somewhat similar, just as today most English names in England have that unmistakable English look about them, no matter what the names might have been originally: Celtic, Danish, Angle, Saxon, Frisian, Norman, or the people who built Stonehenge.

We've even developed a distinctive accent. It is broad, full-toned, and very clear. After we have pruned back the polysyllabics, we speak what's left clearly. In part the weather demands it, hot or cold; in part the lingering momentum of Anglo-Saxon imprinting given us in grade school is always at work in us. Our accent has become as distinctive for us as has the harsh accent for the New Englander, or the soft accent for the Alabamian, or the cocky accent for the Texan. It's because of our accent that so many Siouxlanders have been chosen as radio and television announcers – Eric Sevareid, Tom Brokaw, Harry Reasoner, Jack Van Valkenburg (president of CBS).

We've also worked out a special kind of morality, having to do with honesty, a sense of fair play, spirited competition without too much greed, of allowing every citizen to live his own kind of life so long as it does not intrude too much on a neighbor's well-being.

Further, we've worked out our own kind of justice, which isn't necessarily what lawyers think it is, or what ministers think it should be, or what social workers want for us. Our justice is not narrow, but filled with much compassion. It can even be said of our men of law, our lawyers, that they are not yet as greedy as metropolitan lawyers. They go to the same church as the rest of us, have coffee breaks with us, and could suffer from negative criticism along main street. Much as some of them might like to operate as super-citizens they don't quite have the gall to try it. And the percentage of Siouxland lawyers who try to practice in the manner of a Solon is quite high when compared to those lawyers living in heavily congested urban areas.

We applaud financial success but not to the point where we tolerate excess as the expense of the poor. We work at trying to accommodate and help the poor or the momentarily bankrupt. When disaster strikes a farm family, say the husband is killed by a machine on the yard or out on the field, the neighbors band together and help thresh out the grain crop, or pick all his corn, or make up all his hay—until the widow can work out a program of self-help.

We even tolerate the arrogant for a time, hoping that he or she will come to their senses, and become good neighbors. At the same time we admire those who are proud of their accomplishments but who do not brag, who have what we call a permissable kind of arrogance which helps them "handle" smart alecks coming in from other quarters of our country.

The term Siouxland came about in the following manner. I had pretty much finished the first rough draft of my novel *This Is the Year* in 1946, when it struck me that I was doing a lot of unnecessary typing by always having to mention what state the hero was in, Iowa, Sioux Dakota, Minnesota, Nebraska. Except for one instance, none of my relatives ever mentioned the nearby states they lived in, and that instance had to do

with the butter-oleomargarine war between Iowa and Minnesota
which lasted only a few years. It also hit me that should *This
Is the Year* be read by people on the east coast or the west
coast, they'd think "My God, those poor plainspeople sure have
to drive a long ways to get to Sioux City in Iowa or Sioux
Falls in South Dakota," when in actual fact a distance of only
a few miles is involved. Also those distant readers would have
trouble visualizing that this country here was really all of a
piece. So why not give it a name.

The first thing to catch my eye upon examining a map
was that we all lived and loved in the Big Sioux River valley
and its environs. I tried various names: the Valley of the Big
Sioux, Sioux River Country, Land of the Sioux, Sioux-Land,
and finally, dropping the hyphen, making it Siouxland. I drew
a map of my own, putting in it some of the actual town names,
plus those I invented, and when the novel was finished, I sent
the map along with it. The publisher liked the idea of the map
and it was placed in the end pages of the novel. *This Is the
Year* came out in April, 1947, and within months the advertising people glommed onto the name. No longer did they have
to say over the radio, and later on over television, "Serving
northwest Iowa, southeast South Dakota, southwest Minnesota,
and northeast Nebraska," but instead could simply say, "Serving greater Siouxland." Soon after that various organizations
also began using the term, Siouxland Conference (basketball,
football), Siouxland Furniture, Siouxland Insurance Agency,
Siouxland Museums, etc.

Once the term was in place, in our minds, we could take
pride in various points of interest over the whole area: the majestic Blue Mounds in southwest Minnesota (the butt of what
was left of an ancient mountain range running from Mitchell,
South Dakota, to Mankato, Minnesota, a mountain range as
high as Mt. Everest); the Blood Run Mounds in northwest Iowa
(almost four hundred of them indicating that once a considerable
colony of Indians lived there); the beautiful falls in Sioux Falls
in southeast South Dakota where the Sioux River purls and
drops over purple and bloodred Sioux quartzite rocks; the noble
heights of the Newton Hills near Canton, South Dakota; the
incredible rich black soils of an utterly flat tableland around

Hull and Sioux Center and Orange City, Iowa; the voluptuous sloping landscapes around Sioux City, Iowa; the hauntingly slow climb of blue land toward the height of land known as Turkey Ridge in eastern South Dakota; the rip in the rock and land known as Devil's Gulch near Garretson, South Dakota, where Jesse James was reputed to have jumped his horse across to escape vigilantes.

We all celebrate the sites where famous author Ole Rolvaag lived and dreamed, in Elk Point, in Canton, on a farm in Garretson, all in South Dakota; where Herbert Krause taught at Augustana College and dreamed up his wonderfully detailed and poetic novels as well as conceived of starting the Center for Western Studies; where John R. Milton of Vermillion edited an important literary quarterly and wrote novels and poetry; where L. Frank Baum made a magic thing out of a tornado; where Army officer Hiram Chittenden of Sioux City wrote his classic book *A History of the American Fur Trade in the Far West*; where Hamlin Garland lived and wrote for a time near Brookings; where storyteller Ruth Suckow wrote classic novels and short stories about her birthplace Hawarden, Iowa; where the great painter Harvey Dunn was born and lived near Brookings and who left behind masterpieces depicting early pioneer life; where painter Oscar Howe achieved international fame with his sometimes starkly realistic, sometimes dreamy, paintings of both Indian and white life in Siouxland.

Any one of us living in any part of Siouxland can easily drive in an hour or two to listen to jazz concerts in Sioux City, or symphony concerts in Sioux Falls, or old-time hoedown country music in Yankton. Or see plays put on at the University of South Dakota in Vermillion or in the Community Playhouse in Sioux Falls or at the campus theatre at Augustana College also in Sioux Falls.

The several universities and the dozen or more colleges of Siouxland will over the course of a year invite nationally and internationally famous lecturers. In one year, for example, a person hungry for the newest knowledges in various fields could have heard in Siouxland such diverse men as playwright Arthur Miller, anthropologists Richard Leakey and Stephen Jay Gould, or historian John Van Engen of Notre Dame.

We have twice as much to enjoy as do folk living in, say, New York. We read the East's magazines and newspapers, we listen to their radio and television broadcasts, so we know that; plus we also know about our life here. The New Yorkers have only one cultural leg to stand on; we stand on two. They have but one knowledge; we have two knowledges. And we have this in relative quiet and peace, with clear air always overhead, and sunny skies.

Far from living in a monotonous country, we live where we can enjoy the four seasons, snow in the winter (skiing, skating, tobogganing), planting of seeds in the spring (corn, grain, garden produce), warm sun in the summer (swimming, flowers, jogging), and the mellow golden of autumn (harvesting of corn and grain and pumpkins). As if to emphasize variety, nature now and then pitches in with wild weather: raging blizzards in the winter, tornadoes in the summer, floods in the spring.

Siouxland offers some of the best hunting in all of America. Hunters from all over the country come to Siouxland to get their quota of pheasants, spending near fortunes on guns, garb, food, shelter. I've met hunters who came all the way from California, Tennessee, Florida, Wisconsin, who lusted after pheasant meat. The same is true for duck and goose hunting along the James and Missouri rivers. And since various dams have been built along the great Missouri River, impounding huge lakes, fishing has also become an important sport for the outdoors man and woman.

As far back as 1880, Norwegians living in southwest Minnesota, in what is now northeast Siouxland, built a ski jump on the hill on which I live, Roundwind. Later on they moved the ski jump to the tremendous hills southeast of Canton, South Dakota. When I was in my teens, in the late Twenties, my father once took me to an International Ski Tournament near Canton. Still later, that ski organization moved the jump to Sun Valley near Ketchum, Idaho. Since then all sorts of other ski jumps have shown up in our country; Great Bear, Terry Peak, Mankato Jump.

But for a pocket of civility to survive it must produce new creative minds. And of that we have plenty of evidence. Witness

Pete Dexter who took a course in creative writing at the University of South Dakota and whose third novel, *Paris Trout*, won the National Book Award of 1989. There are many other writers of novels: Michael Doane, *The Legend of Jesse Dark*; Dan O'Brien, *The Spirit of the Hills*; Tim O'Brien, *Northern Lights*; Arvid Shulenberger, *Roads From the Fort*; Virginia Driving Hawk Sneve, *When Thunder Spoke*.

Poets also abound: Jack Kreitzer, Freya Manfred, Linda Hasselstrom, Kathleen Norris, John Haines, Sylvia G. Wheeler, Dan Lusk, David Allan Evans, David Dwyer, Bill Holm. Any one of them can still earn a lasting national reputation in the American literary arena. We also have our playwrights: the elder citizen Wayne Knutson, Ronald Robinson, Kaarin Johnston, Craig Volk, Joseph Meier, Frederick Manfred, Jr. And beyond these fine writers, young students already in various high schools and colleges show astonishing competence and originality in writing poems, stories, plays.

Just a casual glance at brochures and bulletins put out by various arts councils in the whole of Siouxland will tell a visitor that quite a literate and cultured audience has grown up. Art showcases, bookstores, lecture circuits, musical events, local book discussion groups, our own radio and television programs, indicate that Siouxland audiences have learned to compare their local creations against national productions – and decide, intelligently, what's done very well and what is not. Siouxland taste compares favorably with the best in America. Siouxland perhaps has the same number of knuckleheads as any other place in America; but when someone amongst us decides to make something our creations are as good as any other creations anywhere. In fact, because of the relative freedom from the patronizing airs of the east-coaster or the west-coaster, our works show wonderful independence, originality, and warm understanding, with little cynicism and less despair.

So, fair warning. So while we are "making" our own novels and poems and symphonies and sculptures and paintings, we will also be having a look at the work of the outlanders (if we can think of ourselves as inlanders) and making judgments.

A Conversation With Frederick Manfred

by Laurie Lee, Michael Matecjek, and Shikha Saklani

The bulk of this interview took place at Roundwind, Mr. Manfred's home just outside Luverne, Minnesota. Like the author himself, the house is literally down-to-earth. It is built like a bear's den, wedged into the side of a hill so that three quarters are below ground, leaving only the broad picture windows of one side to peer out on the Rock River valley below. All that is visible from the driveway are the garage and a small hexagonal hut, his writing studio, about fifty feet away. His "tepee," as he calls the studio, is accessible by a spiral staircase coming up from the living area beneath.

On a cold night in January, Mr. Manfred waved us into the garage and greeted us warmly before leading us down below. A fire crackled in the fireplace made from stones he'd gathered himself. Roundwind's high ceilings, lined with roughly-hewn timber, are designed to accommodate his six-foot-nine inches. One wall is covered with the oil landscapes he painted while recovering from tuberculosis in the early 1940's, and abstract paintings by his daughters Freya and Marya hang throughout the house.

Before the interview we sat down to the meal he'd already prepared for us. "Frisians always show their guests what it is they're eating," he said, passing a thirty-inch Alaskan salmon under our noses, "and I made up the recipe for the stuffing myself." Obviously a man who enjoys talking, his manner throughout the meal was unguarded and eager, at times almost boyish, as he touched on subjects ranging from anthropology and etymology to his own Frisian [North Dutch] ancestry. His voice is buoyant and lively, and flows with the urgency of someone who feels he's never said all he has to say. His face, looking at least ten younger than his seventy-nine years, is expressive

228

and at times mischievious. Often a glint would come to his eye as he related a story about the area that was at once bawdy and telling.

He remained forthright throughout the interview, never once sidestepping a question. In fact, his answers were often more expansive than we expected. When at one point we remarked on his exceptional honesty, he responded, "I get so sick of reading these interviews and I think to myself, 'Why the goddamn liar! Either shut up or say it! One or the other!' "

What first led you to become a writer?

It really starts with my Aunt Kathryn. I should probably go back there . . . . She lived with us while she was teaching school nearby, and she used to read to me when I was a little kid . . . . I used to watch where her eyes would go on the page, and I learned to read before I started school—just picking up those black marks there, you know. I mention that because she was really intrigued by the fact that I could read so early, and later on she was my teacher for awhile too. On our parlor table was a little volume, green, with gold lettering, that said *Poems, by Kathryn Feikema*. And that was my mother's prize thing to have on the parlor table, a round table, you know, with those sort of lion's paws. My mother would just glory in that—that she was related to someone through her husband that was a writer. And that's a powerful impression on a young boy to know that there's a book that someone that you're related to has written. And later on, there was another time when I was maybe five or so . . . Aunt Kathryn took me to the northwest corner of the grove under a huge cottonwood tree where there was some nice grass, and she took her tatting along. And in the meantime I'm in the grass there, and I follow an ant that comes out of an anthill, and it goes up a tree and comes down with something in its mouth, and she says 'What a strange boy you are. Any other kid would've been complaining that we're not doing anything, and here you are, you always find something to amuse yourself. I wonder what's ever going to become of you."

And so I asked her what was the best thing to be, and she said, 'Well, I'd rather be a poet than a president.'

That has come back to me many, many times. Who was president when Homer wrote the *Iliad* and the *Odyssey*? Who was president when Cervantes wrote *Don Quixote*? You know, you totally forget the presidents. If you write a good story or a good poem, it'll last probably forever. Systems of philosophy come and go, systems of politics come and go. They're all very temporary.

Was there anyone else in those early years who was an influence on you?

Let's see, Aunt Kathryn was there off and on until the fifth grade and then she left, and the teachers we had weren't all that good any more, so my mother thought that we should go to a religious school. So we moved closer to Doon, Iowa. And there I ran across, in the last two years, a man named Onie Aardema. He turned out to be a wonderful teacher. He right away spotted that I was restless . . . and he also advanced me two classes in one year to keep me busy. He was the one who went to my parents and said, "You have an unusual boy and you shouldn't just let him be a farmer, they don't often come along like this one."

Did you begin to write while in college?

Well, I stayed home two years between high school and college. My mother decided I was too young to go to the fleshpots of Grand Rapids, Michigan *[laughs]*. Actually, they're all Christian Reformed there too, you know. But I started writing stories. There was a station master down on the Great Northern Railroad, he had a lot of magazines there, and I used to go down and read there. And then I asked him one time if I could use his typewriter, and he says, "Sure." So then I'd write in longhand some stories up in the haymow, out of sight of my father so that he didn't know I was doing this. There was a little window there, up in the haymow, behind some piles of alfalfa, and there I made my little study, when I was sixteen, seventeen and eighteen. And I wrote oh, maybe a half dozen stories up there and typed 'em out down at the railroad depot and then sent them off—and of course they came back—to Collier's and Liberty and whatever was goin' on then. I never saved any of those. It's too bad, I'd like to have seen them. You know, it would be fun to see them, wouldn't it? See if there's anything in there.

Can you remember any of them?

Oh, usually it was nothing to do with farmers, you know. It was something bizarre. It had nothing to do with my own life. I had to learn how to come to grips with that. I probably felt that my life wasn't very interesting, see. And all the big things were happening in far away cities, not in Hull or Doon, you know.

Do you think it's essential, then, to write from you own life?

Use it as a jumping off point . . . I realized that when you write an autobiography it's tough to make it seem as if it always was there—objective. I mean, when you read these great novels, it's as if Tolstoy happened to come along and he listened a little while and he wrote down what he heard and then he got a book out of that, as if it was already written before he wrote it. In an autobiography, the author is sort of opening himself up to a lot of hard looks, you know. He's being self conscious and he's talking about himself and he might be boastful. Or he might be over-shy. And so it's difficult to get a full-rounded body out of that—not looking at the work, but at the man; at the hero. You only get about two-thirds of the person, and it's because it's very difficult for a man or a woman to see the dark side of his or her own moon. Someone else might be able to see it, but not he or she.

However, I wouldn't want to throw out *David Copperfield*, by Dickens, which is heavily autobiographical. And I wouldn't want to throw out *Pendennis* by Thackeray, which is autobiographical. And you'd have to throw out all of Hemingway, just about. And Thomas Wolfe is so obviously over-explosive

about himself and about his feelings, and he loves and hates
and his appetites and all that stuff. I could never stand him,
by the way. Sixty pages and that's as far as I ever got into
him. And then I stopped. He wasn't goin' anywhere. Hemingway
at least knows where he's going, but it's heavily autobiographical.
And then you're not gonna throw out the *Sorrows of Youth
Werthers*, by Goethe. That's really about himself, the *Sorrows
of Mr. Goethe*. So I always felt that there was room for that
kind of a novel too . . . that's a legitimate inquiry.

**What is the difference between a novel and what you call
a "rume?"**

I never liked the word "novel." The word "novel" just means
"new." It's a recent word. "Here's something new." It was when
Henry Fielding came along with *Tom Jones*. It was a new thing,
and they called it [*laughs*] "novel." You know, it's a novel thing.
And it's a terrible word. It doesn't point at anything, it has
no core to it, it's nothing. It's just a trivial surface word. Really.
I looked around a long time for a new word for that but I
never found one. But I did think there had to be another word
for those autobiographical novels. And the first thing that occurred to me was "it's ruminant." I mean, they're ruminating
about themselves; they're telling about themselves. So I looked
up the word "ruminant" in my book upstairs, *Etymology of
the English Language [Skeat]*, and there they traced "ruminant" and "ruminating" to the original Sanskrit, or the very
early Indo-European root word. The original word way back
there meant to bray, to rue in anguish. "This is how I feel."
"This is the poem out of my belly," you know. So I got to
thinking about that and I said, "Hey, I gotta use that." It's
spelled "rhu." I didn't like that "h" in there too well, but I liked
the word ruminant, and then I saw the word "rune," which
is in a sense that too, because you're putting down strokes:
"I was here," you know. "I was here and I made these marks.
This is me. I made these marks here in stone." And so I thought
I'd try different versions, and finally I wrote down "rume" and
I thought, "Hey, that's a new word." And I looked for it all
over, and I couldn't find it and I thought, "Hey, we'll use that.

Green Earth is a rume, and *Wanderlust*, parts of it, is a rume." And *Boy Almighty* is a rume. And then, of course, the problem is if you're any kind of artist at all, you will try to build it up so it becomes a work by itself. You know, apart from you, really, finally, and stands by itself. You can totally die and it'll still be pretty good.

If you measured *Boy Almighty* against his "rume aesthetic," would you say the book was successful?

I had tuberculosis once, almost died of it. In fact, I saw my file one time when I was recovering. I was on a gurney, and the doctor brought me to his office downstairs, at the Glen Lake Sanatorium. And then he went out of the office for a minute and I reached over and picked up my file and looked at it, and it said "Terminal."

Anyway, I wrote *Boy Almighty* within a year or two of being dismissed from the sanatorium, mostly because I noticed that I couldn't remember the names of the doctors that were there in my room, and some other people, and slowly but surely I could see that my brain was freezing over .... One time I couldn't even remember my wife's name. It isn't really a novel. That's sort of an exercise in catharsis. A cathartic novel, that's really what it is. There was no attempt to build character there, I don't think. Well, I tried to get away from who I was somewhere toward the end of that book, but that book is really heavily autobiographical.

Where does the autobiographical element stop in a novel, and where does the fictional begin? Maury Grant, for example, in the novel *The Golden Bowl* has some of your characteristics. Did you smoke as a young man, and play the harmonica?

Yeh. Yeh, I smoked once for a couple of years .... Actually Maury Grant was not me at all. I just saw this guy for about five hours. He was a hobo .... He came from the country, so I gave him stuff that I knew about the country. But I wouldn't have left Kirsten there by the crick. And I would have felt guilty about what Maury did with her by the crick. Except that later on, maybe where I come in again is when he felt bad about it, so he went back to her, see. Cause I wouldn't probably do that.

Didn't Sinclair Lewis have some influence in the success of *The Golden Bowl*?

Yeh. I hope that I am like him in that sense, to help the new writers coming along. He had a great time and patience for anyone who was coming up. Especially from this area . . . Lewis found this book, and it had good reviews, by the way. We were startled – it had a rave, not a long review, but a full column in the New York Times Book Review, full of really fine remarks about it. There wasn't a single bad review of that anywhere. And Lewis spotted that, and he bought the book and read it. And then he saw to it that when the American Academy of Arts and Letters settled on two people who would get a Grant-in-Aid, he made sure that I was one of them.

And one day the telephone rings, I'm frying some potatoes and steak. I picked the phone up, answered it, and, "Is this Fred Feikema?" That was my old name, Feikema. "Yes." "This is Sinclair Lewis." And I thought, *yeh* . . . . And he said, "I'd like to meet you. I'm staying at the Leamington, would you be so kind as to come up and see me sometime?" And so I did . . . . I knocked on the door and walked in. He didn't expect me to be so damn big, and he walks around me like a farmer walking around a prize Percheron stallion, and commenting on my size, and then, "Sit down." And what I did is took along the first couple copies of *Boy Almighty*, my second novel, and then I had bought his *Cass Timberlane*. He said, "What have you got there?" and I let him have it, and he said, "Oh, here, you autograph your copy to me and I'll autograph my copy to you." And so that's what he did. Then we did go up there [Duluth, Lewis' home] for a week, my wife and I, and had a good time up there.

Could you say something about your writing method, about how a book actually takes shape for you? Are there consistent patterns in your writing that you established early on?

The first book, *The Golden Bowl*, actually I first started writing that in '36, '37. It didn't come out til '44, so I spent seven, eight years thinking about that before it became a book. *Boy Almighty* was almost immediately after the experience, and that's why it doesn't show the look of a novel .... But then by the time I started *This Is the Year*, I had a notebook full of preparations for the novel. And after that. [the notebook for a particular work] was usually ten, twelve or more years old before I began writing a book. Now, by the time you get around to doing such a novel, a skeleton starts to show up in all that stuff. It's a little bit like Trilobites. When life first appeared on Earth here, none of the creatures had backbones; they were just flat, empty and had an inlet and an outlet. And they laid over each other and ate each other up. You know, they looked like little bandaids. But finally one of them developed cartilage. That became a backbone and there's where we come from. Well, it's the same way with all those notes. If you wait long enough, a cartilage or a backbone will show up in all those notes. And then I know what to discard and what to keep. And it writes that way.

So it evolves from all this matter, these notes.

Yes. Finally you have so much stuff there .... In the old days I used to have little pieces of paper in my pocket, and on the way into town I'd think of something and pull over and write it down. The next day, before I began writing, I would enter it in what I thought were the proper files or the proper pots on the stove, let's say. And by the time you get around to doing them, you know, it's really thick. And they sort of all fit together. You're like the general with about twenty armies that you're running.

Now when you're gonna write a story, before you begin, you have to have a pretty good idea of the kind of dialogue that's gonna take place in it, 'cause you've heard it somewhere and you've taken notes on it. And you have to have a very clear picture in your head of what your character looks like. Not only what they feel like to you, but what they look like physically. You know, their clothes and eyes and hair and all that sort of stuff, if they've got little dimples and so on, characteristics that are peculiarly their own. And then give them a problem, a problem that you've had in your life that you've been unable to solve. Because there you're gonna get in a lot of angst and it will really start taking on meaning because of it. But even then, you still mustn't write. You must then put everything in motion and see it. And it's gotta be really clear, you see it in your mind so it's stronger, even, than a movie. And once that's done, all you have to do then is to be a recorder. It'll write itself, because you're seeing something that's alive in your head. You've got everything clear in your head and it'll write itself.

It's a total focus on story as story, then, allowing the content to determine its own form?

That's right. I'm just a clerk, taking it down. That's why it writes easy, too. Once I start, they all just sort of run easy. Unlike my friend Nelson Algren, he said that he's always in the dark until he starts putting a sentence down. He doesn't know what's coming next at all.

I didn't want to write a book just to write a book. I would have these things in my head and pretty soon they made their own style. It makes it alive. And you see it. And it helps you write it. Algren told me that he never knew what the next sentence was gonna be about, and his books show it—they're staccato. Whereas, I think, when you read my books, once you get into 'em, you're sucked along. There's a real flow sucking you along all the time. That's because I have a tableau. It's alive, and people are moving on it.

When you begin a novel, it sounds as though you have a fair idea of where you're going. It isn't like some who prefer to discover more as the novel progresses.

I discover a little too. And I try not to look at that notebook unless I absolutely have to for a certain phrase, or something, that I don't remember. I'll know pretty much what's in there, but I try to follow what seems to come out of the writing

I'm doing. There's an interesting thing that goes on when characters start showing up and you think they should go this way and they have their own notion. You always follow where they want to go. Never force it, cause then it's wrong. Sharp readers'll pick it up right away. And I don't aim at any particular, specific ending either . . . . I'm just now learning how to write, by the way. I feel a little bit like Rubinstein who said at seventy he had just learned how to play the piano.

That brings to mind the accomplished sculptor in *Milk of Wolves* who preferred to be called a stonecutter so that he would always have someplace to aspire to.

It's as if I've finally learned what my voice really is, and it took all that time to do it. . . . People tell me that when they read my novels they can hear a voice through it all; that it's consistently through all of the works. I'm not aware of that voice. Even when I read my own things, I don't hear that. The voice doesn't hear itself. Even if I hear it on the tape, I'm always surprised at how it sounds.

And so in some ways I'm glad that I wasn't born into an intellectual family, you know, and too sophisticated. I was glad I was born sort of naive, and primitive, and a farm boy. Because in the process of learning to overcome it, you learn an enormous amount about yourself – where your powers are, where they're not, and all that. You resist people who try to tell you where to go, and you follow your own feelings. Whereas if you're born in a family where everything's pretty well worked out intellectually and sophisticated, then you're sort of caught. It's hard to escape that. The animal in you is gone.

In *Milk of Wolves* you have Jules equate the artistic drive with the sex drive. Is that anywhere close to your thinking?

Yeh, the two go together. Oh yes. *[laughs]* I've tried to hide that for some years. I have problems with the morality, you know, that I was raised in. But the truth is, that I'm very sexual – minded. But, I thought, what I'll do is just take the surplus and put it into novels . . . . It's part of animal health,

really. Part of animal health would be that you have a good
sex drive, you see.

Flowers of Desire **deals with sex within the context of
a highly religious society . . .**

Natural desires arise, and the church and society suppress
them, and I was trying to show that when natural desire goes
awry, look what happens. She [Karla] gets raped by these men,
but she doesn't do much about it.

She lets it happen.

Sure.

**And afterward she's naturally afraid that her strict Chris-
tian parents won't accept her. What surprised us was that
they forgave her much more quickly than we thought they
would.**

Well, it's their daughter. This is what I've noticed around
here. They'll be mad for one week. And then, well, "it's our
daughter."
I went to a wedding a week ago today. A girl in college
was very pregnant, and was going to get married in Luverne.
But I was curious, 'cause that's sort of Karla's story in a way.
The church was full, not of gossipers, really. Lot of women
there, some men, doctors and so on. 'Cause they all knew that
family. But you know they took a sort of pride in the fact
that this was a wedding that went off nice and they were married. And no one was pointing any fingers. They were probably
mad for about a week or two, you know. And I guess the father,
he says he's not gonna walk down the aisle with his daughter.
But the whole family converged on him and made him go. His
parents and his wife's parents. So, they don't want it to happen,
but if it does, they're still family, see? This is the way Siouxland works.

In *No Fun On Sunday,* Sherm's natural desire is undercut by a farm accident, as if the gods were somehow punishing him for trying to escape Siouxland's strict religiousness. Yet up to the accident you've described this desire—this need to play baseball—so vividly that religion has long before paled in comparison. There seems to be a bit of contradiction.

I've had that thrown at me before. But this is my answer, which I had beforehand, not after. You'll notice that he always likes to play slick, well. When he's farming he does it really well. He has the sense of discipline in him. Everything has to be neat. So when he's riding that corn picking machine, the very thing that's gonna lick him is himself; that he is super neat. He doesn't want that cornstalk bobbing around in there. It's an intrusion in his idea of neat-running machine. And he plays shortstop that way too, no errors. And so he has to have the cornstalk out of there. So it's his own sense of perfection that defeats him.

Is it pride?

Pride would be a piece of it. But the self-destruct is sitting with him all along. And the reason it's in there is because of the background he came from.

So he was never able to escape his background because the very seed of it was still in him. Do you find that true of yourself?

No, I escaped. And I don't mind going back to it because I know how to handle it all now. And I also like 'em and I understand that this is the way they are and there isn't much I can do about it. I'm not gonna argue with them. Let's live together.

Siouxland brings to mind D. H. Lawrence's idea of magnetism, or what he calls "spirit of place."

I would agree with that. Animals show that. You take a cat out of here and move it seventy miles, that cat's gonna be unhappy until it goes back to where it was born and raised.

There's something about a particular region that shapes a particular type?

It feeds you. Here's a story. We moved to this big half-section of land. Rats all over the place. The previous man tried to kill 'em and shoot 'em and poison 'em and so on. Well, my father was there a couple of weeks, and he says, "I know how I'm gonna get them." He says, "I'll bring some cats in here." Well the cats were there one day and they vanished. So then he thinks awhile and he says, "Well, I'll get a cat that's pregnant, and just about to have kits, and I'll put her here. And where those kits are born, those cats'll stay." And they did and the rats vanished. There's a real example of place at work.

Was the creation of Siouxland influenced by Faulkner's Yoknapatawpha?

No. The reason I invented Siouxland was, where I live along the Big Sioux River and the different little rivers that contribute to it *[draws an imaginary map on the table]*, here's the state of Minnesota, here comes South Dakota over here and Iowa sits over here. And I would be describing when I was writing *This Is the Year* that somebody drove from Bonnie instead of Doon, to Worthington, Minnesota, or from Bonnie to Sioux Falls, South Dakota, or from Bonnie to Sioux City, Iowa. And to a strange reader that would sound – they would say, "God, these people must drive for miles to get groceries!" When actually it's just a half hour drive or twenty-minute drive. And no one ever mentioned states over here. We'd just say we were going to Norfolk. That means Nebraska. And I thought, "Why don't I just drop all that state stuff and give the name for that Big Sioux River drainage basin?" So I went through a bunch of different things like "Big Sioux River Country" and so on, but I finally settled on Siouxland. And I drew up a map, which is in the end pages of the book *This Is the Year*.

I drew that up in '46, when I was finishing typing the book, and in '47, in April, when it came out, it was in the end pages. And within two months, all the advertising guys in Sioux City and Sioux Falls glommed onto it because it saved them from having to mention all these states. "Serving Siouxland," or "Serving Greater Siouxland" . . . that's all over the place . . . . So unlike Yoknapatawpha, which has never been picked up by anybody else except Faulkner, mine was taken by these people. It helped them a lot. Then I became aware of Wessex and Hardy. And I went back and looked it up, and then I became aware of Yoknapatawpha and John Steinbeck's Salinas Valley and so on. But I did it for a practical reason. I got sick of typing those states over and over again.

Faulkner said that the reason he was a novelist was because he was a failed poet. Do you see a connection between writing poetry and writing prose?

I think probably I started out as a poet in my head. I don't think I'm a very good poet, though. They tell me I write some good stuff, but I'm always careful about those remarks. Tom McGrath had several times told me that he wished I would write more poetry. He had seen a couple poems of mine, 'cause we visited over there in Madison with [Robert] Bly on Bly's farm . . . . My impulse is poetic, but I'm also a storyteller. 'Cause I had stories told to me all over the place. When you see *Of Lizards and Angels*, which is coming out next year, I have every now and then a chapter called "Stoop Talk," when the family sits out on the stoop in the evening in the summertime. And the sun is setting on the west side of the house there, and the east side, the shadow side, you know it's cool there, and pretty soon everybody starts talking. And endless stories were told on the stoop. Even if nothing happened during the day, they'd make it up—where they were in the day. And we had two words for that. Was it *wierheit*? Or was it *grapje*? *Wierheit* meant it was a true story. *Grapje* meant, "You're makin it up." These are Frisians. And Frisians are kind of a family-oriented iconoclastic people amongst others. They are quite a tight family. When you read the book you'll see that: they're

really tight. So story telling is a big part of me. And I do
tend to invent stories.

**Why are most of your stories and novels set in the past
rather than in the time when you were living?**

Well, it's because I've lived so goddamn long. I do like
to go into the previous history, you know. I had in mind
doing a history in fiction of Siouxland from 1800 to the day
I died. And I slowly have been filling in that whole long hallway
of murals, novels, poems, short stories, you know, to fill in
the little corners and so on. The new one, *Of Lizards and Angels*,
starts in 1880 and goes to 1960. And the one I'm writing now
goes up to the very day I quit writing. See, so I will cover
the whole world. And I hope to get to the year 2,000. Because
I have two more projects beyond the one I'm on now that I'd
like to have at it. They're gonna be very contemporary.

But I'm having a little trouble there. My ear for contemporary dialogue isn't all that keen anymore, because it isn't
related to my life so much. My father, he made a remark about
the reason he wanted to die after his third wife died. He said,
"I got nobody to talk to anymore." "Well you've got us, dad."
"Ya, but I had to have you. There's nobody that I worked up
to have as friends of my own," he says. "Everybody that I
can talk to about the old days is gone." And I wrote that quite
a few years ago, and my god, it's come to haunt me. I have
been eager and willing to make friends with new people, provided they're brainy and creative. I don't want anybody that's
just an ordinary critic. But somebody that's creative, I do try
to cultivate them, often misunderstood, by the way, which I
can't help either. I'm gonna have trouble with that, I think,
to really learn what's goin' on in your mind, for example, in
her mind and your mind. I'll have trouble with that. I don't
have your common experiences. Look at the experiences I had
as a boy. You know, I grew up with nothing of so-called modern
civilization. No telephone, no radio, finally a phonograph one day.

**Your writing style has remained consistent over the years,
despite literary movements that have come and gone. Did you**

ever have debates with friends of yours, such as William Carlos Williams, over the way you should write?

Well, I used to have some fierce arguments with Allen Tate. And then in the letters, there's one in there to John C. Ransom, which is really terribly disrespectful. I had sent him some short stories at the *Kenyon Review*, and he had sent them back to me, saying they really weren't for him—they were rustic and primitive and had country vernacular and Siouxlandisms and so on. So then I thought about that and I wrote him and I said, "Well, it's too bad you didn't take 'em, I thought probably it would be good for your magazine," I said. "The other day I was reading one of your stories and I was having an awful time with it—it was so structured and so intellectual and all that. And finally in there they used the word 'beer' and I had to shout to my wife and say, 'Wow, the story's a success!' " *[laughs]* I was really stickin' it into him, you know. But in that sense, I did argue with a lot of those fellows. Robert Penn Warren . . . Warren, though, was wonderful with me. He kept telling me, "I don't like it that you've got so much autobiographical stuff in your things, but then that's up to you, you're who you are. Don't let anybody tell you that that's wrong." He had a lot of Modernist ideas when you were discussing with him. He knew that world far better than I did.

Were you not influenced by them at all?

I'd listen, but it didn't take. *[laughs]*

Now, let's see, when *Lord Grizzly* came out, I was at an English Department party [at the University of Minnesota] and a guy named Morgan Bloom—who went to Kenyon College and was trained by Ransom and Allen Tate and all those fellows—and Tate were there that night. And I was in one corner of the room and I heard—see, I have quite good peripheral eyes, and I saw them lookin' at me, and I was picking it up, sort of off to one side while I was busy with somebody else. And, then, after a few minutes, I heard them saying that "He wrote *Lord Grizzly*" and so on. And one of them said, "Well it was quite good reading," and well, Tate wasn't sure, the form wasn't really quite right. And then Morgan Bloom says, "No, the whole point-of-view of the thing is wrong. In whose mind are we finally looking at all this? There should be, like Warren does in *All the King's Men*, a commentator, who can talk about things here. But suddenly you're over here, and how can you be in this man and still be objective about it?" Well, to myself I thought, "I know now what I'm doing, and I'm doing it right. And people read it, and they get lost in it when I write it right."

You know, some people, when they get into *Lord Grizzly*, they just can't stop. Or *Conquering Horse*. Or *Scarlet Plume*. So I didn't say anything there, but I started thinking this over and talking to Maryanna. Now Maryanna was an extremely bright woman, and she was very impatient with me and what crazy ideas I'd come up with. But she listened real carefully that night. She said "I had the same problem. How could you give us Hugh Glass and be in him, and yet not be in him?" And that's a good observation, you know. And I said, "Well, when I wrote that book, I was in Hugh, but at the same time there was another pair of eyes just behind his head *[laughs]*." And it's all together, but its another pair of eyes sittin' over here, behind his head. This pair of eyes is my eyes sittin' behind his head in the story, see. And that's how that thing was written.

It's a cinematic approach.

It really is.

You had some experiences with moviemaking, didn't you? Do you feel the movies are compatible at all with serious writing?

I got a rumor that somebody was interested out there in Hollywood. Sammy Goldwyn Jr., he wanted to make a movie out of *Lord Grizzly*. So Waring Jones, my friend, he and I get in the car and we drive out there and we spend some time.

And this was what one of the movie stars they approached to take the role of Hugh Glass said, "Who do I act against?" And I said to myself, "What a hell of a question that is. I had to make interesting for two hundred pages, a guy who was alone!

And that's on the paper, but pictorially that should be easy!" You know, if you're any good at all, you can act out of yourself instead of against somebody. So I mentioned that one time to Sammy Goldwyn Jr., and also a guy named William Froug, who was the executive director of the CBS Dramatic Department in Los Angeles.

And then we met one time in the Cock and Bull, and I told him who I was. See, Froug read the book and wanted Walter Brown Newman, who was known as the dean of all screenwriters in Hollywood for a long time, to write the screenplay. And then Newman said well he had difficulty with this and that, and I said "Goddamnit I'll write a screenplay for you guys. But that's the only one I'm ever gonna do." And Froug kinda laughed a little bit. And I went home then, and I wrote the screenplay and I sent it to him. And about three weeks later the phone rang, and he says, "Oh my god," he says, "This is wonderful. The only trouble is your fade ins and fade outs aren't in there." All that technical stuff.

So then I went [back out] to see Bill, and he and I would discuss it in the evening, and then during the day I'd work on the script and put in the stuff that was for the director. After three weeks, we put it all together, and he started parceling out scripts, and they said they would be interested in doing it, provided they got Burt Lancaster. So then we approached Ben Benjamin, Burt Lancaster's agent, and Benjamin had read the book by this time, and he got all excited. And he said, "Don't worry, that's a lock. We'll have Burt in there." And we had everything going, and then Burt Lancaster decided to do *El Hombre*. There went that dream.

It sounds like Hollywood was too much of a hassle.

Besides, it's an entirely different way of doing things. When you're writing a novel, you're trying to make that page come alive, up off that page, what's going on in there [points to an imaginary book]. When you write for Hollywood, it's what do you put up on the wall there? And that's an entirely different way of thinking, and I didn't want to learn to think that way too much. I'm a novelist, not a screenwriter.

Are there any contemporary novelists that you read today?

Saul Bellow writes animated essays, from my point of view, and not fiction at all. That he should get the Nobel is just one of the — and meanwhile here's Robert Penn Warren, brilliant poetry at the end, and at least two great novels, *All the King's Men*, and *Meet Me in the Green Glen* is a marvelous novel. But his poems are great. And then there's Frank Waters, who was really pretty good, and then Vardis Fisher, who should have been recognized. And then Wallace Stegner probably should have had the Nobel by this time too instead of Bellow.

And I can't stand John Updike. He reminds me of a pretty boy that's loved by his mother and every now and then he has to shock his mother by using a four letter word. I met him one time. And it absolutely fit with what I thought of his books. I met him at an International PEN convention. I'm wandering around alone, didn't know anybody there, and all of a sudden a newspaper woman stopped me and said, "I'm from *Life* and I'd like to take your picture. And I said, "Oh, god, what for?" "Well, you're an interesting looking man, and," she says, "I'd like to have you take a picture with John Updike, he's behind that pillar there." "Well," I said, "All right." So we walk over there, and she tells him where she's from, and he says — he said it diffidently — he said, "Well, all right," you know *[raises nose]*. But as she was taking pictures, he kept circling around me. And I said, "What the hell's the matter?" "Well," he says, "she's gonna take my bad side." Wow. I thought, "Well you poor bastard. I have no good sides at all! And even if I did, I wouldn't be worried about it. The hell with it." He lost me forever. I was gonna give him a chance before that. So I haven't read his *Rabbit Run*. I've tried to, but I can't stand him. And also, he went through the New Yorker discipline, you know. And they pare you off. Anything that sticks out is pared off.

And Minnesota writers, do you read them? Garrison Keillor, for example.

I'll tell you, he's not a very good writer. He's a marvelous raconteur, though. On the air he sounds great. I used to love his programs. And a very bright man, and that whole town of Wobegon. Except he should've spelled it with an "E." Not Wo-begon, but W-o-e-begon. Yeah. Should have had really the whole word there. But I never dared to tell him that. I met him one time. I bought a book of his and had him autograph it, the first one, *Lake Wobegon Days*. And all he did was: "This is the first book of a whole series before I can match you." On the number of books, see. And they were all claiming that he was the new Mark Twain of our era, you know. But his stuff doesn't go over, to me. I tried to like it, cause he's from Minnesota. I did read the whole thing, and I read part of another one, and then I stopped. I'll give a guy a hundred pages. And if he doesn't win me over, it's too bad for him.

Has J. F. Powers won you over?

He's a precision writer, and very good. I've got all his books. I've read them all carefully. With *Wheat that Springeth Green* I wasn't convinced, though. It was as if it was a book that had been interrupted many times, so the emotional core is broken continually. A book should feel as if it's a solid core of emotion all the way through; be all of one piece. And that book is interrupted. On the surface it looks connected, but when you let the thing work on you then you think oh my god where's this going? I don't feel this. And then you have to read four or five pages and you don't pick it up. Course, if he takes ten, twelve years to write it, you know. . . .

Some say his short stories are his best work.

Oh, by far. I like all his stories. In fact, when I start writing stories here in a couple years I'm gonna study how he went about his. His and Wallace Stegner's, and that woman from the south, Eudora Welty. Who talks too much. Yeah, in her books, if you read her stuff it's talky talky talky talky. The author hardly ever says anything and the landscape doesn't

say much, you know. But I still want to study her because
she's very good.

What about John Hassler?

Oh, yeh. There's a guy. He really started writing a little
late. He was in his forties. And it's marvelous what he's done.
But the bloom of youth is out of it. It's not there—the passion
of youth. It's sort of a measured passion. But I have told him
that if he wrote ten books like the first one, *Staggerford*, I
said, "You'll push Sinclair Lewis aside." And I think he might.
'Cause it's solid recording in fiction, you know. And it's all really quite good. And good dialogue, and good characterization
and so on. But there's something missing there. Passion or
verve or something. Well, I haven't read the last two. And
somebody tells me that they're wonderful. The last one is really
fine. Dave Wood [*Minneapolis Star Tribune*] is nuts about him.
He's always mentioning him in his pages, you know. And that's
great. And Dave has made a success out of him. He's become
a bestseller and he's sold to Hollywood. So Dave is to be highly
complimented for doing that, and I'm all for it. I think Dave
has gotten the impression, when he looks at my age, "Well,
he can't do anything after fifty," you know. And so he's hardly
given any attention to my stuff in the last while. He always
gives it to some mediocre fellow from South Dakota who doesn't
know what the hell I'm doing.

How do you deal with critics?

Someone should say, "Hey, there's this book out here. I
don't like it, but there's this book." That's okay. Because I used
to say the same thing about Faulkner, I couldn't stand him
until I got *The Portable Faulkner*. And when I read that I
changed my mind about him. So it's possible to change your
mind. But I kind of go along with Brendan Behan about the
critics. He says they remind him of eunuchs. They watch how
its done all day long, but they still can't do it themselves. To
call attention to things is probably why you need them. I suppose if I hadn't written I would have become kind of a sourbutt
kind of critic.

You mentioned before how some of your books have been criticized for being overly macho, overly male. How do you respond to that?

Well I can't help it. Too bad. The hell with ya. You know, if you think I'm really bad, then you should lock me up. Shoot me, see. I don't want to lock you up, or shoot you, for whatever you happen to be. Chaucer is a great example for me. Thank god he only had to write for John of Gaunt and his court, just a few people. Just a few copies around, see. He didn't have to worry about a damn public . . . . He felt free to write about the Wife of Bath and the Miller. That was a great relief, to know what he had been doing when I started reading him. Oh, that was an explosion.

What is your favorite Frederick Manfred book?

I like 'em all, really. Let me put it this way, I thought I drove the deepest in *King of Spades*. Many people object to that book because I brought in the Oedipus complex. But I wasn't thinkin' about the Oedipus complex. I was thinking about an article I ran across in a Rock Rapids, Iowa, paper, which told about a doctor who killed his wife and his son and then committed suicide. And then I found out that when he married her she was thirteen.

See in those days, in the pioneer days, any woman – the moment she was nubile – she was a candidate for marriage, or at least to get the attention of a male, see. So many women, like in Kentucky, got married when they were thirteen, fourteen years old. So then he was around thirty when he married her. Suppose that instead of all three dying, all three survived but didn't know about each other surviving. And have it happen that the shooting takes place when the boy is six. Now, when she's about twenty-eight, thirty, her boy's seventeen. And he'll probably wear a beard. And she looks like she's about twenty-three, and he looks like about twenty-five, so if they accidently met, what would happen? Would they recognize each other instinctively? Would their animal and animus recognize each other.

The other part of the answer is writing about my family—
my father and mother, and then myself and my brothers in
Green Earth. Those aren't really my favorites, I just seemed
to have put more into those two than any other two.

Do you consider them your best then?

Well, I'll tell ya. Until I wrote *Of Lizards and Angels*, up
until four years ago, I would have said to you, "I'll never beat
King of Spades." But I think now I've gone past that. The
[Oklahoma Press readers' responses] seem to agree with that too.

**How have you changed from when you were first writing?
Have you changed a great deal?**

Well, I'm more comfortable with what I'm doing, and I
don't worry anymore about what people that I'm related to
might say, or people in the area. Also, I'm no longer really
writing for them anymore. When I was first writing, I thought
if I could only write something that would please my wife and
John K. Sherman, the book reviewer for the *Minneapolis Star*
at the time, and possibly even get Edmund Wilson to say
something nice—that's who I wrote for. But then I decided
hey, that's wrong. I shouldn't worry about what they think.
Pretty soon they'll die. Then there'll be new people who'll come
along.
    Then I thought, I'm gonna write a book that I'd like to
find in the library, discover a new author. I used to do that;
go down the stacks and see if I could find somebody that no
one had ever heard of before—"I'm first at him," you know.
Then I decided one day, that's wrong too, because then I'm
aiming at something, some kind of an invisible ideal or an invisible audience.
    Then I thought, well, at least I'll write a book to please
myself. And then I decided that maybe that's wrong too. I
should just be the scribe and let the book write itself and not
worry about what I think. And there's the big difference from
when I first started and where I am now. It's like skins that
you shed, see, 'til your real skin comes to the surface. It took

a long while. That's why I can say I feel like I'm just now learning to write, because I don't worry about all those little concerns I used to have. And I'm quite comfortable with it.

Dr. William Harry Jellema
1893-1982

Early in September of 1930, my father drove me from Doon, Iowa, to Perkins Corner, Iowa, where I was to catch a ride with Edward Bierma, Chris Gesink, John DeBie, and Johan TeVelde in an old Ford sedan bought for one dollar. Bierma was a junior and a pre-law student at Calvin, Gesink was a senior and a pre-seminarian, and DeBie, TeVelde, and I were to become freshmen.

It was Bierma who had kept in touch with me during the two years I stayed home from school, 1928-1930. Bierma loved baseball and his Sioux Center church team and the Doon church team often clashed at church picnics, most notably on the Fourth of July.

I'd become restless working on my father's farm east of Doon after graduating form Western Academy in Hull, Iowa, in 1928. I did manage during those two years at home to keep up on good reading. A doctor's wife, Mrs. E. J. Bild, when she learned I loved to read supplied me with mint copies of the complete Jack London and the complete James Fenimore Cooper. With cornpicking money I bought from Sears Roebuck the complete (though bowderlized) Shakespeare and I managed to read him complete too before taking off for college.

After those two years I couldn't see myself as a future farmer of America who liked to read in his spare time. I saw myself as someone who might try to write a classic or two myself. I still remember walking across the farm yard carrying a bushel basket of earcorn for the hogs savoring the reading of the night before and muttering to myself: "You know Jack and James for all their reputation still don't give me the 'really real.' And someday when I write my novels the reader is going to forget how they were written and instead feel the grit and blood of real life as if they're lost in it up to their neck." It was going to be vivid and true and poetic. If possible.

But as we five rode toward Calvin what college life was going to mean to me of that I didn't have the least notion. Stories told by our ministers who'd gone to Calvin, or told by Bierma and Gesink, still didn't give me much of a picture of the campus, of the kind of students I'd meet, or what the prevailing weather was like in Western Michigan.

The first couple of days I went around in a numbed state of mind on the campus. I was given an upstairs room in the dormitory. I was dumbfounded by all the bright literate talk during the meals and out in the lobby. Where were the cornstalks? Where were the Iowa birds? Where were the lovely rising and falling slopes of what I later on called Siouxland? I could literally feel people staring at my six-foot-nine frame, at the suit that really didn't fit, at the shoes that were too small for me. At the age of eighteen I had a size sixteen foot and the biggest shoes made until then were twelves by Florsheim— so a person can imagine how my feet hurt on each step and how I longed to walk barefoot. I also had two cowlicks one of which I had to mash down with grease.

It was Gesink who took pity on my bewilderment. He was a dormitorian and he took me under his wing. When he discovered that I only had fifty dollars for money, he urged me to go see President R. B. Kuiper and tell him about it. Kuiper saw me right away, listening with those sparkling dark eyes of his. He decided he liked me and he arranged for a well-to-do relative of my father to help me out. "Now that you're here, Mr. Feikema, we're going to keep you on the campus." Later on he found a job for me as one of three janitors in the Dorm.

Gesink next took me by the arm and led me to the Hekman Library and helped me work out my class schedule. "You should get the prerequisites out of the way the first two years. After that you can major in what you like best." And one of the classes he registered for me was Logic taught by Dr. Harry Jellema. "He's the best man here. And besides, you better learn to think straight right away. Around Calvinists who are fiends for logical thinking you'd better know about logic."

So it was in Logic that I came upon the teacher I instantly recognized as a great man. He taught his class gently but firmly. He had a warm heart-smile. He was patient with fumbling questions. After a while he made me feel that I wasn't such a fumbler after all. Good thinkers all begin with fumbling inquiry, looking for the right thought and then the right words (the two often arrived in the mind simultaneously) and then summoning up the courage to express oneself in front of one's peers, let alone the wise teacher.

From my freshman year on I took all his classes. He had to give me a C in Logic, and I saw the logic in that. What a vast difference there was in the things he was telling me and the complexities I learned on the farm: driving spirited horses, of picking corn by hand, of sawing wood for the stove in the house, of planting of crops, of fending off the gibes and jeers of farm and smalltown fellows who couldn't understand why I loved to read and why I had even tried several times to write "really real" stories for *Liberty, Colliers,* and *Wallace's Farmer.* Actually, I learned more in that class than I was given credit for with that C. I learned that to write well you had to think well. I learned that perhaps while the pursuit of philosophy was one of the most far-reaching and all-embracing of human mental endeavour, the most poignant and pointed and glittering of human gifts was the creation of poetry, "poetry" in the larger sense of writing plays, stories, poems. It was Dr. Jellema who later on engendered in me the possible thought to see that the creation of a good epic, a good story, a good play far outlasts theories of political science, of theoretical scientific inquiry. Who remembers who was president when Homer wrote the *Iliad* and the *Odyssey*? and moving on to later times who was president when Cervantes wrote *Don Quixote*? when Camoens wrote *The Lusiads*? when Goethe wrote *Faust*? And moving to a still later time, who have been our greatest presidents? They were the writers Thomas Jefferson and Abraham Lincoln, because they were artists first of all. To write well you have to think well. (And I stress that word "well.")

One morning in late March 1933, first hour class, after entering the classroom as he stuffed his ever-present pipe into his jacket pocket and dropped his leather briefcase on his desk,

Dr. Jellema announced: "Today we will try to a different tactic to understand what we were discussing in our last class." From his briefcase he extracted the last issue of the student publication *The Chimes* (March 2, 1933), and began reading from it. One line into it and I knew instantly he was reading my short story, "A Harvest Scene." I almost exploded. Instantly I managed to freeze a solemn expression on my face because I didn't want my classmates (and friends) see me preening myself in vain pride. But I could feel all those startled eyes on my right (I was sitting by the window) stabbing at me.

When he finished the reading, he went on to say that we had in that story an example of clarity of vision. Everything was vividly presented, as if the reader was there watching the young boy making his precise rounds with the binder in an over-ripe oatsfield. Reading the piece the reader was given the first knowings of a harvest time, a prolegomenon, an introductory observation about farming, told in the form of a gripping story. When a philosopher enters a new field he takes a look around to see what the situation is, what are the givens. The same would be true for the scientist or the theologian.

Well, later on, back in my room in the dorm, I knew two things: one was I could write, and the other was I was probably deeper than I'd realized.

I'm sure that because of what happened that day the word got around to the members of the Plato Club. That was *the* club on the campus. The members were the crown princes of deep thinking. One didn't dare to apply to get in, even hint at it. If one did, he was forthwith dismissed forever as a possible candidate. Before the end of my junior year that spring, I was told that I'd been elected to the club for the next year. And at about the same time I was elected president of the literary Pierian Club.

That Plato Club and how it was "run" by Dr. Jellema our faculty sponsor became the model for my writing classes later on, at Macalaster College in St. Paul, Minnesota, at the University of South Dakota, and at Augustana College in Sioux Falls, South Dakota.

Usually there were twelve members in the Plato Club. Each member was assigned to write one paper for the year, a paper that was to be mimeographed (we didn't have the new copying machines) and a copy given to each member at least a week before he was to present it. Then on his night, which began at seven-thirty, he was to furnish coffee and doughnuts and arrange for a meeting place. Sometimes we met in a private home, sometimes in the back of the dining hall in the dorm.

Dr. Jellema was always there with his pipe and his waiting smile and his patient final remarks after each brisk exchange. Sometimes the argument became quite heated. I remember once I argued that Plato was wrong to demand the death penalty. (Our papers, by the way, took different ideas from Plato for a text.) I said killing was killing even if the state committed it, and all killing was wrong. A wonderful fellow student named Curley Magaw took my side. Finally, after listening to all the heated exchanges, Jellema pointed out that the dignity of the state in certain cases did demand the death penalty. There are some crimes that were totally inhuman and totally unchristian and so had to be punished. I remember that Curly and I remarked that only God could say, "Vengeance is mine," and not human beings who might be kings or presidents or premiers.

Later on in the writing classes I conducted I told my students they'd be marked only on two things: 1) their final paper which had to be copied beforehand and handed around to the other members of the class, and 2) their part in class discussions.

Of course, I also leaned heavily on my memory of how Dr. Jellema conducted his classes, especially his warm disciplined manner.

Somewhere along the line, both in the Plato Club and in his classes, Jellema often remarked when a student questioned the existence of God, that the question was already answered by the question. "All philosophers agree that we are born into a situation. One cannot escape that. I happen to believe that that situation is God as Universe. Trying to deny it is like trying to deny that one has been encased in a body. One is in it to begin with. Or rather, one finds oneself in it. We grow up in an environment that is God and, like fish out of water, we would die without Him." That statement by Jellema has given me much freedom in my pursuit of learning, in my reading, in my writing. Since I am already safely caught up in that overall construct, and since I was also given a vigorous inquiring mind, it allows me to question everything, and so gives me the satisfaction of learning how great Creation, the Universe, really is. The findings of Einstein, Bohr, Shrödinger, Dirac, Guth et al. don't in the least disconcert me. Assuming there is a God, I'm sure He'd want me to discover in great detail just how great He is.

Because of the electrifying experience of hearing Dr. Jellema read my story, "A Harvest Scene," in his philosophy class, I finally dared to ask him about something that had bothered me for some time. I'd noticed that certain classmates of mine, the really bright ones, were getting A's while I was getting only B's. I didn't think they were that much brighter than I. I knew in talking to them after final examinations that I'd come up with the same answers they had. So after I'd finished my exam paper in late May of my junior year, I appended a little note: "Professor Jellema, how come I don't get A's when I know I have all the right answers?" Those who took classes from him may remember he had only one question for us to interpret and to explicate. It was usually a long and searching question. He gave us the cord out of which we were to make a rosary of the year, that is, string the different beads, the different points discussed for that semester, onto that cord. Some of my classmates not only filled an entire bluebook but sometimes half-filled another. I usually had my explication, my notion of the rosary, finished in a few pages.

When I got back my bluebook with its usual final mark of a B, this is what I found at the end of it in his handwriting: "Dear Mr. Feikema: Yes, you do have all the right answers. But you arrive at them intuitively, not philosophically, and I have to mark you on your philosophical ability and not your intuitive ability."

Well, he was right. But he was more right than he might have realized. Or, perhaps, he actually did know. I was already a poet, a teller of tales, perhaps even a bard of some note.

Several years before he died, when I happened to visit the Calvin College campus, I received a message from him. Would

I have time to visit him, have a cup of coffee with him? Of course. It was arranged that I'd see him one morning.

He looked like he was in excellent health. His hair was white but still thick. He had on a pair of dark-rimmed glasses, dark tie with a thick knot snugged up into the collar of a dark shirt, somewhat rumpled jacket, and his pipe with its wisps of smoke. We retired to his book-lined study. He inquired about my family; and I his.

Presently we began to talk ideas. He was still the wonderful raconteur, both in delineating an idea as well as recounting a happening with students. He asked me endless questions about why I had written certain of my books. What had been my intention when I started writing a book. What was I trying to say. Soon it was noon. To my surprise he'd arranged for someone to bring us sandwiches, doughnuts, and coffee.

Later in the afternoon, I had a question for him. Had modern philosophers finally gotten around to accepting the findings of those of us who had "arrived at the right answers intuitively?" His face wreathed up in a great wide smile. He remembered. Yes, he said, they had. His only worry was they might not be thinking clearly with their kind of logic, if logic it was. Clarity was still the thing in all human discussion and inquiries.

Then I had another question for him. Reminding him of that story of mine he'd read in class, I asked, "Was it possible to consider the writing of a first-rate play say by Sophocles, or a first-rate epic say by Homer, or a first-rate novel say by Melville, as a legitimate form of philosophical inquiry? Would the modern philosopher accept such a proposition?"

Again there was that wide smile and those alert eyes. "That's an interesting question, Feikema. I've occasionally wondered about that myself. It's probably too late in life for me to dig into that. I'll leave that to the younger philosophers."

"Say, an Alvin Plantinga?"

He nodded.

Late in the afternoon his relative stepped into the house and in a gentle manner suggested that perhaps it was time to end the talk.

As I got to my feet to leave, I asked, "Have you ever looked into the findings of the quantum mechanic fellows?

Einstein, Bohr, Planck, Dirac, Guth? Who think they've found out about the fundamental nature of the universe?"

He smiled some more. "What they've found doesn't much change the original structure of things. Like you and me, they too are caught up in God as Universe, and they may just have come up with some new terms."

I didn't sleep well that night. It was a good state to be in after that wonderful day with a great man.

Prognosis: *Terminal*

Reading Stephen S. Hall's review of Frank Ryan's *The Forgotten Plague* stirred up some old, haunting memories. (Re: *New York Times Book Review*, August 1, 1993.)

In April of 1940, I had just finished washing dishes in a teahouse on Washington Avenue, in Minneapolis, and had almost reached my boarding house on 316 Walnut Street, S.E., near the University of Minnesota, when suddenly I began to cough up blood, and moments later such a powerful cramp seized my chest that I fell down on the sidewalk.

It happened that some of the college fellows who were boarding with me in the same house saw me. They ran out and carried me into the house and up to my bed. And it further happened that a pre-medic named Howard Johnson who also roomed at 316 came bustling into my little room to see what all the fuss was about. He sat a while beside me helping me catch my breath. After my breathing steadied, he asked me to spit into a brown wax cup. He particularly asked me to cough deep to catch phlegm coming from my lungs.

That night he came into my room and told me that he had examined the sputum under a microscope and found that I had tuberculosis. My spit was full of tubercle bacillus. He told me it was against the law for me, an active case, to walk around in public and that he felt he should call a doctor at the Lymanhurst Clinic about me. He said, "Not only is your life at stake, but also the welfare of other people." I told him to make whatever arrangements were necessary to have me sent to a sanatorium. Soon an ambulance took me to Lymanhurst, where it was confirmed that I had tuberculosis. They asked me to sign a pauper's oath, which gave me free hospital care, and then the same ambulance brought me to the Glen Lake Sanatorium at Oak Terrace, Minnesota. All I remember of that ride was that I noticed the maple trees had just begun to bud out.

They didn't right away put me in a room. I was left out in the hallway on the second floor and some screens were placed around my bed. That evening an orderly named John brought me a tray of food. Much to his surprise, but not to mine, I ate all the food. Later on when I overheard John talking to a nurse I learned that the doctors weren't sure I'd make the night. That was why I'd been left out in the hallway. But I knew something about my raging fever. I'd always been able to eat when ill, with the flu, a touch of pneumonia, or streptococcus. I knew that my cast-iron stomach would carry me through.

After a week I was given a bed in a room. I had two other roommates, both old and both farmers. I learned from them that the man who'd occupied the corner I now had had been a chronic whose lungs wouldn't heal and he'd finally died after sixteen years of bedrest. Sixteen years. Actually I was down so low in my bones that the figure meant little to me. I now had a good bed, with clean white sheets, with lovely nurses to watch over me, and with regular food. And soon I had my own staff doctor. Sumner Cohen, M.D. What Dr. Cohen didn't know was that I'd been unemployed for almost a year, and when my unemployment checks ran out courtesy of the *Minneapolis Journal*, I didn't eat well. Working at the teahouse gave me one meal a day.

I was weighed and discovered I'd lost some fifty pounds. My six-foot-nine gaunt body registered at 175. Every morning an orderly came by to pick up our sputum cups. At first my cups was almost always full. But after a month the amount of sputum slowly lessened. Meanwhile x-rays showed that I had shadows in my right lung and possibly a hole the size of a golfball in my left lung. They had some difficulty seeing the cavity in the left lung, due mostly to the fluid caused by pleurisy. It was the pleurisy that had caused me to fall down on Walnut Street.

One morning an orderly came along and announced that he had been instructed to bring me down to Dr. Cohen's office. He helped me slide onto a gurney and wheeled me downstairs.

In the midst of all that slow death Dr. Cohen always managed
a kindly warm smile. He was balding and had a pair of wise
owl's eyes. He reviewed my case. While doing so the phone
rang. He listened a moment and then hung up. He excused
himself saying he'd be back shortly. I lay there quietly for a
minute, all the while staring at my file where he'd placed it
on his desk. I'd learned from the head nurse on my floor that
the last page of one's file had a heading called Prognosis. I
reached over and flipped to that last page. And there, in Dr.
Sumner Cohen's immaculate penmanship, was a single word:
Terminal. I put the file back on his desk. I lay back, nuzzling
my head in my pillow. So. That was the verdict. Well. Well.
Memory of all those wonderful baseball games I'd played,
memory of all those great books I'd read would soon vanish forever. At that particular moment, though, I was quietly pleased
to see that I was taking it quite calmly. There wasn't much
life left in my bones to get excited about losing it forever.

Four months later, my sputum turned negative. Gone was
the little yellow fleck of pus in the saliva. During that interval
I had a half-dozen new roommates – some of whom went home
for a time, some of whom died. And finally I was fortunate
to have two doctor roommates, Merriam Fredricks, a der-
matologist, and Harry Wilmer, who later went back to the university to get his degree as a psychiatrist. From that point on
the members of the San medical staff often visited our room,
and from their talk I learned much about the sanatorium and
about tuberculosis.

Somewhere in August of that year, I surprised the nurse
who came by to weigh us. I'd suddenly in a few weeks picked
up ten pounds. My temperature leveled off at 97.6, which turned
out to be my normal level. I was given the right to stand by
my bed for ten minutes, even drag my feet to the window and
look out at the green lawns and the evergreen trees. Soon after
I was given the right to walk to the bathroom. Gone was that
utterly revolting business of sitting on a bedpan – especially
as it happened that with my huge size it was a little like balanc-
ing an elephant on a dinner plate.

By January 6th of 1941, when I became twenty-nine years
old, I was startled to learn that I'd gained one-hundred-four

pounds, that I weighed two-hundred-seventy-nine pounds. And I looked quite good with all that weight. It was probably what I should have weighed all along. The gaunt hollows and the fallen-in belly were gone.

It took a year before I was allowed to take short walks. And it took another half year before I could walk a mile.

All that time Dr. Cohen asked me not to do any writing. It was too exciting for me. But I could write letters. Which I did. I'd met Maryanna Shorba near the x-ray room one day and we began to correspond. She was a junior at the University of Minnesota majoring in journalism. They never found any bugs on her but she had shadows in both lungs and as a precautionary measure asked her to take the cure. Bedrest for at least a year.

I also corresponded with my father's family, with my brothers, and with Peter DeVries. I did write a few poems, mostly about Maryanna.

Best was that with my good eyes I could read. The librarians at the San got me books of all sorts: Spengler, Darwin, Plato's *Dialogues* (which I read through twice), Hemingway, Faulkner, Dickenson, Melville, Chaucer (I can read him with ease because I know the Frisian language), Steinbeck, Frost, and many others. It was an endless feast – great food on the tray table and great food in the books.

When I was allowed to leave the San for a few hours, Maryanna, who was released early, came to get me in her Ford and I once again saw the countryside around Lake Minnetonka.

And I must not forget my father's visits. Here I was his oldest son, whose real name should have been Frisian, Feike Feikes Feikema VII, just as his name legally was Feike Feikes Feikema VI, and I lay dying. The possible end of the direct line of Feikemas. He always came in with a quietly reassuring smile; and then would sit with tears running down his tan cheeks while holding my hand. It was a two-hundred mile drive up from Doon, Iowa, to the San. About then I had just finished reading Homer's *Iliad*, and Pa's sitting by my bed crying always reminded me of Priam of Troy weeping over the body of his son Hector.

I still had three months to go according to Dr. Cohen, legally, but I decided I'd had enough. My bright doctor roommates had left, Maryanna had gone to live in Minneapolis and had started going to classes at the University. So I told Cohen I was going. Could he assign me to the halfway house, the Sarah Hurst Home? He had come to know me and knew that once I'd made up my mind about something I did it. There was going to be no stopping me. I spoke to him as gently as I could, yet firmly. After all, as he said, I was his pet patient because of what my body had overcome. And you had to be a damned stubborn fool to still want to write novels and poems. He did make one firm request of me. "Fred, don't go back to the hectic life of the newspaper world. Write if you must, but do it in your spare time after you've worked at little spare-time jobs."

The last month at the San I had been allowed to go to the dining hall and eat with patients who'd soon be leaving. I said good-bye to all of them, to the nurses who'd been sweet to me, to social worker Margaret Ridler who'd told the FBI to leave me alone (I'd earlier refused to register for the draft), and who'd further listed me (without my permission) as 4F because of my T.B. and because of my height. She told the FBI, "He's a sore bear in his bed and all you'll do is rile him up and that'll make sure he'll die."

Shortly after I'd arrived at the Sarah Hurst house I got a part-time job writing medical briefs for *Modern Medicine*. And then next I persuaded Maryanna into marrying me. We went to the Little Brown Church in the Vale. She was a Catholic and I was a member of the Christian Reformed Church. We thought that going to the Little Brown Church was a good way to satisfy our past history as Christians.

Every day I walked two miles to work across town in the morning and two miles back home early in the afternoon. It took months before I got used to that regimen. I studied books on diet. I learned to eat hearty uncooked food such as green peppers, tomatoes, carrots, broccoli, apples, oranges, and apricots. I also drank skim milk and ate boiled eggs and broiled lambchops. As time went on muscle replaced fat and my weight dropped from two-seventy-nine to two-forty. Today as I write this, I weigh two-twenty. I live alone on six acres of land out in the country on a high hill, and keeping the weeds down and caring for a large garden and taking four-mile walks keeps me in good shape.

Shortly after we were married, I wrote an article about Hubert Humphrey who'd lost in a run for the mayor of Minneapolis and about Harold Stassen, governor of Minnesota. In it I predicted that Humphrey might become President some day, but not Stassen. Humphrey was warm and brilliant; Stassen was cold and brilliant. I titled it "Report From Minnesota" and it was published in *The New Republic*, October 11, 1943. It was my first publication outside the newspaper world.

Talking with Hubert and Muriel, my wife and I decided we should throw a party. Hubert had dreams of running for the United States Senate the next year. Parties usually get me all worked up; and it happened again that night. And you can imagine my mortification when I couldn't remember my wife's name when I wanted to introduce her to a friend of Hubert. Quickly, before I began to stutter, I turned to her and said, "How shall I introduce you, honey, by your nickname or by your given name?" "Well, of course," she said, "by Maryanna." (I've used that little conversational trick many times when I couldn't remember a friend's name.)

When I went to bed that night I began to wonder about my memory. There had been other memory lapses. I'd run into former San roommates, with whom I'd spent bedpan hour, and couldn't remember their names. A deep freeze was setting in. It was time I did something to break that up, all the more so if I still intended to write novels. Thus one day I decided to recall how I landed in the San. I started writing about the time I fell down on Walnut Street. My memory was reluctant to help me out but I persisted. Slowly I managed to describe in some hundred pages my life from the falling down to the day I learned I was going to make it. I showed it to my wife Maryanna and she wondered if it wasn't the start of a novel. I had just finished writing the seventh and last draft of my first novel, *The Golden Bowl*, which after dozens of rejections in New York had been accepted by a small press in St. Paul, Minnesota, the Webb Publishing Company.

Finishing the T. B. book led to problems. It was too much of an account of a catharsis to be shaped into a novel like my first novel. So I decided, the hell with it, let it be a narrative story about a fellow who'd almost died from the white plague. My editor at Webb, Paul C. Hillestad, despite misgivings about the book's form, decided to publish it. I chose the title *Boy Almighty*. There has been only one American edition of 2,500 copies. It was published over my family name of Feike Feikema. Later on, after I discovered that the name Feike and Frederick came from the same Sanskrit root of "pri-tu," meaning "first born" and "free," I changed my writing name in 1952 to Frederick Manfred. I had finally got so sick of having Feike Feikema mispronounced, "As "Fee'ke Fee-ke'ma," as well as hearing several vulgar puns on it, that I legally changed my baptismal name of Frederick Feikema to Frederick Feikema Manfred, the name I now use in the copyright line.

Once I was writing full time, I began to wonder about some things. Had any of my relatives ever had tuberculosis, on my father's side, on my mother's side! It turned out there were none. I was the only one. Where did I get the bug? I happened to drive to Sioux Falls one day, and curious to see the people I once boarded with, I discovered that they had all died: husband and wife and child, and brother of the husband. And they had all died of miliary tuberculosis. I remembered they were always coughing, but I thought at the time they just had colds. I used to babysit their baby. I ate from their plates. I went to movies with them. The unmarried brother had spent some time in a T. B. sanatorium in the Black Hills. Well that, plus being out of work and having only one meal a day (and sometimes no meals at all), I was bound to go under.

Today at this writing, I can look back on having thirty books published, most of them novels and stories. Not bad for someone who was once considered a "terminal" patient by his doctor. Of the thirteen roommates I had, all but one died, some in my room 176, some after five years once they were released. The mortality rate in those days was seventy-five percent. If you could live five years out in "life," you had a chance to survive a dozen years. But you survived almost as a cadaverous chronic.

I've twice had serious operations since then, once to give me a steel knee, once when I suffered a blocked bowel. Each time I was given a mantoux test. Both times my test was negative. Both times the doctors wondered if I'd really had tuberculosis, and both times I told them about what I'd read in Dr. Cohen's file on me as well as told them that I'd seen my bugs under a microscope. "Well," both of them said, "that's really not possible." Thanks to genetics I am still here and writing every day. I have another book (a miscellany) coming out this fall. I have two more novels finished. And am well into yet another.

So when I meet someone who doesn't particularly care for my work or me and who says, "Hey, I thought you'd be dead by now," I think to myself, "No, and what are you going to do about it." But I don't say it. I nod and smile, and go my way.

Acknowledgments

The Foreword was printed in *Contemporary Novelists*, St. James Press, London, 1972.

"The Evolution of a Name" was printed in *Names* 2:2 (June 1954).

"West of the Mississippi" was printed in *Critique* (1958).

"Doon, Iowa: Magic Place" was published in *Through the Years with Bonnie Doon*, on the occasion of Doon's seventy-fifth anniversary of incorporation.

"Our Old Mother River Has Diarrhea" was printed in the *St. Paul Sunday Pioneer Press*, May 14, 1972.

"Place" appeared in *Publishers Weekly*, October 23, 1973.

"What Makes a True Soul Mate?" appeared as the Introduction of *King of Spades*, Gregg Press edition.

"Space, Yes: Time, No" was given as the Presidential Lecture at the University of South Dakota, March 31, 1981.

"Interview with Frederick Manfred – I" appeared in *Finding the Words*, by Nancy Bunge, Athens, Ohio: Swallow Press, 1985.

"Interview – II" was made in two sessions in 1989, the first at Southwest State University, Marshall, MN, the second at the author's home, Roundwind, near Luverne, Minnesota.

"The Making of *Lord Grizzly*" was presented at the Western History Association conference, Salt Lake City, Utah, October 14, 1983. It was published in *South Dakota History*, 15:3 (Fall 1985): 200-216. Copyright © 1986 by South Dakota State Historical Society. All Rights Reserved. Reprinted with Permission.

"The Little Spirits, or Deons" was printed by the Institute of Indian Studies, University of South Dakota, 1984.

"Old Voices in My Writings" was printed in *The Prairie Frontier*, edited by Arthur R. Huseboe, Sioux Falls: The Nordland Heritage Foundation, 1984.

"Dinkytown" was published in booklet form by Dinkytown Antiquarian Bookseller, Minneapolis, 1984.

"Calvin in the Early Thirties" appeared in *The Calvin Spark*, 31:4 (December 1984).

"Frederick Manfred, Outsize Man and Writer" was printed in *The North Dakota Quarterly* 55:2 (Spring 1987).

"A Conversation with Frederick Manfred" was printed in the *Agassiz Review* 2:1 (Spring 1991).

"Dr. William Harry Jellema 1893-1982" was printed in *The Banner* 127.13 (April 6, 1992).